Dog Friendly Britain
Cool Places to Stay with Your Dog

Dog Friendly Britain

Cool Places to Stay with Your Dog

cool places

Contents

WHAT MAKES A COOL PLACE DOG FRIENDLY?

Going on a trip, however short, is always harder if you have to leave the dog at home. And if you're holidaying in Britain there's really no need, as there are not only plenty of places to stay where you can take your dog, but more people than you can imagine who love dogs as much as you do – and who maybe even want to meet yours!

As a specialist in UK travel, it felt like the right time for Cool Places to publish a guide to Dog Friendly Britain. Just as travelling with children is no longer the handicap it once was in Britain, taking your four-legged friend has in recent years also become more acceptable, with hotels, B&Bs and self-catering cottages often going the extra mile to accommodate dogs and their owners while being careful not to alienate their non-dog-owning patrons.

Really, it's about time. Dogs aren't for everyone, and there are plenty of establishments that are better off dog-free. But the vibe at many British hotels is often so perfectly suited to dogs that it would be a shame to exclude them, and we've yet to find a country inn that's not enhanced by the presence of a hound or two dozing in front of the fire. Location, too, plays a part. It's always a pity to arrive somewhere beautiful, with fabulous walks as far as the eye can see, knowing how much your dog would enjoy it – if only he or she were here!

Of course, some places are more dog friendly than others. In publishing this book, it's our intention to highlight properties that don't just keep a couple of their less desirable rooms for dogs and their owners but who actually seem to like having dogs around. The properties we feature positively embrace the fact that some people prefer not to leave the family pet at home, offering beds,

bowls and treats for lucky pooches, and employing staff who like dogs too. Often they're located in stunning countryside – by the sea, in the middle of lavish country estates or in one of the country's national parks; a few are in towns or cities and will have lots of tips on the best dog-friendly bars and restaurants or the nearest park for a walk. Some are frankly dog bonkers, laying on so many goodies for dogs that you may be jealous of the attention your pet is getting!

Overall, though, we have been careful to include not just places that are keen on dogs but also places that humans will want to stay in too – selecting some of the country's best hotels, pubs, and B&Bs, most beautifully situated glamping sites and cosiest cottages, to ensure that everyone has a good time, not just Fido!

Wherever you go, hopefully you'll be reminded that dogs tend to bring out the best in people, making them ideal participants in the British holiday experience. We hope you, your travelling companions and of course your faithful friend all enjoy your stay.

Martin Dunford,
coolplaces.co.uk

DOGGY DETAILS

We've given contact details, accommodation details and prices for all the properties featured in this book. Prices for hotels, inns and B&Bs include breakfast unless stated otherwise; prices for dogs are either per night or per stay. Prices for self-catering cottages, lodges and glamping include dogs unless stated otherwise.

NINE MILLION PEOPLE CAN'T BE WRONG!

Britain is a nation of dog lovers. Over nine million people have a dog in the UK and it has become more important than ever for owners to be able to take their dogs on their travels. We set up our website to list places that would accept dogs with open arms, and shortly after we started DogFriendly magazine to review the very best dog friendly places around the country. We now have over 100,000 members but the need to discover truly dog-friendly accommodation is more important than ever, especially when so many properties are 'dog tolerant' rather than 'dog friendly' – which is not the same thing at all! With that in mind, we were delighted to work with Cool Places on this book: their team have come up with a range of places to stay that don't just tolerate dogs, they love them, and in the pages that follow you should find the most amazing locations to enjoy with your dog in what is a genuinely useful and inspiring new resource for dog owners.

Steve and Linda Bennett
Dog Friendly Magazine, dogfriendly.co.uk

WHY STRETCH TWO LEGS WHEN YOU CAN STRETCH SIX?

We love dogs and really enjoy being out and about with our pals in the great outdoors – whatever the weather! We think they add essential dimensions of energy, fun and emotion when we are exploring together. With the help of our very own Julia Bradbury, Britain's favourite walker, we have shared some of our favourite dog-friendly walks around the many and varied landscapes of England, Wales and Scotland. Hopefully you'll enjoy them as much as your four-legged friends. As Julia once famously said on a doggy walk, 'Why stretch just two legs, when you can stretch six – or ten…or more?'

The Outdoor Guide and Julia Bradbury
theoutdoorguide.co.uk

BEST DOG FRIENDLY WALKS

COOL PLACES TO STAY WITH YOUR DOG

Country cottages, luxury hotels, cosy gastropubs, boutique B&Bs, yurts and cabins... These are Britain's best places to stay with your dog....

COUNTRY HOTELS

Mr L. J. Burrows is licensed to sell intoxicating liquor of all descriptions for consumption on or off the premises.

SEASIDE AND WATERSIDE HOTELS

TOWN AND CITY HOTELS

B&BS AND GUESTHOUSES

PUBS, INNS AND RESTAURANTS

GLAMPING

COUNTRY COTTAGES

SEASIDE AND
WATERSIDE COTTAGES

CABINS AND LODGES

LONDON AND
THE SOUTHEAST

London casts a long shadow in Southeast England but it's striking how
quickly you can be in deep countryside whichever direction you travel in,
whether it's the wilds of the South Downs, the Kent Coast or Oxfordshire
and the Thames Valley. Don't forget, either, that there are one or two
special hotels in the capital that welcome four-legged friends.

Alkham Court Farmhouse

A luxurious boutique farmhouse B&B that's dog friendly and also has two shepherd's huts.

There's nothing like staying on a farm, but it's a fact that not all farmhouse B&Bs are created equal – indeed you'd be hard pushed to find a B&B anywhere, of any description, that comes up to the high standards of Alkham Court Farmhouse in Kent, one of our favourite B&Bs in this part of the world. A five-star luxury guesthouse, it most recently won a national award for England's 'Best B&B', and has in past years also won Tourism South East 'Beautiful South' awards for 'Best B&B' and also for 'Best Glamping' for their associated Greenhill Glamping business, which has two cosy shepherds huts with wood-burners.

Owned and run by Wendy Burrows and her husband Neil, they genuinely enjoy sharing the delights of their Kentish farmhouse with other people – something that can't always be said. There's a personal welcome on arrival together with a slice of homemade cake, which you can enjoy in the garden or by the wood-burner indoors depending on the season. Wendy is a big dog-lover and always keen to share her favourite walks, cycle rides and nearby attractions, from walking the White Cliffs of Dover to visiting Dover Castle; it's a five-mile walk to Dover Castle, three miles to the Battle of Britain Museum and just under a mile to the local 12th-century church and village pub. Wendy can even arrange for you to explore the nearby bridleways and countryside on horseback if you wish. There's a lovely spacious sauna and hot tub in a converted barn in the garden; they serve legendary, award-winning breakfasts, and provide optional packed lunches and evening snacks.

What about the guest rooms? There are just four rooms, three on the ground floor and one upstairs, each individually designed and furnished but all equipped with high-quality bed linen, robes and slippers, tea-making facilities, a Nespresso machine, still and sparkling mineral water, a Freeview TV and DVD player, digital radio and mini fridge, and (a nice touch, this) fresh flowers on arrival. The bathrooms have been recently refurbished and have posh toiletries. The Garden Room is the farmhouse's dog-friendly room, with direct access to the garden and bowls, towels, treats and poo bags provided. There's also an outside area for washing muddy paws, if required.

Their two shepherd's huts are lovingly restored vintage affairs for two people, with retro fittings combined with modern-day functionality such as electricity and hot water, and they have a small holiday cottage which also accommodates two adults and two dogs. If there is a better or more dog-friendly place to stay in this part of Kent, or a more comfortable or versatile one for that matter, then we have yet to find it.

CONTACT Meggett Lane, South Alkham, near Dover, Kent CT15 7DG · 01303 892056 · alkhamcourt.co.uk
HOW MUCH? Double rooms £140–£170 a night, shepherd's huts from £125 a night, cottage from £110 a night, dogs £20 per stay.
ACCOMMODATION Four B&B rooms, 2 shepherd's huts and a holiday cottage for two.

Bailiffscourt Hotel

The beautiful Bailiffscourt Hotel is somewhat misleading. Sitting on the West Sussex coast just behind Climping's pebble beach, this sprawling hotel is all leaded windows, huge wooden doors and crumbling old sandstone, yet what looks like a smattering of ancient buildings is in fact an ostentatious 20th-century creation dreamed up by Lady Moyne (part of the famous brewing family) and built by architect Amyas Phillips, who travelled the country to seek out original medieval features. The result is an incredibly atmospheric construction with a history dating back just 90-or-so years. Beyond its intriguing origins, the hotel has plenty to please. Walks along the coast or among the 30 acres of gardens are a pleasure. The spa is sublime with its heated outdoor pool, from which you can hear the sea crashing on the pebbles nearby, and the restaurant has a trio of excellent menus offering locally sourced produce and exceptionally fresh seafood. Service is seamless, dogs are fussed over and the warren of lounges in the main building is a cosy place to while away an afternoon by the fire.

CONTACT Climping St, Climping, West Sussex BN17 5RW • 01903 723511 • hshotels.co.uk
HOW MUCH? Double rooms from £265 a night; dogs £25 a night. Ask about their 'Sandy Paws' package (£415).

The White Horse

Located just off a B-road, seemingly in the middle of nowhere, the White Horse in Chilgrove is a fantastic little country pub with rooms. There's prime walking territory right from the front door – laminated maps available on the bar will guide you on a 4.5-mile circular hike over the hills, through the woods and back to the cosy pub. But much of the action here is centred around shooting on the nearby Goodwood Estate. There's a shooting party here almost every week, but even if shooting game birds isn't your thing, it's worth coming here for the hot tubs and great hospitality alone. Dogs are welcome too, as they are at most shooting pubs, and they get a bed, bowl and blanket of their own. Bedrooms are modern and comfortable, with faux-fur touches and funky décor, and some even come with hot tubs under a gazebo in their own private garden. All but 2 rooms have direct access to the communal lawn, and the restaurant serves pub classics like ale-battered fish and chips, or game favourites such as local roasted partridge and pheasant.

CONTACT 1 High St, Chilgrove, West Sussex PO18 9HX • 01243 519444 • thewhitehorse.co.uk
HOW MUCH? Double rooms from £85 per night (or £175 for the hot tub rooms). Dogs £15 a night.

South Lodge

Set amid rolling hills and farmland, South Lodge is an idyllic country house built by Frederick Du Cane Godman, a Victorian collector and explorer. What began as a fairly modest dwelling, though, has today morphed into a huge estate with vast grounds comprising manicured lawns, big open fields and even a glassy lake. It's a sensational, luxurious stay for you and your dog, with amenities to please both 2 and 4-legged guests. Many of the rooms are dog friendly and have direct access to outside space. Dogs are well looked after, with plenty of fuss from the staff, a toy to play with and a bowl and bed in the room. Humans can find pampering opportunities in the spa, a modern space with a brilliant gym, nail bar and a heated outdoor hydrotherapy pool. The indoor pool is great for a swim, but the absolute highlight is the UK's first heated wild swimming pond, packed with reeds and aquatic plants that naturally filter the water. There's also sublime 2-AA-rosette food in The Camellia restaurant, 3-AA-rosette tasting menus at Tom Kemble at The Pass, and plant-based Mediterranean cuisine in the spa eatery, Botanica.

CONTACT Long Hill, Lower Beeding, Horsham, West Sussex RH13 6PS • 01403 891711 • exclusive.co.uk
HOW MUCH? Double rooms from £285 a night, dogs £50 per stay – no limit on numbers.

Ockenden Manor

Old meets new at Ockenden Manor in Cuckfield, as this grand old Elizabethan mansion is paired with a beautifully modern spa whose exterior is almost industrial in design. The elegance of the main house isn't diminished, though, as its lavishly decorated bedrooms and homely lounges and bars make a wonderful countryside retreat. Well placed within the South Downs, this is the place to come for long walks, fireside G&Ts and long soaks in the outdoor heated pool. There is an excellent restaurant, with local produce transformed by the award-winning chef, and the afternoon tea is an indulgent treat. Dogs are allowed everywhere, except in the restaurant and spa, and can be left with reception staff while you relax in the spa. Ockenden Manor is in a great spot, too, not more than 20 minutes' drive from some gorgeous Sussex gardens – Wakehurst Place and Sheffield Park among them – or, to the south, the pretty village of Ditchling and the South Downs. Whether you'll actually want to leave the hotel grounds, though, is an altogether different matter.

CONTACT Cuckfield, West Sussex RH17 5LD • 01444 416111 • hshotels.co.uk
HOW MUCH? Double rooms from £189 a night, dogs £25 a night (maximum 2 per room).

The Jack Russell Inn

The Jack Russell Inn has long seen weary travellers drop in for a kip in its cosy bedrooms, as it sits on what was once a busy trade route from London to the west. Today it's very much a country inn for country pursuits, set within the village of Faccombe and surrounded by several large estates. This is shooting territory, so it's not uncommon here to see the bar area overrun with men dressed all in green, and the main soundtrack if you take the dog for a walk on nearby footpaths is that of game birds clucking from the bushes as you walk by. The pub itself is a lovely little hideaway, though, whether you're into shooting or not. The food in the restaurant is very game-focused but there are also favourites like pork belly and steaks, and the property boasts some decent eco credentials too. You can feel good about bringing the dog here, as the hotel's electricity comes from a wind turbine, heating is powered by a biomass boiler and the water comes from a borehole on the Faccombe estate. What's more, dogs get gravy bones, a bottle of dog 'beer', a blanket and a map of the local trails.

CONTACT Netherton Hill, Andover, Hampshire SP11 0DS • 01264 737315 • jackrussellinn.com
HOW MUCH? Double rooms from £100 per night, dogs £15 per stay, no limit on the numbers per room.

The Master Builder's

Dating back to 1729, this historic hotel – as the name suggests – once housed the Master Builders for Lord Nelson's Navy. Today it is a small but luxurious hotel, bar and restaurant set close to the river Beaulieu in the ancient and unique shipbuilding village of Buckler's Hard, whose houses form a quaint avenue that leads down to the water. The rooms are all smart and comfortable, and some have views of the river. Buckler's Hard is a busy place for sure, but if you stay the night and enjoy the area after the daytrippers have gone home you'll really feel transported back in time. The hotel accepts dogs in 5 of their 'Posh Classic' rooms and indeed is so welcoming it won UK 'dog friendly hotel of the year' in the 2016 'Good Hotel Guide'. They even have a doggy room-service menu and offer bowls, beds and treats in guest rooms, and dogs can dine with you in the bar. Plus of course there are any number of great walks in the local area – above all into the heart of the nearby New Forest, for which Buckler's Hard makes a convenient and very comfortable base.

CONTACT Buckler's Hard, Beaulieu, Hampshire SO42 7XB • 01590 616253 • themasterbuilders.co.uk
HOW MUCH? Double rooms from £100 a night, dogs £20 a night.

Elephant Hotel

A hive of activity for Pangbourne locals for the last couple of hundred years, you can't miss this quirky former pub and manor house near the Thames. There's a huge metal elephant on the front porch and an equally impressive elephant inside, carved from wood and dressed in Indian regalia. Elsewhere, it's all antiques and intrigue with a décor that bears more resemblance to an Indian Raj-era home than a countryside hotel in Britain, but it's all the more striking for it. Bedrooms are charming, with heavy antique beds, Indian art and bathrooms with rain showers over bathtubs for a soak after a long walk and dog-friendly rooms that open out onto the garden. The modern, industrial-chic bar is perfect for post-stroll tipples and there's a cocktail lounge for something more sophisticated. Dogs are welcome everywhere except the restaurant, where the stone fireplace has a a log-burning grill cooking a daily changing menu of sharers like chateaubriand and porterhouse steaks, but you can eat the same food in the bar with your dog. You'll be grateful to have those big old beds to collapse into.

CONTACT Church Rd, Pangbourne, Berkshire RG8 7AR • 0118 984 2244 • elephanthotel.co.uk
HOW MUCH? Dog-friendly doubles from £105 per night. Dogs £20 a night, maximum of 2 dogs per room.

The Fox at Willian

Situated in the pretty Hertfordshire village of Willian, The Fox is a revamped pub that does everything a country inn should do: it has a set of very comfy guest rooms, recently decorated in crisp contemporary style; it serves excellent food that's very moderately priced; and it's not a bad place to pop in to for a pint either. There are 8 rooms in all, all turned out with crisp, retro designs and with king-size beds, good wifi, Freeview TVs, digital radios, coffee-and tea-making facilities and modern bathrooms with aromatherapy toiletries and rainfall showers. The 5 garden rooms are dog friendly, with their own outside entrances with patio seating in front, and they are provided with treats, bowls and beds. Dogs are allowed in the bar, where you can eat either from the simple bar menu or from the fancier next door restaurant menu. Both are relaxed places to eat, with stripped floors and lots of light; there's an emphasis on locally sourced ingredients and lots of things are homemade. There are also plenty of walks in the surrounding area, a couple of which take in a decent pub or two along the way.

CONTACT Willian, Hertfordshire SG6 2AE • 01462 480233 • foxatwillian.co.uk
HOW MUCH? Double rooms from around £100 a night, dogs £10 a night.

The Greyhound Inn

A proper dog-friendly contemporary village inn with comfy rooms and top-quality food.

The Greyhound is the type of place that welcomes you with open arms – owners Martyn and Catriona took over the Grade II-listed Georgian property in 2014 and lovingly refurbished it. Set in Letcombe Regis, a pretty village in south Oxfordshire, not far from the Wiltshire border, it's a proper pub that serves top-notch food, with eight tastefully decorated bedrooms above if you're looking for a weekend retreat in the countryside.

Awarded CAMRA's White Horse Region 'Country Pub of the Year' from 2017-2019 and Muddy Stilettos 'Best Destination Pub' (voted by the public), the inn is a relaxed place for an ale, craft beer or cider, while the rooms upstairs provide a comfy space in which to unwind. Each has an en-suite bathroom and is individually decorated, retaining the character of the building while adding more moden touches such as bespoke headboards, snazzy cushions and local artworks; each also comes complete with a pocket-spring mattress, flatscreen TV, Roberts Radio, and Bramley bath products – plus fresh milk and homemade biscuits – a thoughtful extra.

For guests looking for something special for their loved one, flowers or a bottle of fizz can be arranged for their bedroom., and if you don't want to leave Fido at home then you can bring him with you, as at least two of the rooms are dog-friendly. If you're after a family suite, that's no problem either – opt for 'Lambourn' or 'Oxford'.

Much importance is placed on food at The Greyhound – the regularly changing menu is bssed on an array of locally sourced produce, with imaginative dishes such as twice-baked Cheddar soufflé (a popular mainstay); rabbit boudin with warm lentil and tarragon salad; chestnut and bacon velouté; or pork loin with pork nuggets, English prawns, orange braised chicory, black pudding and hazelnuts. But if pub classics are more your thing, go for the beer-battered haddock with chips, homemade tartare sauce and mushy peas, or the burger with bacon jam, smoked Cheddar and fries.

Finally the area is the ideal spot for long country walks with your hound – the ancient Ridgeway National Trail (described as Britain's oldest road) is close by, as is the Thames Path, and the friendly staff are more than happy to help with routes and have several of varying lengths and difficulties mapped out for guests in advance. For those after something a little less strenuous, the historic market town of Wantage is just two miles from the inn and the Uffington White Horse (a 100-metre-long prehistoric hill figure formed from deep trenches filled with crushed white chalk) is just 15 minutes away by car, and is viewable on a roughly 7-mile circular walk across the downs. Then it's back to the pub for a pint in the bar followed by dinner in one of the cosy dining rooms.

CONTACT Main St, Letcombe Regis, Wantage, Oxfordshire OX12 9JY • 01235 771969 • thegreyhoundletcombe.co.uk
HOW MUCH? Double rooms from £105 a night, dogs £15 a night.
ROOMS Eight individually decorated rooms – with a bath, a shower or both.

The Kingham Plough

Great food and dog friendly rooms in a terrific Cotswolds village pub.

This 17th-century Oxfordshire pub with rooms has undergone quite a makeover in the last ten years or so. Just over a decade ago you couldn't get so much as a cheese roll in what was a typical village boozer; then Kingham's Plough became a gastronomic temple that drew people from far and wide, driven by 'Great British Menu' winner Emily Watkins. More recently, it has reverted to being a bit more of a pub – albeit one that serves really good food and has half a dozen very comfortable rooms upstairs for those who want to stay over. Our kind of place, in fact – welcoming and relaxed while making a big effort to make your stay extra-special.

Katie and Matt Beamish took over the place in early 2019 and want to retain the foodie heritage of the Plough but are also keen to put their own stamp on the place. It remains a gastropub at heart, however, and Matt and Katie, having worked with the likes of Raymond Blanc and Fergus Henderson, continue to source local, seasonal ingredients for both pub classics and more adventurous British dishes, which you can enjoy from an all-day bar menu or lunch and evening à la carte menus. The food is splendid and rates include an excellent breakfast, lots of it homemade, from the cereals to the baked beans, and relatively unusual options like kedgeree as well as an excellent Full English.

As for the rooms, there are six in all, some above the pub and others in a two-storey annexe next door – each individually decorated and very comfortable. All but one of the rooms have super-king-size beds (the other is just a king-size), with high-quality linen and duvets, tea- and coffee-making facilities and minibars with fresh milk, good wifi and large smart TVs and DVD players. The bathrooms have baths with showers (two have roll-top standalone baths), provided with locally made Bramley toiletries. Two dog-friendly rooms are available, and they each have a dog bed, water bowl, treats and a towel for muddy paws. The overall vibe is one of comfort and relaxation with a quirky twist – lots of grainy wood, flagstone floors and pubby nooks and crannies, open fires in winter and a sun terrace for summer, and contemporary British art on the walls, some of which is for sale.

Finally Kingham is a lovely, typically Cotswolds village, and the pub sits rather idyllically on the village green. There are lots of walks that you can do in the surrounding countryside, but to be honest you and your dog might have everything you need right here – Kingham has a main line station a 15-minute walk away so you don't even have to bring the car. If you do, though, the village is also a good base for exploring this part of Oxfordshire – Chipping Norton and Charlbury are a short drive away, as are the Rollright Stones and Daylesford, renowned for the original posh Cotswolds deli – Daylesford Organic.

CONTACT The Green, Kingham, Oxfordshire OX7 6YD · 01608 658327 · thekinghamplough.co.uk
HOW MUCH? The two dog-friendly rooms start at £145, dogs £10 per night.
ROOMS Six en-suite double bedrooms, all but one with super-kingsize beds, two of which can be used as twins.

The Milestone Hotel

An imposing, originally 17th-century building with a wide range of rooms and suites, this cosy and enticing London 5-star is extremely welcoming to dogs and their owners, with a perfect position for walkies opposite Hyde Park and Kensington Gardens. The hotel's 62 rooms are decorated in a classic style with fine fabrics, fresh flowers, antiques and rare artworks that will have you feeling at home in no time. Almost all are open to dogs, with no maximum number and no restriction on size. The hotel has its own 'Pet Concierge' to make your dog's stay a memorable one, organising everything from dog-walking to visits to the vet; indeed they will know all about your dog's needs already if you have filled in your 'pet preference' form before you arrive. Your dog will have a bed, toys, food and blanket waiting so they can get comfortable while you pop down to the hotel gym or spa. When you go down to breakfast, they can choose a 'pooch pancake' or 'mini omelette' from the dedicated dog menu, which also has main courses and snacks at lunch or dinner. Scooby Doo Spaghetti, anyone?

CONTACT 1 Kensington Court, London W8 5DL •
0207 917 1000 • milestonehotel.com
HOW MUCH? Double rooms from £375 a night, dogs free.

The Pilgrm

This snazzy pooch-friendly spot may have no front desk, room service, baths or mini bars, but don't let that put you off. Situated in a convenient location opposite Paddington Station, the hotel has 3 dog-friendly rooms on the first floor, and its stylish rooms offer some of central London's best-value accommodation – fusing contemporary and vintage, decorated with cast-iron reclaimed radiators, soothing tones, handmade mattresses and Egyptian cotton sheets and towels, original artwork, Freeview TVs, real plants, USB sockets and Marshall bluetooth speakers. Guests can grab a tea or coffee from the Pantry on each floor and water from self-service water stations (just ask for your own recyclable bottle). The ground-level Workshop Coffee café is a casual setting for a steaming cup of Joe, while the first floor lounge serves breakfast and lunch. The hotel is also in an excellent position not only for dog walks (on nearby Norfolk Square) but also for exploring London – handy for public transport and also close to Notting Hill and Hyde Park.

CONTACT 25 London St, London W2 1HH •
0207 667 6000 • thepilgrm.com
HOW MUCH? Bunks start at £99 for 2 people per night, up to £129 for a 'Large' room. Dogs £30 a night.

The Hoxton Southwark

The latest addition to the burgeoning Hoxton group, which has 2 other hotels in London, this Southwark hotel is maybe the coolest place to stay south of the river. It has 195 rooms spread across 14 floors, ranging from small doubles to lovely light corner rooms that are the spacious match of any hotel in London; bathrooms are reasonable sizes and all have tea- and coffee-making facilities and water as complimentary, along with comfy beds, Freeview TVs and good wifi throughout. The first and second floors are home to the dog-friendly rooms, and dogs go free, as well as being provided with a dog bowl, bed, treats and toy and a dog-friendly guide to the local area – something all the Hoxton hotels do. Rather sweetly, they also ask the dog's name so they can give him/her a proper welcome. The ground-floor lobby, bar and restaurant all merge into one and are deliberately sociable spaces; dogs aren't allowed in the ground-floor Albie restaurant or in the top-floor Seabird restaurant but you can order food with your dog in the ground-floor bar or in the comfy (and quieter) mezzanine bar.

CONTACT 32–40 Blackfriars Rd, London SE1 8PB • 0207 903 3000 • thehoxton.com
HOW MUCH? Double rooms from around £200 a night, dogs free.

The Ampersand Hotel

One of very few privately owned five-star hotels in this part of London, The Ampersand is not only an extremely comfortable place to stay in a great London location but more than half the rooms are dog-friendly, and hounds get a bed, bowl, treats and a toy as standard. Despite an official rule of one dog per room, they are also refreshingly relaxed about the number and the size of the dogs they admit. Ranging from small doubles to deluxe studios and suites, there are 111 rooms in total, and although each is individually styled they all boast extremely comfy beds with bespoke headboards, tea- and coffee-making facilities, Freeview TVs, robes and slippers and either bath tubs or walk-in showers in spacious bathrooms with high-end toiletries. The dog-friendly rooms are the more expensive Deluxe rooms, which are very spacious, with chaise-longues at the end of king-size beds, and walk-in showers as well as baths. The hotel also has a small gym, and they serve food all day in the Drawing Room café, where dogs are always welcome.

CONTACT 10 Harrington Rd, London SW7 3ER • 0207 589 5895 • ampersandhotel.com
HOW MUCH? Dog-friendly Deluxe rooms from £330 a night – dogs free.

Lydhurst Cottages

Luxurious self-catering on a beautiful Sussex country estate – a perfect location for dogs and their owners!

Situated on the edge of the Sussex Downs, tucked away in a beautiful woodland location, it would be hard to find a more bucolic yet accessible country retreat than Lydhurst, let alone one that was quite as perfect for dogs. A set of self-catering cottages on a family-owned country estate in the High Weald Area of Outstanding Natural Beauty, Lydhurst is a very special place to stay, owned and run by Amber and Adrian Baillie, who live nearby: Warninglid village is a short walk away and has an excellent pub, and the cottages here are a perfect place to relax and make the most of nature, with dogs welcome and walks galore through ancient woodlands on multiple footpaths. It's a massive stroke of luck that Amber and Adrian decided to share it with the rest of us!

There's a variety of accommodation dotted around the 400-acre estate, and all the cottages have the best modern touches: the three largest have smart TVs and they all have good wifi, Roberts digital radios, underfloor heating in the bathrooms, big Smeg fridges, Nespresso machines and bluetooth speakers. They have plenty of character too: the listed 16th-century Farmhouse sleeps eight in four bedrooms and has gloriously wonky floors and an elegant, historic feel in a very secluded setting. There are two well-equipped bathrooms upstairs, a big open-plan kitchen with an Aga and a comfy sitting room with a wood-burning stove. Not far from the farmhouse, flanked by woods and fields, Stonedelph Cottages each sleep four and five respectively, and you can rent them individually or together. The decor of one is all arts-and-crafts wallpaper and vintage furniture – very Sussex! – while the other is Scandinavian rustic: ultra-cosy, with original floorboards, a wood-burning stove and a lovely, well-tended garden. Nearby, the Mission House is a converted Victorian church hall and school house: with four bedrooms and a wet room downstairs, it's perfect for wheelchair-users, plus there's an upstairs bedroom with a four-poster bed and free-standing bath. Finally, there's the wisteria-clad Aunt's House across the way, whose generous proportions encompass five en-suite bedrooms, a wonderful kitchen-diner and a light and spacious sitting room – plus there is a brace of shepherd's huts back near the farmhouse, which sleep two couples in cosy comfort.

But enough of the details. What we like best about Lydhurst is its peaceful location and the fact that despite being right up to date these cottages are totally in tune with their gorgeous country setting. You couldn't imagine a better place from which to explore this part of Sussex – on foot, by bike or by car – or indeed a nicer spot to properly unwind in the countryside. Yet you are only an hour from London and less than half an hour from Brighton. We think that's pretty special.

CONTACT The Street, Warninglid, near Haywards Heath, West Sussex RH17 5TR • 01444 464300 • lydhurst-cottages.co.uk
HOW MUCH? Short breaks from £415.
ACCOMMODATION Four holiday cottages sleeping from 4 to 12 people and 2 shepherd's huts each sleeping 2.

The Farmhouse at Redcoats

A homely hotel, restaurant and wedding venue in the heart of the countryside of North Hertfordshire.

A recent revamp of a long-running and much-loved privately owned hotel, The Farmhouse at Redcoats is a very homely sort of place, but one with a contemporary twist. One of the many nice things about the hotel is the fact that it doesn't feel as if it's near anywhere much, yet is deceptively easy to reach – just a few miles from Hitchin, off the A1M, making it the perfect place to escape to for a weekend or short break in the countryside near London.

It has 28 guest rooms, divided between five in the main house, eight more contemporary rooms in the old stables in the courtyard, and a further 15 in the recently re-constructed barn, where the main reception is also located and there is a unique large beamed barn which is used for weddings. The four rooms in the main house are comfy rather than posh, with oak beams and crumbling old fireplaces, while the 8 courtyard rooms in the converted stables are more contemporary with cleaner lines and bolder colours. The rooms in the old barn are the most modern, ranged across three floors, and with spacious bathrooms equipped with powerful showers – the ones at the top are cleverly squeezed in among the gnarly eaves and beams of the ancient barn. All have tea-and coffee-making facilities, complimentary mineral water, TVs, phones and super-fast wifi, and the barn rooms are all air-conditioned too. There are four dog-friendly rooms, two Standard rooms in the courtyard and a Standard and Superior room in the barn, one of which has a sofa bed so could sleep a family. Dogs receive a bed, bowl and mat as standard.

The rest of the hotel revolves around the bar, which is a cosy old room at the centre of the original farmhouse, with mis-matched furniture, old beams and curios, and the restaurant, which is a mainly conservatory-based affair that looks out onto the hotel's well-tended gardens and serves a delicious and moderately priced, contemporary British menu (usually supplemented with a couple of well-chosen specials) based around seasonal and local ingredients; they serve oysters and seafood from Brancaster Staithe in North Norfolk, local game and pork, Hereford steaks and a trio of roasts on Sundays. They also offer a rather nice afternoon tea, which you can enjoy in a cosy lounge next door to the restaurant.

Outside there are four acres of gardens with lovely views across the rolling Hertfordshire countryside, and the country location and good bar and restaurant mean you don't have to do much once you're here other than stroll around the gardens or stride off across the fields in your wellies. And you'll be given a handy map on arrival in case you want to do just that.

CONTACT Redcoats Green, Hitchin, Hertfordshire SG4 7JR • 01438 729500 • farmhouseatredcoats.co.uk
HOW MUCH? Double rooms £140–£170 a night, dogs £20 per stay.
ROOMS 28 guest rooms, taking in Standard, Superior and Luxury categories – 5 in the main house, 8 in the old stables and a further 15 in the re-constructed barn.

Fair Oak Farm

A rural estate set in stunning East Sussex countryside – rustic-chic and truly unique.

It's not often we come across a property as special as Fair Oak Farm, or one that offers so much. Nestled on a private 12-acre country estate in Sussex in the heart of the High Weald Area of Outstanding Natural Beauty, the farm can sleep up to 36 guests across self-catering cottages, barns and high-end lodges. Owners Ian and Penny encourage sustainable tourism practices and they cater for all manner of gatherings. The site also welcomes dogs with open arms, indeed its role as the location for the BBC series 'Nightmare Pets SOS' perhaps best describes just how tolerant they are of our furry friends at Fair Oak Farm!

The vast accommodation is spread around the plot and is perfect for a group of friends or a family get-together. The rustic and super-stylish Farmhouse sleeps 10-12 and has three reception rooms, an open fire and a large well-maintained garden with firepit. The country-chic converted barns (sleeping 10-14) are spread across three buildings – choose the quirky Barn & Cow shed with its three bedrooms and bathrooms, or opt for the boutique one-bed Grain Store or Stable Cottage. And did we mention there's a capacious communal space, a dining area large enough to house all 36 guests? Next up are the contemporary, comfortable treehouses that sit in an ancient tree line, shepherd's huts with log-burners, and the Hay Barn overlooking fields. Each area has its own private parking and scenic views, there's a barbecue for cookouts on balmy evenings – or you can put you feet up and let a private chef do the cooking. Keen to play a game or watch a film? Head over to the table tennis table or the cinema barn. There's also a brand-new boot room and laundry room, which have a dedicated shoe- and dog-wash area.

Ian and Penny really have thought of everything. As well as providing high-end accommodation, they also offer a range of activities exclusively for guests, including wine-tasting with a local producer, clay pigeon-shooting, chocolate master classes, photography classes, trout-fishing and spa beauty treatments on-site in the super-cool, dedicated treatment studio. Be sure also to watch out for the alpacas and peacocks that roam this rural treat.

It's hard to imagine wanting to leave this glorious spot, but for those keen to venture out there's plenty to do, whether it's walking and cycling in nearby Bedgebury Forest, rock-climbing at Ridge, strolling through the medieval village of Mayfield (just over two miles away) or visiting the National Trust's Scotney Castle, where the gardens are lovely and thoroughly dog friendly for well-behaved hounds on leads. Soon enough, though, you'll feel the pull back to Fair Oak Farm.

CONTACT Witherenden Rd, Mayfield, East Sussex TN20 6RS • 01435 884122 • fairoakfarm.co.uk

HOW MUCH? From £6395 for the whole estate for a week in low season, up to £7995 in high season; weekend stays from £4695 in low season up to £5795 in high season. Discounted midweek stays available.

ACCOMMODATION Fair Oak Farm sleeps up to 36: the Farmhouses sleep 10–12, the converted barns (Stable Cottage and Grain Store, Barn & Cow Shed) 10–14. The glamping options sleep 10 (in 2 eco-lodge treehouses, 2 shepherd's huts and a Hay Barn).

Bethnal & Bec

Not far north of London, Bethnal & Bec is a chic, adults-only, dog-friendly venue for weary folk looking to escape for a weekend or even longer and do... well.. nothing in particular. Made up of 2 extremely comfortable self-catering retreats crafted from a former stables, it's easy to reach but feels very rural and away-from-it-all, with countryside views and pretty much every home comfort you could wish for laid on by thoughtful owners Vicky and Chris – wood-burning stoves, bathrooms with rainforest showers and toiletries, robes and slippers, your own hot tub, fast wifi, Bluetooth speakers and Smart TVs if all you want to do is binge-watch your favourite dramas. There's an honesty pantry, stocked with a selection of snacks, drinks, frozen meals and locally made gin and vodka which you pay for on your in-room iPad, and they also have dine-in food which on warm days you can enjoy at your own patio table. You could spend a very happy weekend or longer here, making the most of your retreat, wandering down to your dog-welcoming local, The Bull, or just enjoying multiple country walks.

CONTACT Nottinghams, Cottered, Hertfordshire
SG9 9PU • 07790 901051 • bethnalandbec.com
HOW MUCH? 1 night £220, 2-nights £295–£440;
2-night-min at weekend but no check-out time on Sun.

Winter's Farm Cottage

Just outside the lovely hilltop Sussex village of Mayfield, this beautifully converted former stables is a spacious holiday retreat for 2 people, situated amid gorgeous countryside. It has an open-plan sitting and dining area with a wood-burning stove, a well-equipped kitchen with washing machine and microwave, a bedroom with king-size bed and underfloor heating throughout. French doors open out onto a patio garden, but what really sets this property apart is the fact that it's surrounded by lovely countryside with multiple walks in all directions, making it a perfect spot to enjoy with your dog. There is loads to see and do nearby – a 3-mile circular walk through the countryside around Mayfield, walking trails and cycle routes at nearby Bewl Water and Bedgebury Forest, and National Trust properties like Pashley Manor and Scotney Castle. The Rose & Crown in Mayfield is dog-friendly, as is The Star at Old Heathfield, which serves excellent food, and you should consider also a trip to the shingle beach at Pevensey Bay, 18 miles away, which is dog friendly most of the year.

CONTACT Kent & Sussex Cottages • 01580 720770 •
kentandsussexcottages.co.uk
HOW MUCH? From £430 to £620 a week, depending
on the time of year.

Horne's Place Oast House

This former Oast House on the outskirts of the Kent village of Appledore has been converted to a glorious 10-bedroom oasis of calm with bright spacious rooms, exposed beams and a large inglenook fireplace. They welcome dogs and there is plenty of room for them to run around in its large grounds. The property sleeps up to 25, with 7 bedrooms in the oast house itself, and the rest, all en-suite, in a neighbouring barn. The Oast House's main kitchen-dining room is very much the heart of the place, perfect for big, celebratory dinners; when the sun is shining there's enough space for everyone to eat outside on the deck overlooking the pond and garden, where you can also make use of a built-in BBQ or wood-fired pizza oven. Inside, there's a comfy sitting room with an open fire and smart TV, a games room with table football and pool, and a hot tub. It's very comfortable and hard to leave, but also perfectly placed for getting out and about with your dog, with walks galore on Romney Marsh and the High Weald Area of Outstanding Natural Beauty, and the beach at Camber Sands just 10 miles away.

CONTACT Horne's Place, Appledore, Ashford, Kent TN26 2BS • 07588 379844 • hornesplaceoast.co.uk **HOW MUCH?** £4500–£6200 a week, £3600–£4960 for a 3-day weekend.

The Warrens

Situated right at the foot of the dunes at glorious Camber Sands, The Warrens couldn't enjoy a better location for dog-lovin' folk. It's a lovely white clapboard house typical of this part of Sussex, and can sleep up 10 people in its 5 bedrooms. All accommodation is on the same floor so it works well for guests with relatively limited mobility; there is a shared bathroom with roll-top bath and a further 2 wet rooms; and the well-equipped kitchen boasts a cooker, giant fridge, microwave, dishwasher, washing machine and a large dining table. Among other facilities, there's wifi, digital TV and a DVD player. Outside, a lovely garden faces south and has a BBQ and lots of garden furniture, though you may find that you spend most of your outdoors hours on the beach, which is fabulous for sunbathing and swimming and right on your doorstep. Electric bikes are available nearby and you can eat at The Owl or the Gallivant, while further afield there's Rye in one direction, and the wonderful RSPB reserve and beach at Dungeness, with its quaint fishermen's cottages.

CONTACT 1st Avenue, Sea Rd, Camber, East Sussex TN31 7FQ • 01580 830932 • camberaccommodation.co.uk **HOW MUCH?** From around £950 –£1900 a week. Short breaks available for £700–£1200.

OUT AND ABOUT

Four great walks with your dog

ASHRIDGE ESTATE Explore the stunning woodland and parkland of the Ashridge Estate, with its rich wildlife, diverse habitats and varied history, mostly following well-defined footpaths but occasionally across fields with livestock, so dogs should be kept under close control. Ashridge can be enjoyed throughout the year but it is spectacular in the autumn, when beech, oak and lime leaves turn unique shades. **5.2 MILES**

LITLINGTON WHITE HORSE In the South Downs National Park, this lovely circular walk explores beautiful mixed woodland with wonderful views of the Litlington White Horse. According to the National Trust, it was created in just one night back in 1836 by a local farmer's son with help from a few friends. As you walk through the woodland, you'll meander to the edge of the trees to enjoy far-reaching views across the iconic downland. It's great on a windy day as you can shelter under the tree canopy. **1.6 MILES**

RYE HARBOUR & CAMBER SANDS The area is a wonderful place to walk, starting from Rye harbour and heading south along the river, famous for its colonies of little, common and Sandwich terns. Follow the path to the beach and if you're lucky you may spot ringed plovers, avocets and oystercatchers along the way, before doubling back to take in the low-rise ruins of Camber Castle and continuing across the marshes to the dunes and beautiful beach at Camber Sands. **10.5 MILES**

WATLINGTON HILL Watlington Hill is well known for its triangular chalk 'white mark', carved into the hill, and it offers extensive views over the Oxfordshire plain to the north and west and beech and ash woodlands cloaking the slopes of the nearby hills to the south. There are wildflowers galore and birds to look out for include soaring buzzards and wheeling red kites. **0.64 MILES**

THE OUTDOOR GUIDE

The Bull Inn

A terrific country inn – and a great base for exploring the eastern Cotswolds.

Midway between Woodstock and Chipping Norton, Charlbury is an excellent base for exploring the eastern Cotswolds. It also happens to have a terrific place to stay in the 16th-century Bull Inn – Charlie and Willow Crossley's self-styled 'home away from home', which is a tremendous pub that manages to be both sharp and stylish and ridiculously comfortable at the same time. It's the sort of place where it's impossible not to relax, with all the bells and whistles a good gastropub should have – delicious, locally sourced, unpretentious food, decent ales and an all-round cosy atmosphere – together with a comfortable set of boutique rooms.

There are eight en-suite guest rooms in all, four in the pub and four in a converted barn, each with a distinctive and individual colour palette and extremely comfortable super-king-size beds with high-quality linen and big squashy pillows, upholstered headboards and bold, ample curtains. Everything is right up to date and chosen with care and huge attention to detail – essential in what is a seriously ancient building. Some rooms have bathrooms with either a bath or a shower, some have both, and a couple have free-standing baths in the room itself; every room comes with good wifi, flatscreen Freeview TVs, tea- and coffee-making facilities, complimentary water, bathrobes and Bramley toiletries. Dogs are allowed in four of the rooms (and throughout most of the pub) and get a bowl and a free packs of treats on arrival, as well as a welcome pack with nearby walks.

They serve an excellent breakfast, and at lunch and dinner the menu features the sort of high-end yet well-priced gastropub food you expect to find in these parts – simple and delicious, with great steaks and burgers, fish and chips, sharing platters and homemade bar snacks, and a choice of three roasts on a Sunday, which you can enjoy either in the bar or the restaurant.

There's loads to see and do nearby, and dogs especially will love it. For the energetic, Wychwood Forest offers a wonderful 8-mile-long circular walk, and the Glyme Valley Way passes nearby; for culture-vultures, Winston Churchill's birthplace Blenheim Palace is a short drive away, and although dogs aren't allowed in the main buildings, the park and estate are fine as long as they're kept on a lead. There's also the popular outlet shops at Bicester Village and the remains of a Roman Villa at North Leigh; and Oxford isn't all that much further.

But really the pleasures of this part of the world are aimless ones: country walks, cosy pubs and farm shops stacked with local produce. Days out from The Bull, finished off with dinner back at the pub, are heaven, and it's easy to forget you're just a 90-minute drive from London. Not only that: Charlbury is just over an hour away on the main line from Paddington, so you can just leave the car keys at home.

CONTACT Sheep St, Charlbury, Oxfordshire OX7 3RR • 01608 810689 • bullinn-charlbury.com
HOW MUCH? Double rooms £100–£200 a night, depending on season, dogs £15 a night (maximum 2 dogs).
ROOMS 8 double rooms, 4 of which are dog friendly.

Artist Residence Oxfordshire

Nestled in the Oxfordshire countryside, just a few miles west of Oxford on the eastern fringes of the Cotswolds, Artist Residence Oxfordshire is the ultimate country inn, with 8 comfortable bedrooms (6 of which are dog friendly) and excellent food and drink served in its pub, The Mason Arms. It's the rooms which really set this place apart; they're equipped with large, comfy beds, powerful showers and decorated with the sort of vintage-inspired but contemporary style we've come to expect from this quirky hotel group. They have wifi, flatscreen Freeview TVs, digital radios, Nespresso coffee machines and mini-fridges stocked with local goodies, and Bramley toiletries in the bathrooms, some of which have standalone roll-top baths. The rooms range in size from the compact 'Rabbit Hole' through the more spacious, dog-friendly 'Farmhouse Loft' to the 'Farmhouse Suite', which has a copper bath tub in the room itself. Of 3 dog-friendly rooms in the outbuildings, the spacious 'Stable Suite' has a private terrace and the 'Barn Suite' a unique four-poster bed. Dogs get a bed, bowl and treats.

CONTACT Station Rd, South Leigh, Oxfordshire OX29 6XN • 01993 656220 • artistresidence.co.uk
HOW MUCH? Double rooms and suites £150–£350 a night. Dogs £15 a night.

voco Oxford Thames

Set inside an historic manor house, voco Oxford Thames enjoys a stunning location, right on the riverbank of the Thames in the village of Sandford. It has a series of cosy but modern bedrooms with good mattresses and high-spec bathrooms with steamy showers, and dogs get a bowl and a blanket. Request a Garden Room and you'll get your own private patio with seating that looks right out onto the weeping willows. On arrival, you're greeted by a double-height lobby-bar with huge, dark timber beams and handed some complimentary honeycomb, made on-site by head chef using honey from the bees living in the hotel's grounds. There's a lovely courtyard for afternoon tea and a decent spa for a spot of relaxation, but it's the grounds that steal the show – beautiful lawns tumbling down to the riverside, where the hotel's own 1920s barge sits on the water like a scene out of 'Downton Abbey'. A boat stops on this stretch of river to ferry passengers into Oxford, but if you fancy a walk with the pooch, take the towpath – approximately 2 hours – into the city centre.

CONTACT Henley Rd, Sandford-on-Thames, Oxfordshire OX4 4GX • 01865 334444 • ihg.com
HOW MUCH? Double rooms from £120; Dogs £20 a night

The Swan at Streatley

Sitting pretty along the River Thames, sandwiched between the historic villages of Goring and Streatley, this perfectly positioned hotel is an idyllic escape for a weekend away with the dog. It's just moments from various National Trust properties, where ample woodland and rolling hills make for brilliant walks with glorious views over the Goring Gap. Nearby Beale Park is great for the kids, and a 10-minute drive (or a couple of hours' walk along the river) takes you to the market town of Wallingford, where the ruins of a Norman castle sit just beyond the river. The hotel itself had a much-needed refurbishment in 2019, and the result is a chic property with neutral tones and clean décor that retains its cosiness through plush carpets and comfy sofas. There's a riverside café-bar that opens onto a manicured lawn with deck chairs and picnic benches. There's waterside dining at the adjoining Coppa Club restaurant, and a gym and yoga studio. Ground floor, river-facing rooms have direct access to the lawn, the dogs get a blanket, bowl and biscuits, and those walks along the river are a beautiful way to start the day.

CONTACT Streatley-On-Thames, Berkshire RG8 9HR • 01491 878800 • theswanatstreatley.com
HOW MUCH? Double rooms from £85 a night; dogs £10, maximum 2 per room; breakfast £5–£16.

Minster Mill

Cotswold escapes don't get much better than this. With a small but inviting spa staffed by truly expert therapists, and a fantastic restaurant serving comforting but expertly prepared dishes in a dramatic timbered barn, you might find it difficult to leave. But do try, because there's lots to love about the surrounding area. Set in the chocolate-box village of Minster Lovell, the hotel is right on the edge of the Cotswolds, just 2.5 miles from the market town of Witney. The main draw in the village is the spectacular ruin of Minster Lovell Hall and Dovecote, a crumbling mess of turrets and stairways surrounded by grassy banks and woodland. The hotel's grounds sprawl along the River Windrush, with lawns, trickling streams and patios with firepits. Bedrooms range from cosy first-floor hideaways to ground-floor rooms with patios. The Garden Rooms are best, though, with their own conservatories cloaked in grapevines, private patios and their own parking spaces. Beds, bowls and treats are provided for dogs, and they can be left in the room while you dine at breakfast, lunch or dinner.

CONTACT Minster Lovell, Witney, Oxfordshire OX29 0RN • 01993 774441 • minstermill.co.uk
HOW MUCH? Doubles from £150 a night; dogs £20 a night, no maximum per room.

Tapnell Farm

Beautiful holiday cottages and glamping on a working dairy farm on the Isle of Wight.

Located just outside Yarmouth, on the western side of the Isle of Wight, Tapnell Farm is a family-run farm with 360-degree views, a beautiful rural setting and the best sunsets in the south. It has several high-quality self-catering options, from farm cottages to glamping, along with all sorts of glamping, from safari tents to eco-domes, and is a great option if you're staying with extended family or a group of friends, as all the accommodation is very spacious and there's so much to do on-site. Plus, of course, they love dogs, and all of the accommodation is dog friendly!

At the heart of the farm, Dairyman's Cottage has panoramic views of Tennyson Down and sleeps up to eight people. It's decorated with a rustic, shabby chic feel — sea-grass carpets and wood laminate flooring throughout, beautiful bespoke fabrics, luxury en-suite bedrooms and a high-spec open-plan living area, as well as a garden and patio area with a barbecue and a hot tub that's perfect for relaxing under the stars with a glass of wine. Stockbridge Cottage, on the edge of the farm, sleeps up to 12 and has views over rolling countryside and towards Freshwater Bay. It's also tastefully decorated, and has a large garden surrounding the house, complete with adventure playground. If you need room for an even bigger family or group of friends, there's East Afton Farmhouse, with eight bedrooms, seven bathrooms, a roof-terrace hot tub, cinema room, games area and private courtyard. Or, biggest of all, try Tapnell Manor with ten bedrooms, seven bathrooms, an electric hot tub, and games area and large living spaces.

The cottages are right on the doorstep of several footpaths and within driving distance of Freshwater Bay and a number of dog-friendly beaches, but there's lots to do on-site too. You can pet the lambs and collect eggs from the free-range hens, go clay-pigeon shooting, pedal go-karts and more. The farm is also home to Tom's Eco-Lodge, whose safari tents, cabins, pods and lodges put the glam into glamping, as do their luxurious domes, which also have amazing panoramic views. Each dome has an open-plan living area, a king-size four-poster bed and a cosy lounge with a wood-burning stove, a small kitchenette plus a separate bunk room. Meanwhile, the Cow Co restaurant is open to dogs and has lots of scrumptious beef and dairy dishes, or you can head over to the honesty shed for all those bits and bobs that got left behind (including a handy supply of dog treats). Many people come back here year after year — we bet you will too.

CONTACT Newport Road, Yarmouth, Isle of Wight PO41 0YJ · 01983 758729 · tomsecolodge.com
HOW MUCH? Cottages £800–£4600 a week. Safari tents from around £750 a week, from £495 for a 3-night weekend, from £400 for a 4-night midweek. Cabins from £600 a week, from £450 for a 3-night weekend. Pods from £80 a night, £550–£775 a week, from £300 for a 3-night weekend. Modulogs from £300 (for 2 nights). Domes £625–£727 a week, £400–£500 for a 3-night weekend.
ACCOMMODATION Everything from 4 to 10 bed cottages to 5 safari tents (sleeping up to 8), 2 cabins (sleeping up to 10), 2 pods (sleeping 2–4), 'modulogs' that sleep 4 + 2 on a sofa bed and 5 domes each sleeping up to 6 people.

Bermondsey Square Hotel

A 10-minute walk from London Bridge Station, this modern boutique hotel sits at the end of hip, happening Bermondsey Street, right on the edge of a foodie district of artisan bakers, coffee roasters, brewers and honey-makers. As such, it's a properly trendy place to stay, excellently placed for exploring London and ultra dog friendly too, with most rooms accepting dogs and offering a blanket, bed, treats and a toy to the lucky pooches who stay here. You can leave your dog in your room while you dine in the downstairs restaurant, plus there are lots of good places to eat nearby that accept dogs, in what is a true residential neighbourhood. The hotel's rooms are stylish and contemporary, with the spacious terrace rooms best for dogs, as they have a large shared outside space. They all have complimentary tea- and coffee-making facilities, fresh milk, juice and water, Freeview TVs and good-sized walk-in showers and toiletries. The Family Rooms especially are great value, with plenty of room for a family of 4 on a king-size bed and sofa bed, and great views over the city.

CONTACT 9 Bermondsey Square, London SE1 3UN • 0207 378 2450 • bermondseysquarehotel.co.uk
HOW MUCH? Double rooms from £149 a night, with continental breakfast; dogs £20 a night.

South Place Hotel

Part of the restaurant-focused D&D Group, you'd expect the food at this hotel to be pretty good, and South Place doesn't disappoint. Not only does it have an excellent restaurant on its ground floor, The Chophouse, it also boasts one of only half a dozen Michelin-starred restaurants in the City in Angler – a sleek affair on the top floor where the views are only surpassed by the quality of the food. But South Place is not just about food. The only hotel to be built in the Square Mile in the last century, it has a good-sized gym, sauna and steam room and 80 very comfortable rooms, ranging from entry-level Loft rooms to Studios and Suites. All the rooms have fast wifi, Freeview TVs, digital radios, minibars, Nespresso machines and decent sized bathrooms; they are all dog friendly and mutts are provided with beds, towels and treats as well as a mapbook showing the best walks nearby. Dogs go free in the higher category rooms and the hotel even runs the odd doggie event from time to time – for example dog-friendly film screenings and even a doggie afternoon tea!

CONTACT 3 South Place, London EC2M 2AF • 0203 503 0000 • southplacehotel.com
HOW MUCH? Loft rooms start at £200 a night, dogs free in higher category rooms, otherwise £50 per stay.

The Pointer at Brill

There are many reasons to consider this as a brilliant place for a break from London. First of all, it's not far to come – not much more than an hour by car from parts of north London; it's situated in a pretty hilltop village that has not 1 but 2 village greens and it is at the centre of a number of relatively undemanding country walks; it could even be a base for Oxford, which is a short drive away, and shopaholics can get their fix at nearby Bicester Village. Last but not least, the food here is worth the trip out of town alone and there are 8 guest rooms (4 above the pub and 4 in a cottage across the street): stylishly decorated in a rustic yet contemporary fashion, with exposed beams, soothing greys and creams on the walls, big comfy beds and good wifi, Freeview TVs, Nespresso coffee-makers, biscuits, fresh milk and still and sparkling water. They have roomy bathrooms with robes, toiletries and powerful rainfall showers, and all are dog-friendly, with bowls, beds and treats. Dogs are also allowed in the bar (where you can eat the same menu as in the restaurant).

CONTACT 27 Church St, Brill, Buckinghamshire HP18 9RT • 01844 238339 • thepointerbrill.co.uk
HOW MUCH? Double rooms from £ 120 a night, dogs £20 a night.

Lainston House

There's more to Lainston House than meets the eye. The long, winding driveway leads up to the main 17th-century manor house, which looks out over wooded hills and well-kept lawns. Inside, there are homely bedrooms with classic but tasteful décor and an inviting bar area with bookshelves and a bright and breezy lounge for afternoon tea. But beyond all this, Lainston has a few secrets up its sleeve: a kitchen garden and cookery school, offering classes in everything from Japanese cuisine to fish cookery, and an aviary where birds of prey such as falcons and owls are kept for bookable interactive experiences. Dogs are welcome and get a bed, bowls and poo bag (the Loggia rooms are best), and the grounds make for lovely walking territory, with intrigue aplenty, from old dovecotes to crumbling chapel ruins dating back to the 12th century. Ask for a map at reception and take the dog exploring around the vast estate. There are plenty of activities on offer, from archery to tennis to clay pigeon shooting, and the on-site restaurant, The Avenue, is a fine-dining experience. Book the Chef's Table for an extra-special night.

CONTACT Woodman Lane, Sparsholt, Winchester, Hampshire SO21 2LT • 01962 776088 • exclusive.co.uk
HOW MUCH? Dog-friendly double rooms from £215 a night, dogs £30 per stay.

The Spread Eagle

This West Sussex hotel is the oldest coaching inn in England – and is dog friendly too.

If the opportunity to stay in the oldest coaching inn in England isn't reason enough to book The Spread Eagle, there's plenty more to entice the traveller with dogs in tow. This utterly bewitching hotel was built in 1430 – twenty years before Machu Picchu was founded by the Incas – and it still retains some of its original features, including some astonishingly well-preserved stained-glass windows.

The hotel has had quite the roster of past guests, from Queen Elizabeth I to Vice-Admiral Horatio Nelson, and the bedroom Her Majesty stayed in is now called the Queen's Suite and has one of the last remaining wig rooms in the country.

Sitting right in the centre of the Sussex market town of Midhurst, The Spread Eagle is all timber beams on the outside and dark wooden floors and cosy fireplaces on the inside. And while it's evidently old and filled with antiques, it's not stuffy, with 39 guest rooms that have been sensitively and successfully updated; some have four-poster beds and all have tea- and coffee-making facilities. Bathrooms have been modernized to include large rain showers and roll-top baths and are provided with robes and Temple Spa toiletries.

Among other facilities there's a wonderful contemporary Scandi-style spa with a small indoor pool, hot tub, fitness suite and four treatment rooms. The restaurant serves a mean Sunday roast and a menu during the week which includes relatively informal lunches and a more formal dinner service. It's a historic, atmospheric place to eat, with excellent service, but serves food that is very much in tune with the times – as does the equally historic and very cosy bar, which has an extensive gin menu but is a welcoming place for a post-walk pint.

The great thing about the Spread Eagle is that dogs are allowed pretty much everywhere except the spa and the main restaurant, so you can feel right at home immediately, with hounds encouraged to curl up in front of the fire or join you in the bar or conservatory for dinner. Dogs can also take advantage of the hotel grounds and the immediate area for quick and easy walks, and of course the South Downs are on your doorstep for more strenuous affairs. Opt for the 'Muddy Paws' package and you get the full list of their recommended local dog walks, including dawn walks for early risers, strolls at dusk and well-planned routes through the best of the South Downs National Park which will wear out the most energetic four-legged friend. And if Fido ends up rolling in something unpleasant, the hotel can even organise sprucing sessions with a fully qualified local dog groomer. It's dog heaven, but with plenty to tempt well-behaved humans too!

CONTACT South St, Midhurst, West Sussex GU29 9NH • 01730 816911 • hshotels.co.uk
HOW MUCH? Double rooms from £159 a night; dogs £20, max 2 dogs per room. A Muddy Paws package from £252 includes overnight accommodation for 2 with dinner and use of the spa, plus 2 dogs, bed, blanket, bowls and treats and a 'Ruff and Tumble' drying coat to take home.
ROOMS 39 bedrooms and suites.

THE SOUTHWEST

Home to the country's most venerated coastline, the Southwest is one of England's most compelling and diverse regions, from the standing stones of Wiltshire and Dorset's Jurassic Coast to the moorlands, cliffs and spectacular sandy beaches of Devon and Cornwall.

The Eastbury Hotel & Spa

Traditional but with a modern touch, this is a comfortable dog-friendly hotel with exceptional food.

If you've ever fancied yourself as an 18th-century gentleman (or gentlewoman, for that matter) then The Eastbury might just be the place for you. Situated in genteel Sherborne, the ancient capital of Dorset, it's about as homely a luxury boutique hotel as you'll find: a beautiful Georgian house with a spectacular garden, a terrific 2-AA-rosette restaurant and most importantly 26 guest rooms that couldn't be more comfortable. Not only that: its new and forward-thinking owners added a spa in 2019, equipped with sauna, steam room, hydrotherapy pool, a gym and outdoor hot tub and lots of treatments, deep in the heart of the surrounding woodlands. Dogs are welcome throughout most of the hotel and in around a third of the guest rooms, where they get a bowl, bed and ball.

The Eastbury's rooms range from cosy doubles with wooden beams to larger luxury doubles and five suites fashioned out of the garden's 'Potting Shed': with moss and sedum roofs, en-suite wet rooms and private terraces, these are spacious and contemporary, and also dog-friendly. Each bedroom is individually decorated, and the décor is traditional without being fussy or old-fashioned – think big comfy sleigh beds, pastel shades, antique dressers and Lloyd Loom armchairs; all rooms come with Egyptian cotton sheets, robes and slippers, flatscreen Freeview TVs, tea- and coffee-making facilities and homemade biscuits; a few have four-poster beds, and some have free-standing baths in the rooms, while they all have en-suite bathrooms equipped with White Company toiletries. Dogs are allowed in four of the main building rooms and five of the potting shed suites, and they get a bed, bowls, treats and a ball, plus they get a branded bandana on check-out!

Like all good country hotels, the Eastbury has plenty of public spaces in which to relax – a couple of lounges, a library and billiard room, not to mention the walled garden outside. Dogs are allowed (on leads) pretty much everywhere except some of the tables in the restaurant, which serves everything from hearty brasserie fare to fine dining, with sandwiches and afternoon teas in between. There is also a cocktail bar decorated with unique modern artworks and a glass pod in the garden that acts as an intimate private dining room – a great place for a romantic get-together or special celebration with friends.

Sherborne is a lovely place to stay, an ancient market town with a well preserved old centre – the sort of place that gets used regularly as a film set ('Far from the Madding Crowd' was filmed here recently). You're well placed for seeing not only the delights of Dorset to the south but some of the best of Somerset too – needless to say, like the Eastbury itself, all fabulous places to visit with a dog!

CONTACT Long St, Sherborne, Dorset DT9 3BY · 01935 813131 · theeastburyhotel.co.uk
HOW MUCH? Standard doubles from £155 a night, Potting Sheds rooms £255 a night. Dogs £20 a night.
ROOMS 26 guest bedrooms including single, double and family rooms and a variety of suites. The hotel's newly refurbished rooms are called Victorian Garden Potting Shed Suites.

The Rosevine

This family-friendly Cornish country house by the sea combines the comforts of a luxury hotel with the freedom of having your own studio or apartment. Set in 2 acres of gardens above the dog-friendly sandy cove of Porthcurnick, the hotel is in a brilliant location for walks along the South West Coast Path as well as for the best bucket-and-spade beach days. There are water sports galore at Portscatho, a 10-minute walk away, and you can easily hop on a ferry to Falmouth from nearby St Mawes. The hotel lawns are ideal for impromptu doggy exercise, and for sea-gazing; indeed on a warm day, with the sea a cobalt blue, you can kid yourself you are in the Med, and when the weather is bad, there is an indoor heated pool. The hotel's décor is subtle and understated, with big comfy sofas, an open fire and a mix of antique and upcycled furniture. Dogs are allowed in all the apartments and there is a good restaurant menu featuring local seasonal produce and also plenty of classics to appeal to less adventurous eaters. You can eat with your dog in the lounge or self-cater.

CONTACT Portscatho, Cornwall TR2 5EW·
01872 5802063 · rosevine.co.uk
HOW MUCH? Double rooms £139–£219 a night;
studios, suites and apartments £149–£379; dogs £10.

Godolphin Arms

Looking out to Mounts Bay from the historic market town of Marazion, the Godolphin Arms sits by the water's edge on a 2-mile beach facing St Michael's Mount, a dog-friendly restaurant with rooms decked out in chic coastal style. Coastal hues, local art and wood panelling adorn a glass and zinc extension (that spills out onto an alfresco dining terrace), an upper deck with sofas and a log-burner, and a chilled-out lower deck with a beach bar that opens directly onto the seafront. There are 10 stylish en-suite rooms, 4 of which are dog friendly, with beds, bowls and treats provided, and dogs (on leads) are allowed throughout the public areas. You can kick back over coffee and cake while you soak up the sea views, tuck into divine Cornish cuisine from the all-day menu or sip cocktails, fine wines and local ales as the sun goes down. The food, most of which is sourced from local farms and fishermen, includes everything from hearty Cornish breakfasts and sharing platters (Mediterranean mezzes, shellfish and Cornish charcuterie), to fish and chips, Sunday roasts and crab sandwiches.

CONTACT West End, Marazion, Cornwall TR17 0EN ·
01736 888510 · godolphinarms.co.uk
HOW MUCH? Double rooms from around £160 a night,
dogs £15 a night.

The Olde House

Situated in a popular part of North Cornwall, a hop, skip and a jump across the estuary from trendy Padstow, Penpont Farm has been in the Hawkey family for 3 generations and remains at heart a working farm. It's a beautiful spot that supports an array of bird and wildlife, and we're lucky that back in the 1970s the family decided to convert a series of stone and slate barns into self-catering holiday cottages. They have since renovated further buildings to create a classy collection of 32 self-contained cottages that provides a gorgeous base from which to enjoy this beautiful part of Cornwall. All but 4 are dog friendly, with a maximum of 2 dogs per property, and it's a brilliant place to have a dog; they can run in the fields or stroll the farm trail and there are loads of coastal and woodland walks, including the Camel trail from Wadebridge to Padstow or Bodmin. They have a supply of dog bowls, balls, a dog wash and waste bins on site. Facilities for humans include an indoor pool, sauna, steam room and hot tub, a games room and outdoor play area, tennis courts and a charging point for electric cars.

CONTACT Chapel Amble, Wadebridge, Cornwall
PL27 6EN • 01208 813219• theoldehouse.co.uk
HOW MUCH? Cottages from £480 to £1240 a week.
Dogs £30 a week.

Loose Reins

Tucked away below the Wessex Ridgeway, Loose Reins is a glamping destination with a difference, with 3 cedar cabins and 3 safari lodges designed with a ranch theme in mind. Each sleeps 4–6 people and has just the right balance between high comfort and proper glamping, with decent furniture (Hypnos mattresses, luxury linen, and proper plumbing and electricity), wood-burners and outdoor fire bowls. Dogs are welcome throughout the site and provided with beds, bowls, towels and treats, and there's a handy paddock for lazy loose-lead walks. You can even bring your own horse, with livery facilities and a network of bridleways stretching in all directions. Whether you're on horseback or not, it's a perfect rural location, within easy reach of some of the best walks in the Southwest, with Blandford Forest and the Wessex Ridgeway on your doorstep and the North Dorset Trail Way passing through the nearby village. The Loose Reins folk will be glad to show you where to go, including a choice of routes taking in the best dog-friendly pubs.

CONTACT Ridgeway Farm, Shillingstone, Dorset
DT11 0TF • 01258 863533 • loosereins.co.uk
HOW MUCH? Midweek 2-night breaks £295–£425,
weekends £375–£520, dogs £25 per stay.

Fingals Apart

Cottage apartments with quirky appeal in gorgeous countryside near the River Dart.

Whether you're looking for a romantic haven or an idyllic family retreat, you've really hit the jackpot at this gorgeous collection of luxury self-catering cottage apartments, tucked into a quiet Devon valley near the River Dart. Set in the grounds of the owners' Queen Anne manor farmhouse, the accommodation has a quintessentially English feel and can host anyone from couples to groups of up to 12 or more in beautifully peaceful surroundings.

A 19th-century mill house conversion retains many of its period features (like the brick and stone arch for the mill wheel) and splits into two separate apartments – 'Lower' with two bedrooms and 'Upper' with three bedrooms. There's a lovely, rustic, homely feel here, and you can rent both apartments together for larger parties. There are also four other architect-designed self-catering spaces, namely the oak-framed Barn, the smaller Wisteria Suite, a separate stand-alone house (Barberry Brook) and the beach-house-style Folly. They are all beautifully furnished, filled with oriental carpets, antiques, objects d'art – often quirky – and original paintings by local artists. Each has a sense of light and brightness, with balconies, big windows, sitting rooms and private patios, some of which overlook the gardens, stream and Devon hills. Dogs are allowed into all apartments but the owners prefer that you don't allow them on furniture or beds – which may be something you are used to anyway.

If it wasn't already clear that this is a one-of-a-kind experience, the excellent facilities seal it. There's a seasonal grass tennis court, croquet lawn and table-tennis terrace, gym and exercise space, dedicated games room, and even a piano for anyone so inclined. Best of all, though, is the 8m-by-4m heated indoor swimming pool, housed in a conservatory full of exotic plants and featuring a huge mural painted by an artist friend of the owners. The pool opens out onto a balcony over the stream and onto the patio in the summer, while there's also a sauna with a large window looking over the stream.

Dragging yourself away from here, you're just a mile from Dittisham – a beautiful village sited on the edge of the river Dart that's also reachable by ferry from Dartmouth. It has a couple of pubs – try the dog-friendly Ferry Boat Inn (or 'FBI', as it's known) for lunch or dinner – and the excellent Anchorstone Café, which also welcomes dogs and whose owners run a water taxi service on the river. You could take this or the ferry to Agatha Christie's former summer house and gardens, Greenaway, just across the river – a trip well worth making. There are also plenty of renowned Devon beaches nearby and Dartmoor National Park is only a short drive away. Dogs are welcome year-round at nearby Sugary Cove, Slapton Sands and Beesands beyond, where there's a great foodie pub, the Cricket Inn, which welcomes dogs and their owners.

CONTACT Old Coombe, Dittisham, Devon TQ6 0JA • 01803 722398 • fingalsapart.co.uk
HOW MUCH? From £345 to £1410 for a 3-night stay.
ACCOMMODATION Six cottage retreats, each sleeping between 2 and 6 people.

St Michaels Resort

Located on the quieter side of Falmouth, within a squishy toy's throw of Gyllyngvase beach, St Michaels Resort is inspired by its surroundings, with calming sea blues and sandy hues that flow across the interiors of the hotel. The themed design speaks of the hotel's focus on tranquillity, coupled with the notion that your stay here will be hassle-free and as indulgent as you desire. The dog-friendly beach-house rooms are classically designed for a couple, with a secluded private patio. Bay Suites allow families to cosy up with their furry friend in the separate sitting room. There is also a plethora of activities and foodie options to enjoy: the health club has a gig-rowing area, gym and pool, and dogs can dine with you in the Garden Kitchen, open throughout the day, for a lazy brunch or wood-fired pizza, or sit by your feet whilst you're reading the paper in the captain's quarters-style library. Your dog can accompany you anywhere in the hotel and throughout the landscaped grounds, apart from the main restaurant, which boasts sumptuous cream teas and sustainably sourced fish dishes.

CONTACT Gyllyngvase Beach, Falmouth, Cornwall TR11 4NB • 01326 369787 • stmichaelsresort.com
HOW MUCH? Double rooms from £55 per person per night, dogs £12.50 a night.

The Old Coastguard

The folk behind this hotel cut their teeth on the excellent Gurnard's Head near Zennor and the 2 places have plenty in common, not least a glorious scenic location and great food, with 14 comfy guest rooms, all of which accept dogs and have some sort of sea view. The emphasis is on comfort, good food and relaxation, with big comfy beds in spacious rooms equipped with Roberts radios and posh toiletries, tea and coffee and lots of books to browse. Some rooms have balconies, most have baths, but all are that little bit different. The hotel has gardens that stretch all the way down to the sea, a wood-panelled bar (where you can eat with your dog) and a high quality restaurant. Mousehole itself is an archteypal Cornish harbour village, with a contemporary patina of cafés, restaurants and galleries, beyond which you can pick up the coastal path – St Michael's Mount and the Lizard Peninsula are on your doorstep – or just go to the beach. You're close to the wonderful beach at Sennen Cove (though this only seasonally welcomes dogs) and also Gwenvor beach, which is dog friendly year-round.

CONTACT The Parade, Mousehole, Penzance, Cornwall TR19 6PR • 01736 731222 • oldcoastguardhotel.co.uk
HOW MUCH? Double rooms £155–£260 a night, no charge for dogs.

Fowey Hall Hotel

Built in 1899 for a wealthy Cornishman, and once a frequent haunt of 'Wind in the Willows' author Kenneth Grahame, Fowey Hall is a fantastic location for mum, dad and excitable children, all ready to explore the rugged coastline, preferably with a dog in tow. Welcoming you with an open hearth, gilded gold mirrors and lofty ceilings, Fowey Hall Hotel is all about giving parents a chance to chill out. All the bedrooms in the main house are dog friendly, the largest of which is a suite, allowing a bit more space to relax. Recent renovations have maintained the hotel's elegant feel but now light-panelled walls and mustard and olive tones add a modern twist. Tweed dogs' heads mounted in rooms add a fun element to the crisp design, and in some rooms floor-to-ceiling windows frame the extensive grounds, which are perfect for a game of hide-and-seek. If you fancy a quiet coffee in the library or a soak in the outdoor hot tub, take advantage of 2 hours' complimentary childcare per day; babysitting services are also available. The hotel's favourite dog-friendly walk is to Lantic Bay – a sheltered cove with white sands.

CONTACT Fowey, Cornwall PL23 1ET • 01726 833866 • foweyhallhotel.co.uk
HOW MUCH? Double rooms from £139 a night, dogs £15 a night.

The Gurnard's Head

A short walk inland from one of the most wild sections of the South West Coast Path, The Gurnard's Head is the sort of place where you can kick off your muddy boots by the roaring fire and sip a glass of world-class wine while the dog snoozes at your feet. A glance at the art hanging on the granite walls hints that, despite rustic appearances, this is the sort of place with an eye for the finer things in life. In the downstairs pub there's a menu featuring seasonal, innovative dishes, while upstairs your rooms will have a Vi-spring bed draped with Welsh wool blankets, Roberts radio and shelves stacked with novels to distract you from the moorland views. The briny air, hearty food and comfort levels encourage such a deep sleep that you might not stir until the cows pass to be milked in the morning; but don't stress, breakfast is a lazy affair (home-baked breads, kippers, Full English, local apple juice) and you won't be in a hurry to leave. Dogs are welcome in all rooms, and dog treats are provided at no extra cost. The same people run the excellent Old Coastguard on the south side of Cornwall near Penzance.

CONTACT Near Zennor, St Ives, Cornwall TR26 3DE • 01736 796928 • gurnardshead.co.uk
HOW MUCH? Double rooms £135–£200 a night, no charge for dogs.

The Horn of Plenty

A beautifully located boutique hotel overlooking the lovely Tamar Valley.

Almost bang on the Devon-Cornwall border, high above the Tamar Valley, the Horn of Plenty looks like the house of your richest friend – and if you don't have a pal like that, then you still get to stay in this rather splendid country manor house, enjoying its impeccable service and attention to detail (though you will have to pay!). What's more you can bring your faithful friend too.

Built in 1866, it was the former crib of a local mine-owner, later converted into a restaurant in the 1960s, when its then owner became the first British woman to be awarded a Michelin star. It's now been a hotel for 30 years, and the individually designed guest rooms have more than kept pace with the times. They are spacious and well-equipped, with high-quality beds, sleek bathrooms with all the luxuries you would expect, and sweeping views (most of the rooms have balconies) – indeed the hotel was editor's choice in the 'Good Hotel Guide' for UK 'Rooms with a View' recently, and was one of 'The Times' Top 40 places to stay in Britain last year. The rooms vary in size but all offer Freeview TVs, tea- and coffee-making facilities, bottled water, fresh milk and a minibar, luxury bath robes, hairdryer, TV and wifi. The four rooms in the main house retain their high ceilings, large windows and original fireplaces; the ten rooms in the coach house conversions are pretty stunning spaces with a contemporary country feel.

All of the coach house rooms are dog friendly, with a maximum of two dogs per room, and your dog is welcome in the library but not in the restaurant or drawing room. The hotel offers a 'Bob & Lush' doggie dinner the first night, and a bowl and plentiful treats. There are also five acres of grounds for walkies, as well as loads of walks into the countryside beyond, either in the valley below or further afield to Dartmoor. There's an outside hosepipe back at the hotel for muddy paws and towels are available on request.

The hotel's other facilities include on-site spa treatments and massages, in association with a local Tavistock treatment centre, and afternoon teas served in the restaurant, drawing room, the library or on the patio. The food too is bang up-to-date and is the other star attraction at the Horn of Plenty. You can expect admirably executed and perfectly formed lunch and dinner menus that are full of delicious, original choices, from Creedy Carver duck and Devon roast veal to Brixham monkfish and Dartmoor lamb – and at decent prices too for country-house living: the six-course tasting menu costs around £70 and gets you the chef's best seasonal effort (think venison carpaccio and lobster raviolo), rounded off with some tasty Devonshire cheeses.

CONTACT Gulworthy, Tavistock, Devon PL19 8JD • 01822 832528 • thehornofplenty.co.uk
HOW MUCH? Double rooms £130–£295; with dinner £215–£380, dogs £10 a night.
ROOMS 16 bedrooms, including 4 in the Main House, 6 in the Original Coach House and 6 in the New Coach House.

The Crown & Anchor

Local pubs don't get much better than Ham's Crown & Anchor, situated in a pretty Wiltshire village and welcoming dogs, walkers and cyclists and serving local ales and excellent food. It also has 5 comfy rooms upstairs to collapse into at the end of the evening. These are individually furnished en-suite bedrooms, each equipped with a good quality mattress and bed linen, Freeview TVs, tea- and coffee-making facilities and newly refurbished bathrooms. Downstairs the pub has a short, moderately priced menu that's a perfect blend of local, seasonal and British dishes. Dogs are welcome everywhere – the bar, restaurant, and all the bedrooms, where a bed, 2 bowls and treats await. Towels are available for a post-muddy walk wipe-down and they have a little nook stocked with help-yourself tea, coffee and post-prandial treats for you and the dog. Finally, the location is well placed for Avebury, Stonehenge, the Vale of Pewsey and the real Downton Abbey, Highclere Castle. It's also a perfect location for enjoying country walks, with 3 long-distance paths nearby.

CONTACT Ham, Wiltshire SN8 3RB • 01488 503040 • crownandanchorham.co.uk
HOW MUCH? Double rooms: midweek from £100 a night, weekends from £120 a night. Dogs £10.

The Sheep on Sheep Street

Situated in the heart of the photogenic Cotswolds town of Stow-on-the-Wold, The Sheep is a restaurant with boutique rooms made up of 3 knocked-together honey-coloured cottages. It has a funky reception area, a large, bright downstairs restaurant that serves excellent food and most importantly 22 comfortable rooms, some of which are dog friendly. About half the guest rooms are located in the main building while the others are divided between 2 separate buildings behind. They all come with king-size beds, TV and wifi and tea- and coffee-making facilities, Nespresso machines and mineral water. There are 3 dog-friendly rooms – 1 Standard and 2 Superior doubles – and the bar and café have dog bowls and treats for canine guests. The restaurant features a long bar and a flickering wood-fired pizza oven, which is not just used to make pizzas but for cooking much of the meat and fish too. There are plenty of dog walks in and around Stow-on-the-Wold – a 40-minute round-trip to Maugersby is particularly recommended.

CONTACT Sheep St, Stow-on-the-Wold, Gloucestershire GL54 1AG • 01451 830344 • thesheepstow.co.uk
HOW MUCH? Double rooms £90–£150 a night, dogs £10 a night.

The White Hart

The small Devon town of Moretonhampstead, right on the edge of Dartmoor, is the perfect location for a dog-friendly coaching inn, and the White Hart doesn't let you down, with dogs staying free in their 20 cosy bedrooms and made very comfortable in their public areas as well. The rooms here are all different and have been updated fairly recently, with flatscreen TVs, tea- and coffee-making facilities and en-suite bathrooms with baths and showers. Dogs aren't allowed in the restaurant but the same menu is served in the cosy bar, where there's a roaring fire for dogs to lie in front of after a long day's walkies and a selection of local ales for their thirsty owners. The menu is perfectly pitched at weary walkers: short and sweet and very local, with Dartmoor beef, lamb and venison and local fish alongside pub classics. Moretonhampstead itself is very much the gateway to Dartmoor, with countless footpaths to explore: try the recently opened 'Wray Valley Trail', which follows an old train line for 6.5 miles from Moretonhampstead to Newton Abbot, via the impossibly picturesque Dartmoor village of Lustleigh.

CONTACT The Square, Moretonhampstead, Devon
TQ13 8NQ • 01647 440500 • whitehartdartmoor.co.uk
HOW MUCH? Double rooms from around £110 a night, dogs free.

The Elephant's Nest Inn

First up this is a lovely old pub in a great location. Originally a 16th-century hostelry, it's the sort of place where you can settle down with a pint and easily overlook their 3 very comfortable bedrooms in a separate extension. However, after a stroll across the moor and a meal in the downstairs bar, these can be a very welcome sight indeed. In fact, the Elephant's Nest is a great location for exploring Dartmoor, in particular on foot, with all sorts of enticing walking routes that you can follow from its doorstep. Of course, no walk is really complete without a dog, and the good news is this is a very dog-friendly place, with 2 dogs of its own and a very warm welcome to yours, both in the rooms and the pub, which serves great food from breakfast through to dinner. Each of the rooms is different but all have en-suite bathrooms and are big enough for 2 people. They also all have Vi-spring beds with goosedown duvets, flatscreen TVs and digital radios and free wifi throughout, as well as tea- and coffee-making facilities and a fridge.

CONTACT Horndon, Mary Tavy, Devon
PL19 9NQ • 01822 810273 • elephantsnest.co.uk
HOW MUCH? Double rooms £87.50–£97.50 a night, including breakfast, dogs £5 a night.

Moonfleet Manor

One of the finest family hotels in the Southwest, Moonfleet Manor enjoys a spectacular location right on the Fleet Lagoon, west of Weymouth on the Dorset coast. It's worth coming here for the location alone – there's direct access to the glorious coastal path, which hugs the lagoon, and beautiful views out to sea on clear days. But there are lots of other things to love about this Georgian manor house. Beyond its various bedrooms in the main house – all tastefully decorated and some sleeping up to 6 people – there's also a spa, a huge games room for the kids, and even a crèche (free for 2 hours a day). Afternoons can be spent playing indoor football, air hockey or bouncing on trampolines, or you can swim in one of 3 heated indoor pools. There's an escape room suitable for all the family, tennis courts and lessons available, and a soft play area and outdoor sandpit for your youngest members. And dogs are welcome in most guest rooms and on leads in the lounge areas and outdoor spaces. The 11-year-old house dog, working cocker Snoopy, roams free throughout and will happily share his water bowls.

CONTACT Fleet Rd, Weymouth, Dorset DT3 4ED • 01305 786948 • moonfleetmanorhotel.co.uk
HOW MUCH? Most of the larger rooms are dog-friendly and start from £120 a night. Dogs £15 a night.

Merchants Manor

Well situated high on a hill on the edge of central Falmouth, this hotel is one of the best – and best-value – places in town. Formerly the Green Lawns guest house, it was bought a couple of years ago by Nick and Sioned Parry-Rudlin who have developed not only a stunningly designed boutique hotel, but one with a praiseworthy restaurant and opulent spa. An Edwardian building at heart, the hotel also has a newer wing, and its 39 rooms are split between the two. All come with free wifi, flatscreen TVs, a welcome tray and luxury toiletries. Five of the rooms are dog-friendly, and there's also a gym, spa and a heated indoor pool. The sub-tropical garden is lovely for a stroll before the short walk into town and to let the pup stretch its legs. The Rastella restaurant is fantastic but sadly not open to furry friends, who will have to eat with you in the comfort of your room or try the menu in the bar, where they serve steak sandwiches, cheese and charcuterie sharing boards and lovely cream teas. A welcoming Cornish home-from-home.

CONTACT 1 Western Terrace, Falmouth, Cornwall TR11 4QJ • 01326 312734 • merchantsmanor.com
HOW MUCH? Double rooms from £120 a night, dogs £12 a night.

Mount Haven Hotel

Beyond the narrow lanes of Marazion, the Mount Haven is a smart yet unpretentious hotel and restaurant for all occasions, from a romantic holiday to a pit stop along the South West Coast Path. The main lounge and bar are smart and spacious, and from here you and your furry friend can enjoy the views over St Michael's Mount. Rooms are comfortable and have all the amenities you might need, and the 3 dog-friendly Garden Haven rooms have a few extra doggie treats included. Everything in the rooms is local, from striking photography to handmade bed frames; even the coasters are from a local artisan. Each of these rooms opens up onto a shared patio garden, sheltered from the prevailing winds. Access to the beach through the village takes you onto the South West Coast Path. The restaurant serves up tasty original dishes, but is unfortunately out of bounds to even well-behaved doggies, who must be left in your room while you eat. But if you're worried that they'll jump up and nestle into your plush duvet, don't fret: you can also eat from the main menu with your dog in the upstairs lounge.

CONTACT Marazion, Near Penzance, Cornwall
TR17 0DQ • 01736 719937 • mounthaven.co.uk
HOW MUCH? Double rooms from £150 a night (room-only), dogs £15 a night.

Weeke Barton

Weeke Barton is the ultimate escape from the big city, since that's exactly what its owners, Sam and Jo, did several years ago, when they threw it all in and moved down here from east London. It's a long way from Hackney, for sure, a big, thick-walled stone longhouse that's home to a studied naturalness that almost enforces relaxation – stylishly decorated rooms with big comfy beds and natural stone en-suite bathrooms with posh toiletries; a lounge with squishy sofas and magazines; a cosy snug with honesty bar; and a dining room with a big slate table at which they serve a civilised-hours breakfast and an excellent home-cooked dinner on request. The property is also set in its own grounds so there is plenty of room to properly relax and enjoy the amazing night skies. There is free wifi and Sonos music systems, but interestingly no TV reception – just flatscreen TVs on which you can watch a choice of DVDs from their extensive library. Dogs are welcome in all rooms if you can manage to keep them off the beds, and there's a dog-friendly local pub that does decent food.

CONTACT Dunsford, Dartmoor, Devon EX6 7HH •
01647 253505 • weekebarton.com
HOW MUCH? Double rooms £125–£145 a night, dogs £15 a night.

Devon Yurt and Granary B&B

Two pristine yurts, rolling Dartmoor views and a romantic farmhouse B&B.

Less is more at Borough Farm, which is home to an award-winning glamping site and B&B on the edge of Dartmoor. It's a perfect, natural spot in glorious countryside, with two yurts set in 18 pristine acres of prime farmland on the Devon side of the lush Tamar Valley and a one-bed B&B in a converted granary in the centre of the farm. For families, especially those with pets, it really couldn't be better: there are footpaths leading off in all directions; children are encouraged to seek out and pet the farm animals, and dogs are welcome everywhere – and provided with a bowl and towel, food and treats to make them feel at home. The owners also provide a customised map showing all the nearby walking routes, including the best dog-friendly pubs along the way, and have details of a local 'doggy day care service' for your canine chum in case you fancy striking out on your own.

Situated on the northwestern fringe of Dartmoor, the views from both yurts (named Little Links and Great Links) are stunning, and they both have their own private paddock and freshwater wood-fired hot tub to enjoy them from. Inside, each has a wood-burning stove, rugs and sheepskins to keep you warm, beds are made up with crisp cotton linen, and they also have their own loo, sink and kitchen, which is helpfully stocked with tea, coffee, sugar, milk, condiments and olive oil. Those features aside, the two yurts are quite different from each other. Great Links, as you might expect, is the larger of the two, situated in an elevated meadow a short walk along a solar-lit path from the shower barn facilities. Little Links is smaller and better suited for a couple or those with younger children, with a romantic wood-fired roll-top bath just a few footsteps away, and also located closer to the showers, refrigeration and washing and drying facilities.

If glamping isn't for you then try The Granary B&B instead – a gorgeous first-floor barn conversion that can sleep two people in a big bright and airy room in gloriously romantic comfort. It's basically one big space, again with spectacular views across Dartmoor. Inside, there are exposed oak beams and a French antique bed and double-ended roll-top bath. Next door the vast space of the communal Loft has tables and chairs, wifi, a fridge, kettle and toaster and games and books for rainy days. You can have a coffee or a glass of wine, plan your day, play games on rainy days or just lounge about. Should you wish, you can even have a massage treatment in here or try a spot of yoga. Breakfast, also, is a delicious affair, with eggs direct from the farm's lovely hens, award-winning local sourdough bread, local apple juice and fruits from the garden.

CONTACT Borough Farm, Kelly, Lifton, Devon PL16 0HJ • 01822 870366 • devonyurt.co.uk

HOW MUCH? Yurt £135–£165 per night Friday and Saturday, £575–£870 per week (only weekly bookings taken in peak season), midweek breaks from £295 for 3 nights. B&B rates from £85 a night for 2 people, including a continental breakfast (for a small surcharge they serve a delicious Full English, and pancakes on Sundays). Dogs xxx per stay.

ACCOMMODATION One double room barn conversion with a double bed, plus two yurts.

Stein's at Trevone Farm

Just outside Padstow in the village of Trevone, these 3 properties have been individually converted and designed by Jill Stein and are part of the Stein self-catering property portfolio. As such, they make a fabulous and very comfortable place to stay: with 3 bedrooms and sleeping 6 guests, they're all dog friendly, well equipped with wifi, TVs, DVDs and all the usual kitchen facilities, as well as an outdoor shower, furniture and parking – plus a welcome hamper on arrival. There's a wood-burning stove for cold evenings and lots of games, books and DVDs for when the weather is disappointing. We reckon the location is as good as it gets in north Cornwall, just a few minutes' walk from partially dog friendly Trevone beach – two beaches in reality, one with broad sands sandwiched between sheltering rocks, the other with rock pools and a natural swimming pool at low tide. Trevone itself is an appealing village and there are lovely walks along the cliffs both to Padstow a couple of miles away, and to Trevose Head in the opposite direction.

CONTACT Trevone Farm, Trevone, Padstow, Cornwall
PL28 8QN • 01841 532700 • rickstein.com
HOW MUCH? 3 nights £555–£1017, 4 nights
£659–£1121, 7 nights £882–£2555. Dogs £30.

Moreton House

This beautiful Grade II-listed Georgian mansion close to the north Devon coast is a very special place to stay, family owned and newly refurbished into a series of luxurious holiday apartments that are among the most comfortable and best equipped self-catering options in this part of Devon. The apartments are perfect for families and their dogs, who can frolic in the 5 acres of grounds. They have smart TVs, wifi, digital radios and DVD players and a couple have wood-burning stoves for cosy evenings in; the ground-floor apartments also have their own private outdoor seating area, with a BBQ for when the weather plays ball. Otherwise the grounds have a gazebo, firepit and campfire circle, play areas and swings, croquet and other garden games. There are also bikes/golf clubs/beach kits to borrow and there's a great family (and partially dog friendly) beach a mile away at Westward Ho!, plus it is also very near the Tarka Trail cycle route, which you can follow all the way to the beaches at Instow and beyond.

CONTACT Abbotsham Road, Bideford, Devon
EX39 3QW • 01237 425519 • moretonhousedevon.com
HOW MUCH? Two-bedroom apartments from £900 a week. Shorter stays also available.

Valley Cottages

Set amid 13 acres of gardens, with its own outdoor pool and lots of other facilities, The Valley feels like it's in the middle of nowhere, yet you're right outside Falmouth and within easy striking distance of loads of other places in Cornwall. It's the perfect place to stay with young children – a large complex of mostly 2- and 3-bedroom self-catering cottage properties in all manner of styles, all ultra-clean, nicely furnished and well equipped with kitchens with all mod cons, free wifi and lots of books and games. A dozen cottages are dog friendly – at least 2 for each type of cottage – and you get a bed, blanket, bowl, a complimentary treat pack from 'Bob & Lush' and a tennis ball. They have a designated area for dogs to run on-site, and they also include details of all the dog walks that you can do right from your door as well as dog-friendly places to eat, drink and visit. The complex itself encompasses a fab restaurant, two swimming pools (one outdoor, one indoor), a spa with fitness facilities and tennis and squash courts – all in a lovely peaceful location.

CONTACT Bissoe Rd, Carnon Downs, Truro, Cornwall TR3 6LQ • 01872 862194 • thevalleycornwall.co.uk
HOW MUCH? From £1495 a week; off-peak from £525 a week, short breaks from £365, dogs £20 a week.

Tistocker's Cabin

Situated in a tranquil location on the Somerset-Dorset border, this log cabin ticks a lot of boxes: it's well equipped and cosy enough for the whole year, and not only welcomes people with dogs but is set within 3 acres of its own grounds for fun and frolics. You're supplied with a bed, crate and bowls if required, and there's a hose for washing muddy paws and an external kennel and run if required. The cabin has the sort of rustic features you would expect, combined with exposed steel, cool lighting and other contemporary touches and funky furnishings: there is an open-plan living room and well-equipped kitchen, a comfy sofa and TV, a wood-burning stove for cosy nights in and a separate bedroom with an en-suite shower room. Outside, you can sit on the decked terrace and enjoy the country views while sipping a glass of wine or cooking dinner on the BBQ, and there are 2 bikes for guest-use. There's even a dog-friendly pub within walking distance and lots to do in the surrounding area if you want to explore properly.

CONTACT Hardington Mandeville, Yeovil, Somerset BA22 9PS • 07880 771094 • tistockerscabin.co.uk
HOW MUCH? From £85 a night – minimum 2-night stay.

Cary Arms & Spa

Perhaps the perfect Devon seaside inn, updated as a sumptuous boutique hotel for the 21st century.

Tucked away on scenic Babbacombe Bay, Cary Arms couldn't have asked for a much better location. Perched delicately on the rocks above the pebble beach, at the bottom of a slightly hair-raising descent down a single-track road, this is a seaside inn to die for, brilliantly combining traditional Devon delights with all the style and comfort you expect from a contemporary boutique hotel.

The sister hotel of another West Country favourite of ours, The Eastbury in Sherbourne, the Cary Arms has just ten rooms and suites, plus four restored fisherman's cottages with two-to-three bedrooms each and eight quirky huts for two people down on the beach. The hotel was famously visited by Queen Victoria and Prince Albert, who were apparently rowed ashore here for a cream tea when visiting Torquay, and it remains at heart a coastal inn but with an up-to-date feel that is more New England than the English Riviera. The eight rooms and two suites all have fabulous sea views and their own terraces, along with king-size beds with good-quality linen, smart TVs, tea- and coffee-making facilities, complimentary bottled water and a decanter of sloe gin, and White Company toiletries and waffle bathrobes in the en-suite bathrooms. Two of the ground-floor rooms welcome dogs, as do three of the four cottages, which are a great alternative for couples seeking a bit more privacy, or families. Dogs are also welcome in two of the beach huts and one of the beach suites, right at the water's edge.

You may be reluctant to leave your little capsule of comfort down by the sea, and you could quite happily spend a few days here, pottering around

on the beach, having a pint or two of local ale in the beamed dog-friendly bar while you watch the sunset, or eating in the hotel's excellent restaurant, which serves good simple gastropub food centred on local beef and lamb and the freshest fish and seafood; it's moderately priced. There is a comfy lounge and billiard room, and a spa with a gym, steam room, sauna, waterfall hydrotherapy pool, showers with a soundtrack of tropical birdsong and of course the usual treatments. There's also a decked sun terrace with an outdoor fire and boxes of blankets for winter days.

It is worth leaving occasionally, if only to experience the 1920s funicular railway that takes you up to Babbacombe proper – best known for its model village, which remains one of the area's best-known attractions. Beyond, you can explore the nearby bays of Oddicombe and Petitor Downs, which are connected by footpath. The Petitor cliffs are the source of Torquay's extraordinary marble pavements, while the waters off Oddicombe are a haven for divers who come here to explore the reedy shallows and various nearby wrecks. All in all a very special place for a short break by the sea.

CONTACT Babbacombe Beach, Devon TQ1 3LX • 01803 327110 • caryarms.co.uk
HOW MUCH? Double rooms £245 a night, beach huts from £389, cottages from £495. Dogs £20.
ROOMS Ten guest rooms and suites in the main building, plus 4 2–4-bed cottages, 6 beach huts and 2 beach suites.

Smuggler's Cove Cottages

Midway between St Ives and Newquay, the evocatively named Smuggler's Cove Cottages are the sorts of places you dream of finding in Cornwall – two architect-designed properties, each sleeping 8 people in comfort, perched just above the waves at the end of a fabulous sandy beach. The lower of the two, Beachside Cottage has 4 double bedrooms and a spacious outside terrace overlooking the beach, equipped with an outdoor shower, sun loungers and a large dining table for al fresco evening meals. The second property, Clifftop Cottage, is built into the cliff above, again with 4 double bedrooms and a 70m balcony right around the property with a dining table, sunbeds and sunshades, plus an outside shower for rinsing off after the beach. Dogs are welcome in both properties, as long as they stay downstairs, and beds, bowls and blankets are provided on request. Sadly, Portreath beach is only dog friendly early morning and after 7pm in summer, but beaches in either direction along the coast – notably Mexico Towans and Watergate Bay – welcome dogs all day all year long.

CONTACT Portreath, Cornwall TR16 4NS •
07768 602498 • smugglerscovecottages.com
HOW MUCH? From £995 to £4495 a week. depending on the time of year. Dogs £30 a week (maximum of 2).

YHA Street

Opened in 1931, this cute Swiss-style chalet is the oldest YHA hostel in operation and enjoys a brilliant Somerset location, close to Glastonbury, Wookey Hole Caves and superb walking and cycling through nearby National Trust land. The hostel has recently been completely refurbished and has accommodation ranging from a mixture of private and dorm rooms to dog-friendly bell tents and a variety of dog-friendly glamping pods – some of which even come with roofs that open for star-gazing. The pods have LED lighting, comfy beds and a table and bench outside for al fresco dining. You can also pitch your own tent if you have one, and in the hostel itself there are communal toilets and bathrooms and an open-plan kitchen/diner to prepare your own food. Nearby, it's possible to walk to Glastonbury Tor, a dog-friendly landmark that is worth the climb for the view alone. Not only that: the hostel is also paw-fectly positioned for memorable walkies in the surrounding Mendip Hills and Somerset Levels.

CONTACT The Chalet, Ivythorn Hill, Street, Somerset BA16 0TZ • 0345 3719143 • yha.org.uk
HOW MUCH? Dorm beds from £13 a night, private rooms from £29 a night, pods from £49 a night.

The Atlantic Hotel

Lots of hotels advertise rooms with sea views but very few offer a view of the sea from every room. The Atlantic Hotel is well named, perched on a headland halfway between the centre of Newquay and Fistral beach. It's a large hotel, with 2 pools and a spa, and a sense of old-fashioned glamour that might just be what you came to Newquay for in the first place. They've done a good job of updating, winning 'Luxury Hotel of the Year' 2016 and 2018, and have 57 light and generously proportioned rooms with large beds, flatscreen TVs, decent-sized bathrooms with toiletries, bath robes and slippers and tea- and coffee-making facilities and minibars. Some have their own terraces, while others are in a separate building positioned to take full advantage of the pool facilities. Dogs are welcome throughout and will have a goody bag waiting for them when they arrive and a bed and bowl in their room; they also get extra fuss made of them in the Café Atlantica, where you can enjoy lunch or dinner together after a day on dog-friendly Towan, Tolcarne, Lusty Glaze and Porth beaches below.

CONTACT Dane Road Newquay Cornwall TR7 1EN • 01637 872244• atlantichotelnewquay.co.uk
HOW MUCH? Doubles with breakfast from £135 a night. Dogs £20 a night.

The Seafood Restaurant

Padstow's Seafood Restaurant is the flagship restaurant of Rick and Jill Stein, and as such you would expect it to be pretty good, but we recommend it for what may seem to be two rather obvious reasons. First of all it does great-value packages which include at least one meal in the downstairs restaurant. The other thing is that the views from the majority of the rooms are wonderful, which makes this as stunning a place to stay in Padstow as you will find. Service is excellent, too, and breakfast as delicious as you would expect, whether you enjoy a hearty breakfast downstairs (with lots of fresh fish options available) or the continental option in your room. The rooms are bright and cheerful with a definite seaside feel, all have lovely bathrooms with luxurious toiletries and towels, and come equipped with milk, tea- and coffee-making facilities, biscuits and a mini bar; and some also have their own terraces from which to enjoy those sea views all the more. Dogs are welcome – and they even provide a dog-sitting service if required.

CONTACT Riverside, Padstow, Cornwall PL28 8BY • 01841 532700 • rickstein.com
HOW MUCH? Double rooms from £165 to £320 a night. Dogs £30 for first night, £5 a night thereafter.

Hotel Endsleigh

Situated right on the border between Devon and Cornwall in the glorious Tamar Valley, this fairy-tale hotel is the country cousin of the excellent Tresanton in Cornwall, both of which are owned by the renowned designer and hotelier, Olga Polizzi. Occupying a 19th-century hunting lodge, the hotel's grounds cover 100 picture-perfect acres of formal gardens, streams, woodlands, follies and grottoes. Inside, the hotel has the feel of the country residence of your richest and most stylish aunt, with 19 rooms and suites artfully and individually decorated with a stylish mix of old and new pieces, wooden floors, roll-top baths and book-lined shelves. All are dog friendly, with a bed, towel, treats and bowl provided, and you will want to get out and explore the numerous footpaths that meander through the grounds with your dog. It's a lovely place to return to after a hard day's yomping through the woods, with a cosy lounge and a restaurant that serves very good, well-priced and unpretentious food – just what you need after a day in the Great Outdoors.

CONTACT Milton Abbot, Devon PL19 0PQ •
01822 870000 • hotelendsleigh.com
HOW MUCH? Classic rooms £190–£265 a night,
Repton and Bedford rooms £250–£330. Dogs £20.

The Scarlet

Almost exactly half-way between Padstow and Newquay, by Mawgan Porth beach in a pretty, lesser-known bay, The Scarlet hotel is a sustainably minded, adults-only, pet-friendly hotel that features all sorts of wow-factor features – designer rooms, clifftop hot tubs, a solar-heated pool, a state-of-the-art spa and a swanky restaurant serving only the freshest local produce. Huge glass windows let in the glowing evening sunlight, illuminating the restaurant and lounge. Nestled just below its family-friendly counterpart, the Bedruthan, it's equally accessible from the beach or coastal path. The serene interior combines open spaces and fireplaces with a dog-friendly lounge with wonderful sea views, and its dog-friendly rooms come with eating and drinking bowls, a blanket, poo bags and homemade doggie treats. One of the most outstanding features is the hotel's spa, where there is a pool, a hammam and private, cushioned pods in a dune garden overlooking the ocean. Later, try the seasonal menu in the restaurant or the vegan tasting menu, with accompanying vegan wines.

CONTACT Tredragon Road, Mawgan Porth, Cornwall
TR8 4DQ • 01627 861800 • scarlethotel.co.uk
HOW MUCH? Double rooms around £230 a night, dogs
£15 a night.

Bedruthan Hotel & Spa

The Bedruthan Hotel has over the years become as much a foodie destination as a place to stay, but above all it's a very comfortable dog-friendly hotel – great for families, couples and groups of adults with or without dogs in tow. There are 5 rooms dedicated just to families with dogs, plenty of public spaces that are open to dogs and the dog-friendly sandy beaches of Bedruthan Steps and Mawgan Porth, not to mention the Coast Path, are all nearby. For tiny tots there's indoor soft play and an adventure playground, plus kids' clubs, so fraught parents get time out for some pampering in the hotel's spa and pool, from where you can enjoy memorable sea views. During school holidays there's entertainment across the board, from crafts to cookery. The guest rooms are all comfy and contemporary, and many have sea views, and there are 2 restaurants, one of which – the Wild Café – is perfect for families and everyday food and lunches, while the other – The Herring – is a more sophisticated seafood restaurant, serving higher-end, grown-up fare that earned it the title of Cornwall's 'restaurant of the year' a few years ago.

CONTACT Mawgan Porth, Cornwall TR8 4BU •
01637 861200 • bedruthan.com
HOW MUCH? Double rooms from £145 a night, dogs
£15 a night.

St Enodoc Hotel

Set in spacious grounds overlooking the Camel estuary, the St Enodoc is a real delight, with 20 rooms and suites that are bright, modern and cosy, many with far-reaching sea views. There's a spa, beach life right on the doorstep, one of Cornwall's best hotel restaurants, and dogs are accepted in almost half of the rooms, with beds, bowls and treats provided. It's a relaxed, chic sort of place, with slate floors and bright, contemporary fabrics, and a calm, almost Mediterranean vibe, with a lovely lounge area with a wood-burning stove. There are 16 double rooms and 4 suites, all bright and light and stylishly decorated; quite a lot have sea views and they all boast big comfy beds, tea- and coffee-making facilities, bottled water and fresh milk. There's satellite TV and wifi, the hotel spa offers a range of treatments, plus there's an outdoor pool and games room. The beach is a stone's throw from the hotel, and dogs are allowed on Porthkilly, Rock and Daymer beaches all year round. You can also explore the Coast Path or follow the Camel Trail all the way to Bodmin.

CONTACT Rock, Cornwall PL27 6LA • 0 1208 863394 •
enodoc-hotel.co.uk
HOW MUCH? Double rooms from £170 a night, £200
for a sea view, dogs £15 a night, additional dogs £7.50.

Soar Mill Cove Hotel

A fabulous hotel in a gorgeous part of the South Hams with stunning views down to its own cove.

This South Hams seaside hotel has been owned by the Makepeace family for three generations, and the welcome is warm and the service and hospitality genuine and traditional. But there's nothing old-school about the Soar Mill itself, whose rooms are well furnished and thoughtfully equipped, with big bathrooms, free wifi, books and games, and even binoculars for enjoying the spectacular views (and maybe spotting a dolphin or two). You can almost hear the waves, and the glorious coastline is just a step or two away.

It's no surprise, either, that the hotel was recently declared one of the Top Ten Dog Friendly Hotels in Devon by a national newspaper. Four-legged guests receive a share of the hand-made treats that are enjoyed by the hotel's own Labradors, Daisy and Farley, bed and blankets are provided on request, and there is also an outside wash spot with warm water for cleaning muddy paws. The beach is dog friendly as long as you clear up after your hound (there are two bins) and dogs are allowed in the reception, bar and café (but not the restaurant).

Accommodation is spread across several options – all with beautiful views across the rolling hills or down to the cove. Some larger rooms and suites are ideal for families, while those looking for a little more privacy can stay in one of the self-catering retreats. All but one of the 22 rooms are dog friendly, with direct access to the gardens, as well as three of their self-catering properties. As well as walks and beach-lounging and swimming, there are lots of activities right on hand – a decent indoor heated, spring-fed, saltwater swimming pool and a spa and gym, while there's also tennis in the grounds and a games room with snooker and table tennis. Soar Mill has an award-winning restaurant that offers a seasonal menu full of locally caught seafood and fresh Devonshire delights which you can enjoy from tables overlooking the bay. They say it's where 'fine dining meets family friendly' and what's certain is the chef is all about local sourcing and ingredients (you have to try his delicious pastries and treats), while the Castaways Café is ideal for younger guests to kick back and relax.

But really the beauty of Soar Mill Cove lies in its position, just outside Salcombe in a gorgeous part of the South Hams; it's right on the Southwest Coast Path and in a perfect location for great walks throughout this beautiful part of Devon. The beach at Soar Mill Cove is dog friendly year-round, as are those at nearby Thurlestone and South Milton Sands. What else? Well, the nice thing is that if (heaven forbid) anything's amiss, you can talk to the owners themselves – something we think is pretty special these days, rather like the hotel itself.

CONTACT Near Salcombe, Devon TQ7 3DS • 01548 561566 • soarmillcove.co.uk

HOW MUCH? Double rooms £159–284; family rooms and suites £209–389. Self-catering from £950 per week. Dogs £15 a night.

ROOMS Choice of country-view or cove-view double/twin and family rooms, plus extended family suites and one 'Hideaway' room with its own private balcony.

Mullion Cove Hotel

Purpose-built as a hotel at the turn of the century, the Mullion Cove Hotel looks every inch the Edwardian resort – and in many ways it hasn't changed since the days when visitors travelled here by rail to enjoy the bracing air of the Lizard Peninsula and its glorious coast. Perched on the cliffs above rocky Mullion harbour and cove, it's one of Cornwall's most romantic hotels, with cosy public rooms that are great for lazing around in with your loved one, doing nothing in particular. It's also had a thorough makeover since the old days and offers a proper 21st-century hotel experience, with an excellent restaurant and well-equipped guest rooms, and a set of brand-new luxury apartments nearby if you'd rather self-cater. The hotel is dog friendly, with a special dog-friendly lounge for you to relax in together, or you can have your dog by your side while you dine and enjoy the view. Dogs also get their own welcome pack and there's no additional charge for dogs during low season. Be sure to check out the many local walks, and of course the nearby beaches, some of which allow dogs all year round.

CONTACT Mullion Cove, Lizard Peninsula, Cornwall TR12 7EP • 01326 240328 • mullion-cove.co.uk
HOW MUCH? Double rooms £100–£185 a night. Dogs £9 a night or free in low season.

Symonds Yat Rock Lodge

Set in the Wye Valley Area of Outstanding Natural Beauty, it's hard to imagine a better place for a dog-friendly break than these 6 stylish self-catering apartments, which look out over the Wye Valley in one direction and the Forest of Dean in the other – and sit under the darkest of dark skies. Each sleeps 2 people and you can walk straight into the Forest Of Dean from your front door. The apartments are open-plan, contemporary and comfortable, with spacious living areas and fully fitted kitchens; all have Freeview TVs, CD and DVD players and wifi, and wood-burners for cosy nights in. There's a communal garden where you can light up a BBQ, take in the stunning views or pick herbs and fruit. Symonds Yat Rock viewpoint is just a mile away, you can walk or cycle the Peregrine Path, the 7-mile 'Dog and Muffler' or the 3-mile 'Highmeadow Woods' – or just take a canoe down the Wye. There are also plenty of dog-friendly pubs nearby, for example the New Inn, which is just a mile's stroll through the forest. Then it's back to Rock Lodge for some star-gazing.

CONTACT Hillersland, Coleford, Gloucestershire GL16 7NY • 01600 773220 • rocklodge.co.uk
HOW MUCH? Two-night stays £160–250; additional nights £40–80.

Gooseford Farm

A small working farm set smack bang on Dartmoor's north side, this 16th-century farmhouse B&B is all about the old beams, wonky floors and comfy beds. There's wifi throughout but you'll soon be distracted by the views, the cows, or the farm Jack Russell who sleeps in the tractor. Visitors are welcome to watch the cows being milked at 4pm each day, and if you want to walk them back to their pasture that's okay too. The B&B has 4 rooms, and although dogs aren't strictly allowed in them, they are welcome to sleep downstairs in their own beds or on a special doggy sofa. Dogs are also welcome in the apartment next door, which has a small self-contained garden at the back. Blankets are available, and if you forget their food your host Mary will always rustle something up. Speaking of food, there is tea and homemade cake if you arrive in the afternoon and breakfasts are outstanding. Mary makes bread daily, there's homemade jam, and milk and honey from the farm. No surprise, then, that they won Channel 4's 'Four in a Bed'!

CONTACT Gooseford, Whiddon Down, Devon EX20 2QQ • 07929 627717 • goosefordfarm.co.uk
HOW MUCH? Double rooms from £85, cottage from £90 a night for 2. Dogs £6–£10 a night.

Byron Apartments

Byron's boutique beachside apartments tick all the boxes you need for a perfect seaside holiday. They're 150m from the beach, come in a range of sizes and have lots of facilities – parking, a heated pool, gym, sauna and games room, and many of them accept pets. Around half have sea views and most have balconies or private patios to enjoy them from, while décor-wise they are furnished in a crisp contemporary style, with well-equipped kitchens, open-plan living/dining rooms with floor-to-ceiling windows, good wifi, smart TVs and washing machines. Each apartment also has its own 'surf shed' so you can leave your stuff on the beach. The block has its own restaurant too, Brundle's – a bonus in a village not exactly inundated with good places to eat. Finally there's the beach, which provides reason enough to stay – either Woolacombe's huge main beach, the rocky cove of Barricane Beach to the right, which has a tremendous beach café, or Putsborough Beach, at the far end of Woolacombe's strand, which also has a good café.

CONTACT Beach Road, Woolacombe, Devon EX34 7BS • 01271 871643 • byronwoolacombeholidaylets.co.uk
HOW MUCH? 2-person apartments £425–£950 a week, 4-person £500–£1700, 6-person £725–£1900.

OUT AND ABOUT

Four great walks with your dog

HOLNICOTE ESTATE This beautiful short walk delivers great views across National Trust's Holnicote Estate in Exmoor, starting at Webber's Post carpark and heading along moorland and back down through the wooded valley. In all, the Holnicote Estate has some 150 miles of footpaths and bridleways to explore, and this modest walk makes a great introduction to Exmoor's unique landscape. **2.6 MILES**

HOLYWELL & CRANTOCK BEACH Treat your dog to a trio of North Cornish beaches, with golden sands and towering dunes to explore on this unforgettable circular stroll. Start at the village of Holywell and follow the beach with the coastline on your left, walking around Kelsey Head to the brilliantly named Porth Joke beach. Continue on the South West Coast Path towards Pentire Point West, with stunning views, and on to Crantock Beach. **5.2 MILES**

THE LIZARD This walk explores the southern tip of The Lizard Peninsula, taking in the coves and rocks of the coast and pretty inland villages. Pirates and shipwrecks are part of local lore, and you can spot dolphins, porpoises and whales out to sea. It makes for a lovely day's walking – not too difficult but with the odd steep stretch. **12 MILES**

PADSTOW TO GUNVER HEAD This spectacular circuit takes you through sweeping countryside, over wild cliffs and along the banks of the Camel Estuary. From the quayside head through Chapel Stile field and follow the footpath, cutting diagonally through farmland to the coast at Gunver Head. Trace the coastline back past Butter Hole and the collapsed sea cave of the Pepper Hole until you veer back into the mouth of the estuary. **5 MILES**

THE OUTDOOR GUIDE

Talland Bay Hotel

A luxurious dog-friendly hotel tucked into an idyllic bay between Looe and Polperro.

Slap on the South West Coast Path, the Talland Bay Hotel reckons it's Cornwall's most dog-friendly hotel, and with good reason. It's deliberately relaxed when it comes to canine companions, and aims to be as welcoming to four-legged guests as it is to humans: all the guest rooms except for one are dog friendly, and dogs are provided with welcome packs that include bowls and a blanket and their own stock of handmade treats. For humans, too, the Talland Bay Hotel is all about pure relaxation. Forget the trappings of spa treatments, indoor pools and sports facilities – here the focus is on glorious sea views, sub-tropical gardens, fine Cornish cuisine and lounging around in a quirky but luxurious environment, furnished in a distinctive and at times slightly crazy fashion, with an oddity around every corner.

The rooms and suites are spacious and have been individually decorated, and there's an airy seaside feel throughout, with a roll-top bath in one, a sleigh bed in another. Many also have gorgeous sea views as well as direct access to a patio, terrace or garden.

The hotel reception has bowls with water for thirsty dogs, and towels for muddy ones. It also has a pretty big collection of local and international artwork, both in the rooms and public areas and dotted around the gardens. The hotel has two restaurants serving the same 2-A-rosette menu, and dogs are welcome to eat with their owners in the sea-view conservatory or on the terrace; they're offered a sausage for breakfast and chicken for dinner. There's a very comfy bar too, which, like the rest of the hotel's public spaces, is dog friendly.

The hotel's staff also have lots of recommendations for places to eat and drink nearby – and places to visit, too – that are dog friendly, and plenty of printouts of the best dog walks.

Just as well: this is prime territory for strolling with your faithful hound, a short walk away from glistening Talland Bay, which has a lovely beach that is dog friendly all year round. From here the South West Coast Path runs west to Polperro (2 miles away), where dogs are also welcome year-round, and east to Looe (3.5 miles away) where there are more dog-friendly beaches. Also close by are the Cornish harbour town of Fowey and the Eden Project.

Sweeping up a grand tally of awards, including 'Best Small Hotel in Cornwall' a few years ago, and 'Best South West Restaurant' in 2017, this former family home proves that location, style and cuisine are all you need to relax and embrace the natural beauty and lifestyle this part of the world offers. They really get it that dogs are properly part of any family, but to be honest the fab clifftop location and ocean backdrop are fabulous whether you have a dog or not. Cornish hospitality at its best.

CONTACT Porthallow, Cornwall PL13 2JB • 01503 272667• tallandbayhotel.co.uk
HOW MUCH? Double rooms £160–£250; £240–£330 including dinner. Dogs £20 per stay.
ROOMS 19 rooms and 4 suites, nearly all dog friendly.

The Inn at Fossebridge

As you enter the Fossebridge Inn you are likely to be welcomed by Gibson, the resident black Labrador who is a much-loved local institution with his own Facebook page and annual birthday party. It's clear that Gibson sets the tone here, and there are dog treats and water bowls in the bar and in the extensive grounds, which are over 4 acres in size and contain a lake and a section of the River Coln. In winter, log fires in the restaurant are cosy and in summer up to 200 people can be found dining alfresco from the extensive menu; particularly popular are the Inn's range of pies (try the roast shin of beef or Breton chicken pies) and there is a good choice of vegetarian and vegan options. The pub is conveniently situated on the ancient Fosse Way and well placed for visiting Cirencester and Cheltenham, and just up the road is the National Trust's Chedworth Roman villa, one of the grandest Roman dwellings in the country. The Inn's 9 rooms are all dog friendly, and they can provide local walking maps too, with a 2-mile circular trip from the Inn particularly popular.

CONTACT Stow Rd, Fossebridge, Gloucestershire GL54 3JS • 01285 720721 innatfossebridge.co.uk
HOW MUCH? Double rooms £95–£135 a night; dogs £15 a night.

The Noel Arms

Situated in one of the most picturesque villages in the Cotwolds Area of Outstanding Natural Beauty, the Noel Arms is steeped in history – it is even said that Charles II stayed here during the Civil War. It's also very dog friendly: all 28 of its guest rooms are dog-friendly, even the 2 with grand four-poster beds, and there are water bowls and dog treats in both the bar and café. The hotel hosts up to 20 dogs at a time and fluffy friends are welcome throughout the hotel and on its terrace, which is a sun-trap in the summer. Its nearby sister property, Cotswold House, has a further 10 dog-friendly rooms and a garden that is ideal for pets. The surrounding countryside is stunning and the hotel provides walking maps for guests – plus the popular 'Cotswold Way' long-distance footpath begins nearby. The hotel is particularly well-known for its Indian food: its chef has been named Best Curry Chef at the Great British Pub awards on 3 occasions and his Curry Nights attract up to 100 guests. Oh, and the homemade cakes and pastries in the cafe are not to be missed either!

CONTACT Lower High St, Chipping Campden, Gloucestershire GL55 6AT • 01386 840317 • bespokehotels.com
HOW MUCH? Doubles from £99 a night; dogs £15.

The Wheatsheaf Inn

This 17th-century inn in an archetypal Cotswold village boasts 14 seriously stylish rooms and a top-notch restaurant with a range of local delicacies, and the management are 'happy to welcome dogs as much as people'. They're not kidding. Dogs – both locals and tourists – can be seen in the bar and restaurant contentedly munching on bowls of dog treats. Dogs even get a welcome bag complete with branded bandana and natural shampoo products. The area is full of glorious walks and walking maps are provided to guests – a recommended 4-hour round-trip is particularly popular. Dogs can wander (on a lead) in the garden, which has a pizza oven and bar and is packed in the summer. As for the rooms, they are the epitome of rustic chic and come with B&O TVs with FreeSat, complimentary wifi and Bramley and Acqua di Parma toiletries. Power showers come as standard and the larger rooms have baths as well. This is also a place for children, with a fun kids' menu illustrated by local school kids, as well as rows of child-size Hunter wellies.

CONTACT Northleach, Gloucestershire GL54 3EZ· 01451 860244· cotswoldwheatsheaf.com
HOW MUCH? Double rooms from around £120 a night; dogs £15 a night.

Hare & Hounds Hotel

Dogs are top at the Hare and Hounds, a boutique country house hotel in the Cotswolds, just outside the small market town of Tetbury. Set in its own extensive grounds, it's a thoroughly comfortable place to stay. Although dogs aren't allowed in their 2 AA–rosette restaurant, which serves excellent food in a formal environment, they are permitted in the bar, where they can eat with their owners and enjoy their own special doggy menu; you can also eat with your hound on the outside terrace, overlooking the lovely gardens. There are 42 guest rooms in all, of which around a quarter are dog friendly; they divide between the main house, where the rooms are quite traditional, and a newer block with more contemporary rooms. There is also a cottage for 2 in the grounds with a hot tub and its own garden. Finally, the location is great, with extensive grounds for off-lead walks and the amazing Westonbirt Arboretum just around the corner – home to the country's largest collection of native trees and a perfect place to wander with your hound once you've exhausted the delights of the hotel.

CONTACT Bath Rd, Westonbirt, Tetbury, Gloucestershire GL8 8QL · 01666 881000 · cotswold-inns-hotels.co.uk
HOW MUCH? Double rooms from around £125 a night. Dogs £15 a night.

Watergate Bay Hotel

Taking the concept of luxury beachfront hotel to a new level, yet dog friendly too.

With its long stretch of uninterrupted sands, this hotel is a great destination for children, romantic getaways, and dogs alike, all year round. An extension of the relaxing beach life bang on the doorstep, it invites you straight off the sand into stylish accommodation. Not only do many of the rooms and living areas benefit from dazzling views over the two-mile stretch of Watergate Bay's beach, but all the beach activities you could dream of can be arranged at the click of your fingers, and the hotel is located right on the South West Coast Path.

It has a lot in common with its sister hotel, Another Place The Lake, in the Lake District, with an emphasis on luxury and comfort without pretension and a liking for the outdoor life, dogs and families – the perfect place to chill out and relax, safe in the knowledge that you will be well fed and that nothing is too much trouble. The hotel has been here for years but its latest incarnation takes the beachfront hotel concept to new levels, with a 25m indoor infinity pool overlooking the sea, a hot tub and loungers on the terrace and beach-facing boardwalk, a spa and Finnish sauna. Should you feel like you've done enough relaxing, surf lessons are on offer everyday at this very popular surfing spot, and there is also an on-site gym. Babysitting facilities are available, there's a kids zone (for under-12s), brilliant facilities for teens and dogs are welcome in around half the 70 or so rooms – and, crucially, on the beach itself, which is dog friendly year-round.

All the rooms have en-suite bath or shower rooms, with bath robes and Watergate Bay Elements products, plus tea- and coffee-making facilities, flatscreen TVs and DVD players, iPod docking stations or Bluetooth speakers, good wifi and hairdryers. Dogs get a Joules dog bed, there's 24-hour room service and in most rooms they can add a cot or small child's bed so you don't have to opt for a family suite or apartment. All are available with or without sea views, and apart from that the main difference between categories is simply size. Finally, for those who prefer to self-cater, there is a range of beautifully furnished contemporary apartments with open-plan living areas and two double bedrooms. Dogs can be left in rooms and many guests use baby monitors to keep an eye on them.

Among the hotel's bars and restaurants open to dogs are Watchful Mary, the hotel's new cocktail bar and a popular evening haunt with the locals, the Living Space – one of Cornwall's coolest sea view venues for drinks and food – and the Beach Hut, which serves burgers and grills on the beach itself. All in all, they seem to have thought of everything at the Watergate Bay Hotel. If there is a better beachfront hotel in Cornwall, then we have yet to find it.

CONTACT On the Beach, Watergate Bay, Cornwall TR8 4AA • 01637 860543• watergatebay.co.uk
HOW MUCH? Double rooms with no sea view £185–£290 a night; double rooms with partial sea views £230–£340; rooms with sea views £230–£350; family suites £330–£455. Apartments from £620 a night. Dogs £15 a night.
ROOMS 71 rooms, from 'Standard' to 'Best', 'Suites' and 'Family Suites', plus 2-bedroom self-catering apartments.

Hotel Tresanton

A 20-minute ferry hop from Falmouth, the Tresanton looks back from St Mawes on the Roseland Peninsula – a cluster of seafront cottages that was taken on by Olga Polizzi in 1997, who transformed it into one of the area's most famous boutique hotels. The seaside sister of the Endsleigh in Devon, it is the epitome of waterside chic: all of the 30 rooms gaze out to views of St Anthony's Lighthouse, and the hotel boasts a plethora of luxuries, including a cinema, sun terrace and a private yacht – and, as you might expect, a renowned bar and restaurant that between them deal in deftly-executed cocktails and assiduously sourced British and Italian food. There's a beach right in front of the hotel and for all its seaside chic, the Tresanton is a great place for a family holiday, with a number of dog-friendly rooms, kids' activities and a playroom. They also have child-listening and babysitting services for parents who want a quiet dinner for 2, and dogs are welcome to join their owners on the terrace or in the so-called Dogs' Bar, which serves the same menu as the restaurant.

CONTACT Lower Castle Rd, St Mawes, Cornwall TR2 5DR • 01326 270055 • tresanton.com
HOW MUCH? Double rooms £255–£380 a night, dogs £25 a night.

St Petroc's Hotel

Part of the Rick Stein empire, the excellent, casual St Petroc's Bistro has 10 guest rooms upstairs that are simplicity itself – furnished, you have to say, in a way that makes you wonder why all moderately priced hotels aren't done like this, with functional, tasteful furniture (and not too much of it), working fireplaces, and a décor that is just the right side of minimalist, done out in neutral shades with the odd splash of colour. Rooms range in size from 'cosy' to 'generous' but all have en-suite bathrooms luxuriously decked out with high-quality towels and toiletries and equipped with good showers; some rooms have free-standing baths – on the upper floor cosily situated beneath exposed wooden beams. Many have simple four-posters but all have comfy beds furnished with decent cotton sheets and duvets. Most are dog friendly and dogs get their own blanket to take home. Although dogs are not allowed in the restaurant, you can eat with your dog outside in the garden or in the bar. Rates include breakfast served in the bistro, although you can also have a continental breakfast served in your room.

CONTACT 4 New St, Padstow, Cornwall PL28 8EA • 01841 532700 • rickstein.com
HOW MUCH? Double rooms from £125 to £315 a night, dogs £30 for the first night, then £5 a night.

Budock Vean Hotel

Set on a splendid private estate above the lovely
Helford River, this is not simply an engagingly
traditional country house hotel. With a huge
swimming pool and intimate little spa, it is also the
perfect choice for families – both nuclear and multi-
generational – who can enjoy the pool, which has
an open fire and sauna as well as a terrace with a hot
tub. The hotel also has a really good restaurant and
lots of other facilities, including its own golf course
and extensive grounds that are ideal for lazy walks
with the dog after enjoying one of their excellent
breakfasts. As for the guest rooms, over half have been
recently updated in contemporary country house
style, with lush new bathrooms and walk-in showers,
and they are provided with robes and slippers, tea,
coffee and mineral water and Elemis toiletries in the
bathrooms. Dogs are only allowed in the Standard
and Superior rooms, but the hotel also offers a
number of comfortable cottages in the grounds, some
of which are dog-friendly, where you can self-cater
or use the hotel's many and varied facilities – or
maybe both!

CONTACT Mawnan Smith, Falmouth, Cornwall
TR11 5LG • 01326 252100 • budockvean.co.uk
HOW MUCH? Double rooms £95–£150 a night, dogs
£10 a night or £8 for stays of 5 nights or more..

Thurlestone Hotel

With a seaside location to die for, overlooking a
particularly sumptuous stretch of the coast of South
Devon, this is as comfortable a place to stay as you
could wish for. Owned by the Grose family for over
100 years, the hotel is a big white landmark building
in its own grounds with 70 rooms, varying from
deluxe doubles with wonderful views of the sea to
cheaper inland-facing rooms and spacious family
suites. Dogs are welcome in a number of inland
and sea-view rooms and get a goody bag with
treats, poo bags, a ball and details of all the beaches
nearby that welcome dogs, including Thurlestone
itself, which is a huge dog-friendly strand. All the
rooms have comfortable beds, satellite TV, good wifi
and well-appointed bathrooms with Temple Spa
toiletries and robes, and the hotel has numerous
facilities, including children's play areas, tennis
courts, a golf course, spa and pool, a well-equipped
gym and several places to eat, one of which – the
Village Inn – you can eat in with your dog in what
is basically a cosy local pub serving good meat and
fish dishes in a more relaxed environment.

CONTACT Thurlestone, near Kingsbridge, Devon
TQ7 3NN • 01548 560382 • thurlestone.co.uk
HOW MUCH? Double rooms £150–£295 a night, dogs
£10 a night.

Rosehill Lodges

Luxury lodges with hot tubs in a perfect North Cornwall seaside location.

Situated on the north Cornwall coast, halfway between Newquay and St Ives, Rosehill Lodges are a bit of a hidden gem, buried deep in the woods, yet only a ten-minute walk from the Blue Flag beach at Porthtowan. Run by the affable John and Pauline Barrow and their team, they describe themselves as 'luxury lodges' and for once it's a description that is spot-on. Constructed with locally sourced timber, and with sustainable bamboo flooring and grass roofs, they are super-well-insulated and stay cool in summer and warm in winter. They also use reclaimed materials as much as possible – ships's timbers and railway sleepers – and energy comes from solar panels, so they're eco-friendly too.

There are ten lodges, of which six are dog friendly; each has two or three bedrooms and beds that can be configured in various ways depending on what you need, so they're ideal for both families and groups of friends. On arrival you get a pet hamper with a dog blanket, towel, a bowl and treats and poo bags. There's a kitchen with a fridge, freezer, dishwasher and washer/dryer, a decent-sized living area, and each lodge comes with its own wood-burner (and yes, since you ask, seasoned logs, firelighters and kindling are all provided, for free). It's not all rustic home comforts – each lodge also has superfast wifi and a smart TV, as well as an external drench shower with which to properly wash away the sand before you collapse into your very own hot tub on your very own verandah. You'll have worked up quite an appetite at the beach, but luckily there's also a charcoal barbecue for cooking up those all-important alfresco feasts.

As for the location, it really couldn't be better. It's a perfect spot for exploring this part of Cornwall but also interesting and comfortable enough in its own right if all you want to is veg out. Unfortunately mid-May to September there's a timed dog ban on Porthtowan's beach between 10am and 5pm, but there is ample room to play with your dog on the dunes behind, where there is also a stream to splash around in. Try also the excellent Blue Bar and Beach Café which are both dog friendly (and have water bowls for dogs). The lodges are in any case close enough to pop back to now and then, and you're also right on the South West Coast Path so you can set off in either direction to explore the coastline if you fancy a longer walk. Dogs are permitted all year round on nearby Lushington beach, for example.

The village has a shop and surf tuition and the Rosehill Valley is a delight for birdwatchers, as are nearby Hayle Estuary and Godrevy Head, both of which you can reach on the coast path. By car, you're also just half an hour away from some of Cornwall's most iconic attractions – the Eden Project and Lost Gardens of Heligan. If, that is, you can drag yourself out of that hot tub.

CONTACT Rosehill, Porthtowan, Cornwall TR4 8AR • 01209 891920 • rosehilllodges.com
HOW MUCH? Short breaks £416–£1436, £550– £2246 for a week.
ACCOMMODATION 6 2-bedroom lodges, 4 3-bedroom lodge, all with wood-burners, verandahs, BBQs, hot tubs.

Laverstock Farm

Picture this: a long sweeping driveway leading to a grand farmhouse and a group of homely self-catering cottages. Sounds appealing doesn't it? Located on a working farm in the heart of rural West Dorset, Laverstock Farm is a relaxing place to escape, with 6 cottages and 2 shepherd's huts a 15-minute drive from Bridport and less than half an hour from the Jurassic Coast. It's a lovely spot to take a break; all but one of the properties are dog friendly and range from 4-bed Lambrook Cottage, complete with log-burner, open-plan kitchen, dining area and BBQ, to the romantic bolt-hole of Gardener's and 2 cosy shepherd's huts, which boast an outside kitchen with a firepit. There is no electricity, but 4 rechargeable lanterns are provided and there's a shared washroom with a heated floor and fresh towels. Whichever option suits best, there are far-reaching views and roaming animals, plus a large vegetable garden, a children's play area and a games room with air hockey, pool and table tennis – not to mention plenty of good walks right on your doorstep.

CONTACT Laverstock House, Laverstock, Dorset DT6 5PE • 0130 8867866 • laverstockfarm.co.uk
HOW MUCH? Cottages £90–£220 a night; dogs £25 per stay; shepherd's huts from £90 per night.

Highbullen Cottages

These 4 self-catering cottages are part of a lavish hotel complex of the same name, housed in an impressively Gothic country house that was apparently a favourite of actor Laurence Oliver. The 3- and 4-bed cottages are as comfortable and well-appointed as the hotel: 3 of them are dog friendly and they all have lovely bright rooms, high-spec country kitchens with Agas and refurbished bathrooms, many of them en-suite. They also enjoy gorgeous views over the Mole Valley. The really good news, though, is that guests at each of the cottages can take full advantage of the facilities at the hotel, which include a golf course, tennis courts, croquet lawns, a spa, sauna and gym and no less than two pools (indoor and outdoor), along with an impressive range of bars, restaurants and lounges. We wouldn't blame you if you and your dog didn't want to leave the confines of the hotel's 125 acres, and many people do just that. But the location is excellent, well placed for Exmoor and the North Devon coast, yet far enough away to enjoy the sort of peace and quiet you can only find in this part of Devon. No wonder Laurence Olivier loved it so much.

CONTACT Highbullen Hotel, Umberleigh, Devon EX37 9HD • 01272 377432 • myfavouritecottages.co.uk
HOW MUCH? £525–£1495 & £795–£2495 a week, depending on the season.

Bosinver Farm

As an antidote to 'nature deficit disorder', the experience at Bosinver Farm cottages couldn't be more effective. Throwing you and your family firmly into the Great Outdoors, Bosinver Farm offers the chance to follow Farmer Dave to feed the animals and collect eggs from the hens, look out for wildlife and the Gruffalo on woodland trails, ride ponies and light campfires, hunt bugs and build dens on the 'Wild Kids' programme. Bosinver's cottages are set amid 30 acres of wildflower meadows and gardens, and have a bright, contemporary designer style, with wood-burners and all mod cons. With properties sleeping from 4-12 people, there are picture-perfect thatched cottages, a historic farmhouse, converted barns, and even a stylish eco-house. Ten cottages are dog friendly and they are happy to provide personal recommendations for walks and dog friendly attractions, and even a secure kennel or access to a dog-sitting service. The farm also has a heated indoor pool, sauna, gym, play barn and games room, plus outdoor play areas, woodlands and a lake to explore.

CONTACT Trelowth, St Austell, Cornwall PL26 7DT • 01726 72128• bosinver.co.uk
HOW MUCH? Cottages from £540 a week, dogs £40 a week.

Leskernick Cottage

Right in the middle of Bodmin Moor, Leskernick is as remote a place to stay as you could find in England. With 7 acres of its own, but also surrounded by hundreds of acres of open moorland, it would almost be a pity to arrive without a dog. Originally a 17th-century mineworker's cottage, it has been extended over the years, with an extra floor added and an extension that makes the most of the wonderful views across the moor. Thoroughly modernized, it comfortably sleeps 6 people in 3 bedrooms; there's an Aga that supplies hot water and wood-burners to keep things cosy, along with oil-fired central heating. It feels off-grid, and strictly speaking it is, although electricity provided by a generator fires up the dishwasher, washing machine, TV and DVD. There is mobile reception, but it's erratic, and wifi too, although it's only really up to checking emails. Walks lead off in all directions – you won't need a lead! – to bronze age settlements and stone circles, not to mention 'Brown Willy' – at 420m above sea level, Cornwall's highest peak, just an hour's stroll away.

CONTACT Bolventor, near Launceston, Cornwall PL15 7TJ • 07818 407060 • leskernick.com
HOW MUCH? £625–£835 a week, depending on the season.

Artist Residence Penzance

A quirky – and dog friendly – boutique hotel with 22 contemporary rooms and a three-bedroom cottage.

Smack bang in the middle of Penzance, it would have been all too easy to buy up this Georgian mansion and run a traditional hotel with bragging rights about its top location. Not so for the Artist Residence Penzance, where time and effort has gone into a unique boutique design that stands out from the crowds. The elegant townhouse exterior conceals 20 rooms and one suite, each individually decorated by Cornish and British artists, plus there's a three-bedroom cottage, complete with log-burner and copper roll-top bath.

It's a vibrant mix of new and old, from a sea-themed double to chic twin rooms, and a comfy deluxe suite along with wacky street art murals. There's also a three-bedroom cottage, which is the perfect seaside retreat for a family. The key word throughout is comfort. The rooms have en-suite bathrooms with eco-friendly toiletries, flatscreen TVs and free wifi, while the cottage has an open-plan living room and kitchenette with log-burner, and a luxurious bathroom with copper roll-top bath and walk-in rainfall shower. Nine rooms welcome dogs, as do all the public spaces, and it isn't unusual to see some of the staff's dogs chilling out by the fire too. The Cottage is also dog friendly, a self-catering option for larger families with three bedrooms, kitchenette, copper roll-top bath, and a log-burner that is just shouting out for a dog-tired hound to curl up in front of it after a long day exploring the town and coastline. Old railway sleepers and leather armchairs maintain the charm of Cornwall in a different era, while following the hotel's unique style in all the small details. There's a maximum of two dogs per room and all dogs receive a bed, bowl and a bag of treats. Not all of the beaches welcome dogs during summer – try Eastern Green, Mounts Bay or Long Rock, which are dog friendly year-round.

Breakfast is served in the ground-floor restaurant, The Cornish Barn, using fresh local produce, and the restaurant is also open for lunch and dinner, providing a selection of small plates and meat and fish dishes from the smoker. There is a large beer garden complete with table football, ping pong, a fully stocked bar and a barbecue for summer days, and also an indoor bar-lounge with a log-burner and a focus on local ales and cocktails crafted using Cornish spirits. It all adds up to a stunning hotel with unique design, delicious food and a thoroughly laid-back atmosphere – topped off by that central location that, yes, they should still brag about!

Artist Residence Penzance is a refreshingly vibrant place for a break for a couple or small family, especially as it's only a five-minute walk to the Isles of Scilly ferry. And the good news is that Artist Residence have other equally enticing locations in Brighton, London and Oxfordshire.

CONTACT 20 Chapel St, Penzance, Cornwall TR18 4AW • 01736 365664 • artistresidence.co.uk
HOW MUCH? Double rooms start at £75 a night, dogs £15 a night.
ROOMS 20 double rooms, 1 suite and a 3-bedroom cottage.

EAST ANGLIA

Despite being one of England's most accessible regions, East Anglia is relatively unknown, yet there is so much to see here it's hard to know where to start. It's rich in history and landscape, from the rugged glories of the North Norfolk Coast to the historic wool towns of Suffolk and the extraordinary wetlands of The Broads.

Titchwell Manor

A tremendous North Norfolk Coast boutique hotel with great food.

Looking out over the coastal salt marshes, Titchwell Manor is about as comfortable and stylish a place from which to enjoy the North Norfolk Coast as you will find. Fashioned out of a large and not especially distinguished redbrick Victorian farmhouse, it ticks all the right boxes for a short break, with 26 boutique rooms and a reputation for food that puts it head and shoulders above its competitors on a coast that's not exactly short of good places to eat.

First the rooms. There are nine rooms in the main building, four in the cottage annexe, with the rest arranged around the U-shaped stable block 'herb garden' courtyard behind. They're all individually styled, with retro furniture, clean, crisp lines and a bold colour palette that makes you think of the sea. Pricewise, they range from the cheapest 'Good' doubles through 'Better' and 'Best' up to the largest 'Signature' rooms. 'Good' rooms tend to be in the main house and are a bit smaller, with king-size beds. 'Better' rooms are in the stable block and are more contemporary, with king-size beds and (sometimes) sea views as well; 'Best' rooms' are in the cottage annexe and the stable block and they all have super-king-size beds, while four also have a private patio area. 'Signature' rooms, naturally the largest, have freestanding baths and separate showers and complimentary soft drinks, Nespresso coffee machines and bluetooth speakers – and a couple have their own terraces with private hot tubs.

All the rooms have good wifi, flatscreen smart TVs, hairdryers and bath robes, tea- and coffee-making facilities, and spacious and recently updated en-suite bathrooms with White Company toiletries. Around a third of the rooms are dog friendly, and dogs are greeted on arrival with their own bed, towel, biscuits and a map detailings the excellent walks in all directions, including the long-distance Norfolk Coast Path and Peddars Way. And, for humans who come back to their room tired and a little sore, the hotel has the perfect antidote – in-room massages and holistic therapies that will have you in dreamland.

As for the rest of the hotel, it has a sunny coastal feel that is perfectly in tune with its seaside location. There are two restaurants, the casual, dog-friendly Eating Rooms and the more formal Conservatory; you can enjoy their 3 AA-rosette menu in both and on Sunday there's a groaning buffet and a choice of roasts. They serve a delicious breakfast and a popular afternoon tea every day in the Eating Rooms, and the hotel is also behind nearby Thornham's superb fish-and-chip shop, Eric's, which serves both traditional chippy offerings along with halloumi spinach arancini, Japanese-style fish burgers, battered king prawns and more.

CONTACT Titchwell, near Brancaster, Norfolk PE31 8BB • 01485 210221 • titchwellmanor.com
HOW MUCH? Double rooms £130–£230 a night; Signature rooms £235–£325 a night. Dogs £15 a night.
ROOMS 26 guest rooms, 9 in the main building and the rest across the courtyard behind, ranging from 'Good' to 'Better' to 'Best' doubles to 'Signature' rooms, some of which have hot tubs.

Mill Farm Eco Barn

Situated just outside the pretty seaside village of Winterton-on-Sea, the two luxurious barn conversions not only enjoy a superb location, they are also an extremely eco-friendly place to stay. Owners Emma and Neil Punchard used recycled wood and other material in the conversions, a biomass boiler fed with wood pellets heats both houses, and a rainwater tank provides water to flush the loos and fill the washing machine. So not only can you relax in the lap of luxury, you can feel good about it too. The Eco Barn welcomes dogs and has 4 large bedrooms (2 with en-suites), a huge living area and well-equipped kitchen and a separate dining area that leads out onto a large patio area with BBQ; the smaller 1-bedroom Hay Barn sleeps 2 and is also dog friendly. Outside, you can collect eggs from the chickens or hang out in the games barn playing ping pong or pool, and the fabulous dog-friendly beach and dunes of Winterton are a short walk away across the main road. The village has a good pub, too, the Fisherman's Return, where dogs are practically compulsory.

CONTACT Mill Farm, Hemsby Rd, Norfolk NR29 4AE • 07900 376462 • millfarm-ecobarn.co.uk
HOW MUCH? Eco Barn £800–£2000 a week, Hay Barn £300–£575 a week; 3-night minimum stay.

The Brisley Bell

Rescued from permanent closure a couple of years ago, this Mid-Norfolk watering-hole is a proper village pub, but one that just happens to serve tremendously good food and also has some very comfortable guest rooms. There are 6 rooms in all, 2 of which are dog friendly, and they're spacious and well-proportioned and have decent wifi, smart TVs, tea- and coffee-making facilities, complimentary mineral water and homemade shortbread and sloe gin, Roberts radios and underfloor heating. Bathrooms are slick and contemporary and come with complimentary toiletries. The moderately priced, meat-led menu changes daily and features high-quality country cooking that makes the most of local produce. As for location, you couldn't be much closer to the centre of Norfolk than Brisley, which makes a great base for the nearby Brecks. The grounds behind the pub offer the chance to run off a bit of steam with your hound, as does the large village common in front, and there are any number of country walks possible beyond the village.

CONTACT The Green, Brisley, Norfolk NR20 5DW • 01362 705024 • thebrisleybell.co.uk
HOW MUCH? Double rooms with breakfast from £88 to £192 a night, dogs free.

Morston Hall

A former 'East Anglia Small Hotel of the Year', Morston Hall is a first-rate country house-style boutique hotel, just off the main North Norfolk coast road a couple of miles outside Blakeney. The hall itself is mostly 19th century, but its 13 individually decorated guest rooms – most of them named after local Norfolk country seats and split between the more traditional rooms of the main house and the more contemporary 'Pavilion' rooms – are sleek and modern, with thick carpets and heavy drapes. There are kennels in the grounds for dogs, but well-behaved canines can stay in all but 2 of the hotel's bedrooms. Where they can't go is the restaurant, which has a reputation for outstanding cuisine and serves a 7-course tasting menu every night at dinner. The Hall also offers half-day cookery demonstrations and is a popular wedding venue. None of this will impress your four-legged friend of course, but he will be happy with the hotel's location, overlooking the Blakeney National Nature Reserve and right on the Norfolk Coast Path, with blustery walks galore in the vicinity.

CONTACT Morston, Holt, Norfolk NR25 7AA
• 01263 741041 • morstonhall.com
HOW MUCH? Double rooms from £185 a night, dogs £20 a night, maximum 2 per room.

The King's Head

A few minutes from the handsome North Norfolk Georgian town of Holt, this is a great contemporary country pub, serving excellent food and local ales and with 4 comfy rooms upstairs, all of which are dog friendly and furnished in the same cosy but up-to-date style that's in keeping with the building and period, with large comfy beds and en-suite bathrooms with powerful showers. The front 2 rooms are the largest and best proportioned and it's a peaceful, homely place to stay. Downstairs, the pub is a welcoming mix of contemporary and rustic style, with a stripped-down look enhanced by eclectic furnishings and knick-knacks. There's a snug bar for drinkers, a main area devoted to food, which is served all day in summer, and an enclosed garden for alfresco lunches and early morning walks. They bake their own bread with flour from a nearby mill and source most other ingredients locally, including ales from their own brewery. You can reach the coast on the North Norfolk Steam Railway from Holt to Sheringham, or just explore the countryside and coast on foot.

CONTACT Holt Rd, Letheringsett, Norfolk NR25 7AR
• 01263 712691 • kingsheadnorfolk.co.uk
HOW MUCH? Double rooms £100–£140 a night. Dogs £10 a night.

Milsoms Kesgrave Hall

A dog-friendly country house hotel with a cool but relaxed and super-friendly boutique feel.

Situated on the eastern edge of Ipswich, this rather grand building used to be a school and was also once owned by the local Tolly Cobbold brewing dynasty, but nowadays Kesgrave Hall is a country-house retreat that's part of the small but perfectly formed East Anglian boutique hotel group, Milsoms Hotels.

It sits in expansive grounds, and for a place that is so easy to reach retains a strong away-from-it-all feel. It has just 23 rooms, around half of which are in the main house, with the rest in the former headmaster's quarters and various outbuildings. In the main house, the rooms range from 'Standard' (with back view and no separate shower) to 'Best' (which are very large and have free-standing baths and separate showers), taking in 'Superior', 'Deluxe' and 'Principal' along the way. Deluxe rooms upwards have separate walk-in showers while those in the grounds have separate entrances and a secluded feel, and range from 'Superior' to 'Principal'. All rooms have superfast wifi, complimentary water and soft drinks, fresh milk, TVs with full satellite access (including BT and Sky Sports), rain showers and either a/c or Dyson fans.

Downstairs there's a bar and lounge that are relaxed rather than stuffy, and a 2-AA-rosette restaurant, which is deliberately accessible (no reservations, no dress code), staying open all day and featuring stripped pine tables, an open kitchen and a quirky way of ordering – just write what you want on the pad provided. Brunch isn't just for weekends at Kesgrave Hall, which is great if you've done a midweek bunk from work, while summer means drinks on the outdoor terrace, a read of the book

and a stroll in the grounds, making sure you're back in time for a proper afternoon tea, served from 3pm to 5pm every day.

Most of the hotel's outside rooms are dog friendly, and lucky hounds all get towels, bowls, poo bags, treats and a sausage for breakfast – up to 2 dogs are permitted in each room and there's no restriction on size. Dogs are allowed everywhere except the main restaurant and you can eat the restaurant menu in the bar with your dog, or on the large outside terrace, beyond which there is a massive lawned area where dogs can run and kids can kick a ball about while their parents chew the fat. Like we said, it's cool, relaxed and boutique, and super-friendly too.

The hotel also provides maps with the best local walks, and the extensive grounds mean there is a decent early morning off-the-lead run on your doorstep. Once you've walked the dog, treat yourself to a spot of pampering at the brand new on-site Kesgrave Hall Spa, where you can choose from a range of treatments or just loaf about in the huge hot tub or sauna. Failing that, head off to the nearby Suffolk Coast and its beaches and coastal path, or try some of the excellent riverside pubs a short drive away, for example the Maybush Inn in Waldringfield or the Ramsholt Arms on the other side of the Deben estuary.

CONTACT Hall Rd, Kesgrave, Ipswich Suffolk IP5 2PU • 01473 333741• milsomhotels.com
HOW MUCH? Double rooms from around £145 a night. Dogs £10 a night.
ROOMS 23 en-suite double rooms.

The Crown

This pub-restaurant has 34 en-suite bedrooms, located either in the main building or dotted about the various converted barns outside. They're all nicely finished, and are quirkily classified as 'Good', 'Better', and 'Best'. Dogs are welcome in most rooms, and get a blanket, bowl, treats and even something for breakfast; they can eat in the front bar and curl up in the lounge or snug, and there's a dog shower for muddy paws and towels if you need them. Even the cheapest rooms have TV, wifi and well-fitted bathrooms, yet the whole place retains a cosy charm that reminds you it's a converted pub – just what Wills and Kate were looking for when they stayed here a few years ago after attending a nearby wedding and firmly put the Crown on the map. Before you ask, they stayed in the Swan room, complete with four-poster bed and enjoyed an excellent Full English breakfast in the garden room the next morning. The restaurant, incidentally, is very good and the countryside around is great for walks, for example to their equally dog-friendly sister pub, The Ship in Dunwich.

CONTACT The Street, Westleton, Suffolk IP17 3AD •
01728 648777• westletoncrown.co.uk
HOW MUCH? Double rooms £125–£165 a night. Dogs
£7.50 a night.

The Swan at Lavenham

At the centre of this old Suffolk wool town, The Swan is a Lavenham institution, but it has done a pretty good job of reinventing itself over the years, blending the unique character of its ancient timbered building with updates to its rooms, comfy public areas and a discreet spa. The hotel has 45 rooms, most of them blending modern looks with the heritage of the building, with splashes of colour that fit surprisingly well with the ancient beams and creaky floors. Almost all have baths (with showers), and Freeview TVs, tea- and coffee-making facilities, complimentary water and biscuits, wifi and Temple Spa toiletries. They have 7 dog-friendly rooms, and pooches get a bowl and a treat on arrival, and you can eat with them in the Airmen's Bar, in the hotel's courtyard garden or in your room. Dogs can also curl up by the fire in the comfy lounge that wraps around most of the ground floor. The Gallery restaurant serves a fine-dining menu and the Brasserie restaurant serves more workaday food. For exercise, walk to nearby Long Melford, following the old railway line – a 10-mile round-trip.

CONTACT High Street, Lavenham, Suffolk CO10 9QA •
01787 247477 • theswanatlavenham.co.uk
HOW MUCH? Double rooms from £180 a night. Dogs
£12 a night, maximum 2 per room.

The Ickworth Hotel

Ickworth House is one of the most venerable country estates in the country but there's no standing on ceremony here; indeed its aim is to make you, your kids and your pets feel to-the-manor-born at least for a few days. Situated just outside Bury St Edmunds, the 180-acre estate is perfect for exploring with your hound; there are 27 guest rooms, all of which accept dogs, with a good choice of doubles, suites and family rooms. Some are traditionally furnished, others more modern, but all are spacious and have large bathrooms. There's also the Lodge at Ickworth in the grounds, which houses 1-3-bedroom apartments. The hotel has an indoor pool, and de-stressing parents can enjoy this and the spa treatment rooms while taking advantage of 2 hours' free childcare a day, babysitting and baby-listening services, a kids' club and a cinema showing family films. Plus of course the park, woodlands and the grounds in general make for a fabulous, safe environment for families and dogs, with everything from footpaths and cycle routes to geocaching and more.

CONTACT Horringer, Bury St Edmunds, Suffolk
IP29 5QE • 01284 735350 • ickworthhotel.co.uk
HOW MUCH? Double rooms from £95, family rooms
from £165. Dogs £15 a night.

Beechwood Hotel

Situated in the small town of North Walsham, on the northern edge of the Broads National Park, this boutique bolt-hole has long been one of our favourite Norfolk places to stay – and its owners ensure dogs are not only welcome but well looked after. It's pretty traditional in style, with 17 beautifully furnished rooms that hark back to the days of Agatha Christie (who was a regular guest here when it was a private house). There are also 4 more contemporary double rooms in Bay Tree House next door, furnished to a high standard, and all the rooms – in both houses – have free wifi, iPod docking stations, flatscreen TVs and spacious bathrooms (a couple with free-standing baths). The main house is full of Christie memorabilia and there's an easy-going, old-fashioned charm to the place, with a cosy bar and a lovely small garden out the back, plus an excellent restaurant, serving a daily changing menu based on local produce. Dogs can eat with their owners in the back lounge, or they can be left in your room while you dine in the restaurant.

CONTACT Cromer Rd, North Walsham, Norfolk
NR28 0HD • 01692 403231• beechwood-hotel.co.uk
HOW MUCH? Double rooms £100–£175 a night. Dogs
£15 a night, £20 for 2 dogs.

Idle Waters

A delightful and dog friendly waterfront cottage on the river Stour.

Who said you couldn't improve upon perfection? Not only is this picture-perfect 16th-century timbered cottage, situated in a peaceful woodland setting by the river Stour right on the Essex-Suffolk border, about as idyllic a place to stay as you could wish for, it's also owned by the same people who own the fancy Talbooth restaurant across the water. So, uniquely, you can take off your pinny, put down your wooden spoon and enjoy some of the best food for miles around in the restaurant across the river. Dogs are welcomed with their own bowl, towel and poo bags, and you are provided with a map of local walking routes.

The facilities at the Maison Talbooth hotel at the top of the hill are also available to guests, and include a tennis court and sumptuous open-air swimming pool, hot tub and spa, as are those of the nearby Milsoms Hotel, which has a slightly cheaper but still excellent restaurant serving an all-day menu and a buzzy bar and terrace. The cottage is olde-worlde on the outside and beamed inside, but is otherwise right up to date, with an open-plan fitted kitchen and diner and doors leading out onto the garden, a bay-fronted living room overlooking the river complete with inglenook fireplace and squishy sofas, while upstairs there are two double bedrooms, also with views over the river and both with en-suite bathrooms. The cottage has good wifi and a smart TV with Sky, and a hob, oven, microwave, dishwasher, washing machine and tumble dryer – plus the owners leave a breakfast hamper of goodies for your stay.

The cottage is in the heart of the Dedham Vale Area of Outstanding Natural Beauty, 'Constable Country' to give it its other name, and the cottage in fact featured in one of the artist's paintings – 'The Vale of Dedham'. It's a truly beautiful spot in its own right, and you could just stock up on provisions at the excellent nearby farm shop and happily spend your days in the cottage and around, exploring the woods and mucking about on the river, not to mention dining and supping at the two hotels. But you can also follow the river path for 15 minutes to Dedham – a pretty village with a venerable old church and a couple of decent pubs – and stroll across the meadows to another Constable sight, Flatford Mill. You can row on the river, hire bikes or canoes, visit the wonderful nearby Munnings Museum (housed in the 19th-century artist's home), on the outskirts of Dedham village, or just stroll the footpaths and intriguing byways that branch off in all directions.

Idle Waters is a gentle, peaceful and enriching place to stay, and very easy to reach from London. The only drawback is that it is so hard to leave.

CONTACT Gun Hill, Dedham, Essex CO7 6UP • 010206 323150 • milsomhotels.co.uk
HOW MUCH? From £250 (Mon–Thurs) to £400 a night (Fri–Sun); 2 nights (Fri–Sun) £700; 7 nights £1500.
ACCOMMODATION Idle Waters comfortably sleeps 4 people in 2 double bedrooms, both of them en-suite.

Pack Holidays

Gail Adams is a dog-lover like no other. When she started renting her holiday cottage in rural East Ruston in North Norfolk, she was determined they would not just accept dogs but, er, lots of them… and that was the beginning of Pack Holidays, which specialises in dog-friendly holiday rentals in North Norfolk. They have a wide array of holiday properties ranging from seaside cottages to converted windmills and a couple of cabins in the midst of the Broads National Park. Gail is quite picky so you can be sure that all her properties are of a high standard; plus she's local so is on hand to deal with any problems that might arise. It's not all about the dogs either – Pack Holidays properties are in excellent locations that would suit anyone – but they have no limits on dogs and don't charge extra for them either. Above all, this part of Norfolk is the perfect place for a dog-friendly holiday, with great beaches, walks that include some of the country's best long-distance footpaths, and a host of pubs that welcome four-legged friends as a matter of course.

CONTACT Near The Lodge, Honing Road, Dilham, Norfolk NR28 9PN • 07935 375899 • packholidays.co.uk
HOW MUCH? Prices from £400 a week (lots of short breaks available too).

Triumphal Arch

You can play lord of the manor and admiral of the fleet at the same time in the rooms set into this splendid 18th-century Arch. Built to show off to passing travellers, it occupies a prime position on North Norfolk's vast Holkham Estate, within easy reach of one of the finest Palladian houses in the country and with grounds that feature numerous cycle trails and footpaths. You can hire bikes nearby, row on the lake during summer, and, beyond the walls of Holkham Park, follow Lady Anne's Drive down to Holkham Bay's vast dog-friendly beach, and the delicious shady pine woods just behind it. It's a romantic spot, no question. The Arch has just one bedroom at the top of a spiral staircase (there's a kitchen and shower room below), with a roll-top bath, king-size bed and plenty of space to enjoy the views over the park. Not surprisingly it's a terrific place for a dog, too, with high quality walkies all around, though dogs must be kept on a lead in the park. There are good, dog-friendly local pubs nearby too, not least the estate's own Victoria Inn in Holkham village.

CONTACT Norfolk Cottages • 01263 715779 • norfolkcottages.com
HOW MUCH? From £756 to £1289 a week, maximum 2 dogs.

Waveney River Centre

An oasis of activity in what truly feels like the middle of nowhere down in the southern Norfolk Broads, Waveney River Centre has multiple forms of accommodation: it's a well-equipped waterside dog-friendly glamping and camping site; it also has its own pub with (non-pet-friendly) boutique rooms, plus a number of dog-friendly holiday lodges. It has moorings and rents out day boats and canoes at what must be one of the best locations from which to explore this part of the Broads National Park, with plenty of opportunity for walks and cycle-rides. The long-distance Angles Way passes nearby, the Wherryman's Way a little way north, and the countryside around is as peaceful a corner of England as you'll find. The site is partly supplied by solar energy and has an energy-efficient pool, but maybe the best (and greenest) thing they have done is to reinstate the foot ferry across the river to Carlton Marshes – heaven for a dog but also making the car journey from Lowestoft to Waveney about 6 times shorter. All in all, a very peaceful retreat, but with plenty to keep you entertained.

CONTACT Staithe Rd, Burgh St Peter, Norfolk NR34 0DE • 01502 677343 • waveneyrivercentre.co.uk **HOW MUCH?** Camping £10–£38, pods £40–£50, lodges £99–£125 a night, maximum 2 dogs.

The Cabin-in-the-Vines

You don't have to be a wine-lover to enjoy the rather wonderful Cabin-in-the-Vines, you just need to be happy to be the only one spending the night bang in the middle of a Suffolk vineyard. This well-appointed wooden cabin, insulated with sheep's wool and powered by solar panels and state-of-the-art batteries, is the perfect off-grid place for 2 eco-friendly folk to get away from it all. With a living area, bedroom and separate bathroom with shower, toilet and sink, towels and toiletries. it also has its own fully equipped kitchen complete with hob, oven, fridge and everything else you might need. Best of all, you can bring Fido, and the location is so tucked away and gorgeous that you might not want to leave; indeed its outside porch is about as perfect place to enjoy a summer evening with a glass of wine as you'll find – plus there's no wifi (just a DVD player), making it an easy place to switch off from the world outside. Finally, the location couldn't be better, with a couple of pubs within walking distance and footpaths leading off in all directions, as far as the nearby Suffolk Coast AONB.

CONTACT Rumburgh Rd, Wissett, Suffolk IP19 0JJ • 07867 009967 • valleyfarmvineyards.co.uk **HOW MUCH?** Prices from £120 a night (minimum 2-night stay), dogs £20 per stay.

OUT AND ABOUT
Four great walks with your dog

BLAKENEY POINT The iconic spit of Blakeney Point is best discovered on foot, starting at Cley Beach and following the beach and shingle ridge to the dunes at the far end. Here you'll find the National Trust's sheltered Lifeboat House, from where a wooden boardwalk leads to the beach by Blakeney Harbour, where seals bask on tidal sands. Dogs on leads here!
7.5 MILES

BLICKLING ESTATE WALK The National Trust's Blickling Estate includes a Jacobean mansion and magnificent gardens and grounds. Try the Estate Walk, which takes in the best of Blickling's woodland, with stunning views across the lake to the hall – great to explore on your own or with a dog. Blickling is renowned for its bluebells in the spring but there's something to enjoy all year. **3 MILES**

STOUR VALLEY & DEDHAM VALE This walk explores the picturesque Stour Valley and Dedham Vale, an area made famous by the 19th century landscape painter John Constable. Mostly flat, this circular walk follows a section of the Stour Valley path past the hamlet of Flatford and Flatford Mill (painted by Constable) through an area of wildlife-rich hedgerows and wildflower meadows. **7 MILES**

WELLS-NEXT-THE-SEA & HOLKHAM An action-packed walk that starts and finishes in the seaside town of Wells, taking in a bustling harbour, golden sand and pine woodlands before finishing back on the seafront. Wells is famous for its beach huts, but it's the beach and dunes that your dog will want to explore – plus you should save some energy for the stunning pinewoods behind the beach.
4.7 MILES

THE OUTDOOR GUIDE

Woodfarm Barns and Barges

Gorgeous dog-friendly barns with gardens to roam in — plus dog-friendly barges in great Suffolk locations.

If you're looking for a romantic retreat close to London then Woodfarm Barns, deep in the heart of rural Suffolk, might just fit the bill. The accommodation is dog friendly but it's also extremely comfortable for mere humans, with no less than six luxuriously converted barns in a peaceful meadow, each sleeping two people, plus a 15th-century partially thatched farmhouse which sleeps seven. All of the barns are lovely — bright and stylish, with original oak beams and clapboard exteriors with enclosed private gardens; some have ground-floor bedrooms, some mezzanines; five of the six have hot tubs and the only one that doesn't — Granary Barn — has a larger garden and a big bedroom window that offers wonderful country views. They all have well-equipped modern kitchens, but you also get a breakfast basket delivered, complete with coffee, eggs and bacon and more. All are kitted out with Freeview TVs, DVD players and good wifi, and there's also a shed nearby that's full of things you can borrow — from bikes and stuff for dogs to books and DVDs. The farmhouse is wonderfully cosy, with a sitting room with an open fire, a big farmhouse kitchen with an Aga and three spacious bedrooms and three bathrooms with free-standing baths.

You don't have to be a dog-owner to enjoy the accommodation at Woodfarm Barns, but it helps: they make a big thing of welcoming four-legged friends, and once your dog has stayed here once he can stay again for free, having been issued with his own Dog Passports to prove his credentials. There's also a huge two-acre garden for you (and your hound) to gambol in, plus loads of lovely walks and cycling routes from the Barn; and the Suffolk Coast is also less half an hour's drive away.

Consider also a stay on the same owner's two equally dog-friendly Dutch barges, which are just as comfortable as the barns and enjoy superb mooring spots — 'Twee Gebroeders' on the Deben river at Woodbridge and 'Onderneming' on the Alde river right by Snape Maltings. Restored just over a decade ago, Twee Gebroeders is the smaller of the two, with a spacious main saloon, a thoroughly up-to-date galley with a cast-iron oil-fired range which supplies heating, hot water and cooking facilities, and two cabins — one double, one twin. The Onderneming is a beautiful late 19th-century sailing barge so lovingly restored that even the most dedicated landlubber would relish a few nights on board: at 100 feet long and over 18 feet wide, she has all the mod cons you would expect from a regular holiday cottage and can comfortably sleep six people in three double cabins. Again, she's extremely dog-friendly, and just as well — there are few better places to bring a dog than Snape, with gorgeous walks stretching in all directions.

CONTACT Woodfarm House, Stonham Aspal, Suffolk IP6 9TH • 01449 710032 • woodfarmbarns.com

HOW MUCH? Barns from £1030 a week, short breaks from £430; Farmhouse from £1530 a week, short breaks from £650; Twee Gebroeders from £970 a week, short breaks from £410; Onderneming from £1420 a week, short breaks from £600.

ACCOMMODATION 6 barns for 2 people, a thatched Farmhouse sleeping 7 people. Twee Gebroeders sleeps 4 in 2 cabins; Onderneming 6–8 in 3 cabins.

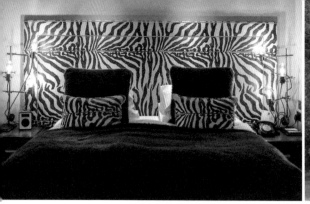

Milsoms

Situated in picturesque Dedham, right on the Essex–Suffolk border and in the heart of Constable Country, Milsoms is the original hotel of one of our favourite East Anglia hotel groups – a smallish property, with just 15 rooms and a vibrant bar and brasserie. Six of the rooms are dog friendly but what we like most about the Milsoms group is the fact that their places are comfortable yet relaxed, they tend to have a good restaurant and buzzy bar on site – and they welcome dogs! This one is no exception, with stylish guest rooms with satellite TV, a minibar packed full of complimentary soft drinks, free wifi and lovely indulgent en-suite bathrooms with nice toiletries. There's all-day dining from morning till night in a large-ish restaurant, and dog-owners can eat with their dogs in the lounge or on the terrace. There are lovely mature gardens outside, and it's a great choice for exploring this lovely village and the countryside around, in particular 'Constable Country', where great dog walks abound. Dogs can stay unattended in guest rooms and get towels, bowls, treats and poo bags.

CONTACT Stratford Road Dedham Colchester Essex CO7 6HW• 01206 322795• milsomhotels.com
HOW MUCH? Double rooms from £150 a night, breakfast not included. Dogs free.

The Bucks Arms

Location, location, location. The Bucks Arms would be a nice pub wherever it was, a welcoming old place serving excellent food to hungry locals and tourists, and with 4 characterful rooms upstairs for those who want to stay over. In fact it sits right outside the Jacobean splendour of Blickling Hall in North Norfolk, so is a very special place, with 2 of its rooms enjoying unique views over the hall's grand frontage while the others look out over the vast expanse of Blickling's country park. It welcomes dogs, and no wonder: there are almost 5000 acres to explore on the estate, so it's really perfect for dog-lovers. The rooms are simply furnished but are generous sizes, all with en-suite bathrooms, and 3 have four-poster beds just to help you get into the spirit of the historic location all the more. There's free wifi throughout and each room has a flatscreen TV. As for the pub, it serves predictably excellent breakfasts, and a full menu at lunch and dinner times – smoked haddock rarebit, a lovely Cromer crab salad or just great steaks, burgers and fish and chips.

CONTACT Blickling, Aylsham, Norfolk NR11 6NF • 01263 732133 • bucksarms.co.uk
HOW MUCH? Double rooms from £85 a night. Dogs £15 per stay.

The Elveden Inn

This country inn is a thoroughly inviting roadside hostelry. Part of the Guinness family's Elveden Estate, it couldn't be better situated for getting lost in nearby Thetford Forest with your dog and has 8 spacious rooms, 4 of which are dog friendly. Sensitively restored, the pub is a family-friendly sort of place too, with mismatched furniture and bare floorboards in its main public areas. The rooms are contemporary but cosy, decorated in neutral browns, creams and greys – a mixture of large family rooms, with super-king-size beds and sofa beds and bath/shower, and doubles/twins with king-size beds and showers only. All the rooms are provided with Freeview TVs, tea- and coffee-making facilities, complimentary water, wifi and Elveden's own-brand toiletries in the bathrooms. Elveden is one of the largest farms in East Anglia, so you're in good hands when it comes to food and drink: they serve just what you need after a full day in the forest, with fish and chips, sausage and mash and game and venison from the estate, and although dogs aren't allowed in restaurant, you can eat the same menu in the bar.

CONTACT Brandon Rd, Elveden, Suffolk IP24 3TP •
01842 890876 • elvedeninn.com
HOW MUCH? Double rooms £90–£140 a night. Dogs
£20 a night.

The Pier at Harwich

Harwich isn't the obvious location for a boutique hotel, but this is as chic and stylish a place to stay as you'll find anywhere on the East Coast. The hotel references Harwich's seafaring past, with both its bar and restaurant and 14 upstairs bedrooms (6 of which are dog friendly) designed to make the most of the stunning sunsets and glorious harbour views. All the bedrooms are equipped with flatscreen satellite TVs, complimentary soft drinks and posh aromatherapy toiletries, and there's wifi throughout. There's an excellent first-floor restaurant that opens out onto the building's elegant period wrought-iron balcony, and although you can't eat there with your dog, you can enjoy their company in the bar downstairs, which serves a menu inspired by the town's Scandinavian roots – open sandwiches, sharing platters and great oysters. Dogs get a bowl, towel, poo bags and treats, and there are lovely walks just around the corner, on the town green and following the waterfront path to nearby Dovercourt Bay and its Blue Flag beach. At less than 2 hours from London, it's a great weekend escape.

CONTACT The Pier, The Quay, Harwich, Essex
CO12 3HH • 01255 241212• milsomhotels.com
HOW MUCH? Double rooms from £145 a night.
Mayflower suite from £225 a night. Dogs £10 a night.

The White Horse

Great food and comfy rooms in a fabulous North Norfolk coastal location.

It's hard to beat the location of this combined restaurant, pub and hotel, which backs straight onto the marshes, lagoons and creeks of the North Norfolk Coast. It's something of a local landmark, a special place to eat and also to stay, with seven airy, attractively decorated, en-suite guest rooms in the main building and eight dog-friendly 'garden rooms' at the back, with sedum roofs to blend with the marshes beyond. Consisting of five doubles and three twin rooms, these have been thoughtfully provided with wooden-floored entrance halls for dog beds and muddy boots, and their own terraces for sitting out and enjoying the marsh and sea views; a couple are large enough for a family of five.

Dogs are provided with handmade dog treats and blankets for the duration of their stay. All of the rooms are spacious and contemporary, with a blue-green décor inspired by the seascape beyond. Some have sea views and the top-notch 'Room at the Top' is split over two levels and has its own viewing telescope with which you can take in the best views of the coastline. Whether you stay in the main building or in the garden rooms, all the guest rooms have large comfy beds, smart TVs, digital radios, wifi and tea- and coffee-making facilities, including Nespresso machines.

The White Horse also offers a great selection of guest ales at the bar, including some from its very own Brancaster Brewery just up the road, and the restaurant is one of the best on a coast that's not exactly short of good places to eat. As you might expect, it serves excellent fresh fish and seafood, including local mussels, crab and lobster, which you can enjoy either in the pub itself or the delightful modern conservatory at the back, which makes the most of the property's position overlooking the sea.

Certainly one of the things that makes the White Horse special is the location. It's a short stroll down to pick up the Norfolk Coastal Path at the bottom of the garden, making it a perfect place to stay for dog owners, walkers, cyclists or indeed anyone who wants to explore this unique stretch of coast. You can reach the RSPB reserve at Titchwell by following the coastal path west for about an hour, while to the east it's only just over six miles to Holkham, with its iconic beach and historic hall and estate (perfect for a wander with the dog), and the seaside town of Wells-next-the-Sea just beyond. And if you're looking for somewhere else to stay along the Norfolk coast it's worth knowing that the same family own the excellent King's Head at Letheringsett near Holt, as well as The Farmhouse at Redcoats and Fox at Willian in Hertfordshire – all of which are featured in this book.

CONTACT Main Road, Brancaster Staithe, Norfolk PE31 8BY • 01485 210262 • whitehorsebrancaster.co.uk
HOW MUCH? Double rooms: midweek £110–£230 a night, weekends £150–£240 a night. Dogs £10 a night.
ROOMS There are 15 comfy and contemporary double en-suite rooms divided between the main building and a sedum-roofed, purpose-built extension close to the coast path.

Rectory Manor

An elegant country house B&B that is like the home of your poshest dog-loving friend.

Tucked away in a little-known South Suffolk village, close to the honeypot towns of Lavenham and Long Melford and just a stone's throw from the delights of Constable Country, Rectory Manor is about as homely a place to stay as you could wish for. Arriving here is a bit like attending an old-fashioned country house party, with an efficient and very attentive butler along with Honey the dog there to greet you. Once inside, there's the chance to take the weight off your feet in the book-lined lounge, where a fire burns in the grate and where you can either tinkle at the grand piano or more likely help yourself to a drink from the well-stocked honesty bar. Ancestral portraits cover the walls, and trinkets and family photos adorn every surface. The furniture is tasteful and, like most private homes, sometimes mismatched. Dogs are welcome and they get their own bed; indeed it's the sort of place that can't help but be enhanced by the presence of a well-behaved pooch or two.

There are three rooms in the main house and four in a converted stable block behind the house, and there's only one that doesn't allow dogs. The main house's rooms set the tone, classic in style yet with contemporary touches – one has a wall-length mural of the Bridge of Sighs in Venice in the bathroom, another features the Baroque ceiling of a Roman church as the headboard of the bed. The rooms in the former stables are a bit more sleek and up-to-date, but they demonstrate the same quirky mix of antique and modern, with reproduction tapestries and more artful bespoke headboard prints. All of the rooms are generous sizes, and they all have wifi, tea- and coffee-making facilities, fresh milk and complimentary water, minibars, and even cut-glass decanters filled with gin and whisky for a nightcap or two. The bathrooms are well equipped, with bath robes, Penhaligon toiletries and little extras like sewing kits and cotton buds.

Rectory Manor's butler is always on hand in case you need anything, while occasionally the owner Frank pops up to talk you through the history of the building and his family, many of whom get a name-check in the breakfast room – intriguingly, they all tend to be war heroes, adventurers and spies.

Other facilities include the gardens that wrap around the house, an outdoor swimming pool (open April–September), a tennis court and a croquet lawn – racquets, balls and croquet equipment are all provided – plus there is a hot outdoor shower to clean your hound's muddy paws. You won't be disappointed if you opt for breakfast, as not only is the butler on hand to serve you but you get to enjoy a very well-stocked continental buffet and excellent bacon and sausages from a local butcher.

CONTACT Great Waldingfield, near Lavenham, Suffolk CO10 0TL. • 01787 372428 • rectorymanorhotel.co.uk
HOW MUCH? From £150 a night for the cheaper rooms (2-night minimum stay on summer weekends). Breakfast £12–£17 on top. Dogs £10 a night.
ROOMS 7 double rooms – 3 in the main house and 4 in the converted stable block.

Maison Talbooth

The flagship of the Milsoms group, this agreeable country house has just 12 gorgeously styled guest rooms. They all come with a range of other goodies and services, such as complimentary soft drinks and snacks, satellite TVs and free wifi, and there's a deliberately homely vibe throughout, with an informal flagstoned reception and a lounge that leads through to a Garden Room and outdoor terrace looking out over manicured lawns and gardens. Dogs are welcome in the lounge and grounds and all rooms, where they get towels, treats, bowls, poo bags and food on request. Outside there are tennis courts and an outdoor heated pool and hot tub; the pool house also has satellite TV, honesty bar, bath robes and an open fire. There's a spa with various treatments on offer, and for dinner you can be whisked off to their fine-dining restaurant, Le Talbooth, 2 minutes' away, which has a lovely location by the River Stour and a fab terrace to enjoy it from during summer. Otherwise, it's breakfast and light lunches in the Garden Room or the Talbooth's nearby sister restaurant, Milsoms.

CONTACT Stratford Rd, Dedham, Essex CO7 6HN •
01206 322367 • milsomhotels.com
HOW MUCH? Double rooms £215–£275 a night, suites £335. Dogs £30 a night.

The Bell Inn

There's nothing like staying in a cosy country inn, and the Bell Inn is one of the best you'll find, situated in the sleepy village of Horndon-on-the-Hill near Southend-on-Sea. It's a lovely old family-owned pub and has been a terrific place to eat for years, plus there are 26 very comfortable guest rooms, some of which – High Brow, Du Barry, Stable and High Tea – are dog-friendly. One of the many nice things about the Bell is that it remains a proper local pub, with plenty of people dropping by just for a drink. But plenty more stay to enjoy the food, either in the busy front bar, where you can eat with your dog, or in the quieter restaurant area at the back. Walks include the surrounding Langdon Hills and Langdon Country Park, or a footpath down to the Thames to indulge in a spot of mudlarking along the 'Sea Wall' path. Or you could just enjoy the food and hospitality and potter about the village, which is a dead end since they built the A13 and has a main street of timbered and clapboard houses. Sit and relax in the garden and enjoy the views...

CONTACT High Road, Horndon-on-the-Hill, Stanford-le-Hope, Essex SS17 8LD • 01375 642463 • bell-inn.co.uk
HOW MUCH? Double rooms and suites £80–£145 a night, including continental breakfast. Dogs £15 a night.

The Crown & Castle

Founded by former hotel inspector Ruth Watson, the Crown & Castle bills itself as a 'restaurant with rooms' and food is very much to the fore here, with the emphasis on local ingredients and the service a perfect blend of attentive and relaxed. What you eat really depends on the time of year, but there's usually a good selection of local fish and seafood dishes, steaks and homemade pies. The rooms, meanwhile, divide between 'Best' rooms in the main house and 'Terrace' rooms in a separate building, plus one suite with its own terrace. All are bright and contemporary and recently refurbished, with super-king-size beds and well-appointed bathrooms; dogs are welcome in the 5 ground floor rooms, which have direct access to the garden. They can curl up with their owners in the bar, or if they're organised enough can get their owners to book the one dog-friendly table in the restaurant. Dogs also get treats, poo bags and towels in their room, plus lots of suggestions for walks both by the sea and in nearby Rendlesham Fore

CONTACT Market Hill, Orford, Suffolk IP12 2LJ •
01394 450205 • crownandcastle.co.uk
HOW MUCH? Double rooms from about £170 a night.
Dogs £10 a night.

The Black Lion

Picture for a moment a picturesque pub in a beautiful Suffolk village. Chances are you are imagining somewhere quite like the Black Lion in Long Melford, which occupies an extremely picturesque location overlooking the village green, next to a medieval church. There can't be too many better places to wake up if you're after a weekend in the country, so it's good to know that the Black Lion not only serves good food but also has a comfy set of rooms to flop into after dinner. This small Georgian inn has been updated beautifully, with wooden floors, artfully mismatched furniture and a comfy lounge with armchairs and newspapers combining to suggest a comfortable house in the country at which you are one of the most important guests. There are 10 rooms, and apart from a couple of cheaper 'Snug' rooms, all are spacious and come with king-size beds, wifi, TVs, tea- and coffee-making facilities, homemade biscuits, mineral water, and en-suite bathrooms with tubs and Noble Isle toiletries. All apart from a family suite are open to dogs, who get a blanket, treats and more.

CONTACT The Green, Long Melford, Suffolk CO10 9DN
• 01787 312356 • theblacklionhotel.com
HOW MUCH? Double rooms £90–£130 a night. Dogs
£10 a night.

The White House

Just outside Burnham Market, the owners of this wonderful flint-and-white North Norfolk mansion have thought of every detail to make your stay more comfortable. The rooms are luxurious and well equipped, with indulgent bathrooms and contemporary-yet-cosy furnishings; they serve delicious breakfasts in a bright and sunny garden room, and if you have a large party and something special to celebrate, you can have the place to yourself. Of the White House's 12 rooms, bedrooms 1 and 12 – the suite – are both dog friendly and come with a dog towel, water bowl, treats and poo bags. All rooms come with ultra-comfy Hypnos beds with silk duvets and goosedown or allergy-free pillows, TVs and Roberts radios, super-fast wifi, tea- and coffee-making facilities, and bathrooms with underfloor heating and 100 Acres toiletries. Best of all, walks head off in all directions, among them one that leads to the Norfolk Coast Path and Brancaster beach, which is dog heaven. They also offer horse livery at the family stables opposite the house, so as well as dogs you can bring the horses on holiday too!

CONTACT 5–7 Sussex Farm, Burnham Market, Norfolk PE31 8JY • 07785 439727 • stayatthewhitehouse.co.uk
HOW MUCH? Double rooms from £150 a night, dogs £10 a night.

The Fritton Arms

Tucked away on the edge of the Norfolk Broads, the Fritton Arms straddles the Norfolk–Suffolk border – a country inn that serves excellent food, has 8 comfortable rooms plus a number of self-catering cottages and woodland lodges. Originally dating from the 15th century and expanded in Georgian times, the Fritton Arms is a deliciously relaxed sort of place, with creaky floorboards, big fireplaces, random works of art and scatterings of books and magazines. The décor throughout is rustic yet contemporary, with squashy sofas in the lounge, comfy chairs around an open fire in the bar and stripped-down pine tables with modish blue chairs in the restaurant. There's a big outside terrace, beyond which you can enjoy the lakeside and the grounds of the Somerleyton estate which not only has great walks but lots of leisure facilities too – everything from boating and wild swimming to tamer stuff in an open-air pool or a spot of tennis. Dogs are welcome in all rooms and the lounges, bar and restaurant, and the cottages are pet-friendly too.

CONTACT Fritton, Great Yarmouth, Norfolk NR31 9HA • 01493 484008 • somerleyton.co.uk
HOW MUCH? Double rooms £110–£200 a night, dogs £15 a night.

Strattons

When it opened nearly 30 years ago, Strattons was the epitome of a new breed of British boutique hotel, with an attractive historic building, a great restaurant and comfortable rooms that were contemporary and welcoming, and a little bit quirky. Tucked away in a courtyard footsteps from what passes for urban hum in Swaffham, it's still a great place to stay, with 8 rooms in the main house, 2 opulent suites, and 2 slick self-catering apartments across the garden. One of these is dog friendly, as are 2 double rooms in a converted cottage, and dogs are provided with food, bowls and poo bags; the hotel will also order fresh meat or bones from the local butchers if you ask in advance and the rooms have mini fridges for storage. The hotel has maps detailing local walks, including the easy stroll through the meadows beyond the churchyard opposite. And although it's not open to dogs, the restaurant is fab and you can eat the same menu with your pooch in the lounge or in your room. Also, their excellent café–deli is dog friendly and open for breakfast and lunch.

CONTACT 4 Ash Close, Swaffham, Norfolk PE37 7NH • 01760 723845 • strattonshotel.com
HOW MUCH? Double rooms from £99 a night, suites from £131, apartments from £154; dogs £10 a night.

Five Acre Barn

Housed in an award-winning barn conversion midway between Aldeburgh and Thorpeness, Five Acre Barn makes a lovely base for seeing the Suffolk Coast. An architect-designed bolthole with jagged roofs, cedar cladding and soaring ceilings it's the ultimate contemporary B&B, with 5 very comfortable and spacious guest rooms, 3 of which are dog friendly. David and Bruce are big dog lovers, and each room has its own stretch of decking with access to no less than 5 acres of garden and woodland. Breakfast is a relaxed and sociable affair and there is loads to see and do nearby: the sea at Thorpeness is just over a mile away, and is easily reached on foot through the woods, where you can pick up the Suffolk Coast Path. You could also walk to Aldeburgh and the wonderful Red House, home of the composer Benjamin Britten, or if you have a sociable dog you could just chill out for the day in the Barn – there's a Sonos music system, comfy sofas, games and books and a wood-burner that will almost make you wish for a rainy day.

CONTACT Aldeburgh Rd, Aldringham, Suffolk IP16 4QH • 07788 424642 • fiveacrebarn.co.uk
HOW MUCH? Double rooms £100–£130 a night, dogs free.

Victoria Inn

Situated just a few minutes' walk from the golden sands of Holkham Beach and at the gates of Holkham Hall, the Victoria Inn is in an ideal location for discovering one of the most appealing parts of the North Norfolk Coast. It has a total of 20 bedrooms – 10 in the pub itself with a further 10 in the so-called Ancient House opposite. They're all individually decorated, with a choice of twin and double rooms in the pub and a selection of suites in the Ancient House. Most of the rooms in the pub are bright and spacious and come with king-size beds, tea- and coffee-making facilities (with fresh milk and homemade shortbread), wifi, en-suite bathrooms with toiletries and robes – and some rooms have standalone baths and separate showers. Dogs are welcome in all the rooms in the pub and throughout the ground-floor areas. As for the food, it's – naturally – estate-sourced, not overly complicated and delicious, and you can eat with your dog in the bar, preferably after a day enjoying the glorious dog friendly expanse of Holkham beach and the pinewoods behind.

CONTACT Park Rd, Wells-next-the-Sea, Norfolk NR23 1AB • 01328 711008 • holkham.co.uk
HOW MUCH? Double rooms from £100 a night, dogs £10 per stay.

The Rose & Crown

Run by the people behind the excellent Bank House in nearby King's Lynn, this ancient inn has been around since the 14th century and in some ways is still a traditional village boozer. But it's also well known as a place to stay, and is everything a pub with rooms should be – delightfully modernised with 16 pretty and very comfortable en-suite guest rooms and a cracking bar downstairs. The rooms are all bright and seasidey and come with good quality beds and linen, TV, fluffy towels and Molton Brown toiletries. Pooches pay a modest extra charge. The walled garden is a sunny spot for drinkers, while the restaurant is first-rate, with proper attention given to local, seasonal ingredients – oysters and mussels, burgers and steaks, and a good Sunday lunch. The pub is also so handy for some of the most alluring stretches of the North Norfolk Coast – the Snettisham RSPB reserve, Sandringham and the pretty villages nearby – Docking, Bircham, Ingoldisthorpe – all of which are lovely links in a perfect country walk with a dog.

CONTACT Old Church Rd, Snettisham, Norfolk PE31 7LX • 01485 541382 • roseandcrownsnettisham.co.uk
HOW MUCH? Double rooms £120 a night, dogs £15.

Weybourne Home Farm

The North Norfolk Coast is so perfect for dogs that it's almost a shame to travel here without the family pet. This complex of holiday cottages couldn't be better situated, on the edge of the small village of Weybourne, a short walk from a dog-friendly pebble beach. There are well over a dozen cottages, sleeping between 3 and 7 people, and several accept dogs. The site itself has an indoor pool, a games room and soft play area and a small gym; there are well-tended gardens for early morning walks, lots of parking and a bike store, plus a dog-friendly pub a short walk away. As for the cottages, they are a mixture of converted barns, flint terraces and detached houses, but they're all beautifully fitted out with stylish interiors, up-to-date bathrooms and kitchens, wifi, central heating and sometimes wood-burning stoves. You need a car to get here but if you want to put the car keys in a drawer for a few days, it couldn't be more ideal: the Norfolk Coast Path passes right by, with the popular harbourside village of Blakeney 5 miles in one direction and the seaside town of Sheringham, 3 miles in the other direction.

CONTACT Holt Rd, Weybourne, Norfolk NR25 7ST • 01264 588334 • weybourne-holiday-cottages.co.uk
HOW MUCH? Short breaks from £420, 7 nights from £495.

Oak Tree Cottages

Just ten minutes away from the sea at Happisburgh, Oak Tree Cottages is a small complex of 3 single storey flint cottages set around an L-shaped courtyard, just outside the North Norfolk village of East Ruston. Family-owned and -run, owners Lauren and Chris Risby are keen dog-lovers themselves so when they took over the business they knew they wanted it to be dog-friendly. There are two 2-bedroom cottages and one 3-bedroom cottage, and another 1-bedroom property on the way. All are dog friendly, and all are brightly restored barns with beams, quarry-tiled floors and lovely big open-plan living areas. Up to 4 dogs are welcome in each property and they provide beds, bowls, dog tags, throws for the furniture, towels for muddy paws, poo bags, treats and even crates if you need them; plus there's an enclosed field for dogs to run around in. It's a great place to visit with a dog, with country walks all around and great sandy beaches nearby – at Happisburgh, Mundesley and Overstrand – that are either completely or partly dog friendly.

CONTACT Church Farm, East Ruston, Norfolk NR12 9HJ • 01692 773259 • oaktreecottages.co.uk
HOW MUCH? Two-night stays from £295, weekend breaks from £425.

THE MIDLANDS

Whisper it – England's Midlands contain some
of the most beautiful countryside in the UK.
From the green hills of Shropshire, Herefordshire
and the Borders to the granite heights of
Britain's first national park and the flat fenlands
of Lincolnshire, there's a bit of something for
everyone in England's rolling heartland.

Walcot Hall

Your very own country estate in the heart of the Shropshire Hills.

Not many people know about Walcot Hall – not many outside the county of Shropshire anyway. And indeed you could pass through the village of Lydbury North and not know that the house was even there, tucked away up a long, winding drive from the main road. It's a 'Georgian gem', and one that you can experience for yourself, with 15 self-catering holiday cottages and lots of interesting glamping options in a variety of buildings and structures, including an old reconstructed chapel in the estate's 20-acre arboretum, which was itself added by Clive of India when he lived here in the 18th century.

With between one and five bedrooms, the cottages and apartments are as cosy as you could wish for, thoughtfully furnished with a classically comfortable feel that will make you believe you really are lord and lady of the manor for the weekend. Walcot Hall can accommodate families, romantic couples or large groups, for example in the beautifully refurbished five-bedroom Garden House or the spacious Styche on the top floor of the main house. The Hall's cottages and apartments all have wood-burning stoves or Agas, and some have private patios or garden spaces. The most recent addition is Norbury Hall, which sleeps 6 and overlooks a kitchen garden tended by women from the local Mennonite community, while the furthest-flung is the Dipping Shed, which sleeps four in secluded comfort. Our favourite, however, is the Chapel, whose two double bedrooms are also wonderfully private among the trees. Dogs are welcome everywhere and get a dog bowl and treats on arrival.

The estate also has a wide range of glamping options – five yurts, a gypsy caravan and two romantic shepherd's huts, two showman's caravans, even a converted fire truck. Some of these have their own facilities, the yurts share a converted henhouse loo, others use a 'long-drop' earth toilet in the woods; and there is a hut with a gas-powered shower. All are exquisitely fitted out in a rustic but very comfortable style with double beds.

Whether you go for the cottages or the glamping, you have all the privileges of a night on the estate, and the fabulous walks you can do here might be enough for you and your hound. You're also spoilt for choice in the countryside around – try the scenic three-mile route to Bishop's Castle, a thoroughly welcoming little market town where you can eat and drink at the excellent dog-friendly Castle Hotel. Closer to home, the village pub, the dog-friendly Powis Arms is owned by the estate and serves good food, while in the other direction you might try the equally dog-lovin' Kangaroo in Aston-on-Clun.

CONTACT Lydbury North, Shropshire SY7 8AZ • 01588 680570 • walcothall.com

HOW MUCH? From £400 for short breaks to £750 for a week in Walcot Hall's 2-bedroom offerings. Larger properties cost from £825 (for a short break) to £1750 for a week. Glamping £120–£200 for a 2-night weekend.

ACCOMMODATION 15 self-catering holiday cottages and apartments, 5 yurts, 1 gypsy caravan and 2 shepherd's huts, 2 showman's caravans and 1 converted fire truck.

The Devonshire Arms

Another fine member of the Chatsworth stable, the 'Dev' is one of the Duke and Duchess's oldest pubs, and very handsome it is too, sitting squarely in the pretty hamlet of Beeley, just a mile or so from the stately pile. It's a pub that's moved with the times but is also strangely unchanged. You can sit (with your dog) in the stone-flagged bar with a pint or eat in front of the fire, but it also has a brasserie these days which serves the same menu – everything from wild rabbit pie to fish and chips and local game in autumn and winter. It's a very cosy place indeed, giving you a warm feeling that continues right up to its bedrooms, 4 of which are upstairs while the others are scattered in various buildings around the village – one of which, Brookside House, is dog friendly. All the rooms have wifi, flatscreen Freeview TVs, tea- and coffee-making facilities and en-suite bathrooms with toiletries, and are very comfortable – the perfect place for you and your faithful friend to discover all the walks possible from the village and of course on the Chatsworth estate itself.

CONTACT Beeley, near Matlock, Derbyshire DE4 2NR • 01629 733259 • devonshirebeeley.co.uk
HOW MUCH? Double rooms from around £100 a night, dogs £10 a night.

Langar Hall

When the remarkable, and remarkably charismatic, Imogen Skirving turned her delightful family home into a bijou hotel some 30 years ago, she was determined to create something that was warm and friendly, luxurious and stylish – and she succeeded in spades. Now run by Imogen's granddaughter, Langar Hall, is located on the edge of the village at the end of an avenue of lime trees. The interior is a canny amalgam of the High Victorian and the modern, with each of its 12 guest rooms boasting an individual style and flavour, from the Bohemia room with its four-poster bed to the rusticated Cricketers with its rocking chair and vintage floor mats. The hotel restaurant is simply outstanding, and although dogs are only occasionally welcome in selected rooms in the main house, they are always welcome in Agnew's Chalet', a prettily designed hut in the grounds with its own verandah, and The Pod beside the croquet lawn. The grounds also provide good opportunties for impromptu walks and well-behaved pooches may receive the occasional treat from the kitchen.

CONTACT Cropwell Bishop Rd, Langar, Nottinghamshire NG13 9HG • 01949 860559 • langarhall.com
HOW MUCH? Double rooms from £150 a night, dogs £30 a night.

The George Townhouse

Located in the middle of the handsome north
Cotswolds market town of Shipston-on-Stour,
and by far the grandest building on the high street,
this 18th-century coaching inn has been the
heartbeat of the town for years. It's had a bit of a
boutique makeover in recent years but remains a
popular local venue for food and drink. Like all
good pubs, it's welcoming to dogs, both in the bar
downstairs and in 2 of the rooms above, which
come with king-size beds, high-quality mattresses
and stylish bathrooms with rainfall showers, plus
Temple Spa toiletries, flatscreen TVs, mineral water
and Nespresso machines. There are 15 rooms in
all, ranging from smallish 'Classic' rooms to larger
'Superior' and 'Deluxe' rooms and so-called 'Deluxe
Plus' rooms, which have a free-standing bath and
separate walk-in showers. There's also a suite right
at the top of the building. Downstairs they serve a
shortish, moderately priced menu with half a dozen
starters and mains, plus good steaks and a few pub
classics – and we challenge anyone to finish what is a
generously portioned Full English breakfast.

CONTACT 8 High Street, Shipston-on-Stour,
Warwickshire CV36 4AJ • 01608 661453 •
thegeorgeshipston.co.uk
HOW MUCH? Doubles £100–£180 a night, dogs £20.

Forest Holidays Sherwood

What child hasn't dreamed of running through the
glades of Sherwood Forest with a bow and arrow?
Well, here they can, at Forest Holidays' superb
woodland site in the heart of Sherwood Forest
in Nottinghamshire. There are 3300 acres of pine
forest to explore, a choice of cabins – including
luxury treehouses (sleeping up to 10 people) and
adults-only hideaways (sleeping 2) – plus a host of
activities, both within the Forest Holidays site itself
and in the forest beyond – there's a visitor centre
a 5-minute walk away that has all you need to
know about the adjacent Sherwood Pines Forest
Park. All the cabins are extremely comfortable,
equipped with TV, wifi (an optional extra), fluffy
robes (standard in the Golden Oak cabins) and dogs
are welcome in many of the cabins. There are great
walks galore, and numerous facilities and activities
from traditional biking and walking trails to Segway
hire, plus a branch of the Go Ape high-wire outfit.
The Forest Retreat centre also has a café and bar,
shop and play area and organizes bushcraft and
wildlife-spotting activities with the Forest Rangers.

CONTACT Sherwood Pines Forest Park, Edwinstowe,
Nottinghamshire NG21 9JH • 03330 110495 •
forestholidays.co.uk
HOW MUCH? Short breaks from £300, dogs £15.

The Castle Hotel

The perfect country bolthole, with comfy rooms, a cosy bar and restaurant and a wonderful Shropshire location.

Once you get to the top of the main street of the tiny town of Bishop's Castle, which is where you'll find the Castle Hotel, you feel like you've really got away from it all. Based at the end of a small cul-de-sac, with glorious views over the surrounding countryside, much of it within the Shropshire Hills Area of Outstanding Natural Beauty, the hotel makes for an inspiring bolt-hole for aspirant walkers and cyclists and is very family and dog friendly.

The Castle has been here since the early 18th century – owners Henry and Rebecca claim local boy Clive of India was once the landlord – and it's just our sort of place: comfy rather than posh, with large and cosy rooms with flatscreen TVs, tea- and coffee-making facilities and wifi throughout. There's also a cottage across the road which you can either rent on a self-catering basis or using the facilities at the hotel. There's a good restaurant downstairs serving great breakfasts and a lovely menu the rest of the day that includes lots of local produce and a veggie option or two; the bar is very convivial and well used by locals and makes a point of serving proper brews from the local area, including the town's two micro-breweries, the Three Tuns and Six Bells (the hotel has special rates on brewery tours for real enthusiasts). There is also a fantastic, almost Mediterranean-style garden that overlooks the Shropshire Hills from its high perch behind the hotel, and which is perfect both for enjoying an early evening glass of wine from its covered arbours or giving the dog a quick early morning walk.

Indeed the Castle is one of the most dog-friendly hotels we know, not only encouraging you to bring your pet for no extra charge but also providing a 'Dog Welcome Box' in the room which includes a blanket, towel, food bowl, lead, treats, poo bags and an ID collar explaining that your pet is on holiday, with a contact number for the hotel. They also include recommendations of local vets and the best walks nearby – and your dog might also like to play with the owners' friendly dachshund, Millie.

Finally, there's the Castle's location, which is frankly glorious and perfect for dogs, with lots of circular walks of all kinds possible from your doorstep, and lots of cycle trails too. The hotel has details of lots of good walks, including the South Shropshire Way, which passes by right outside, and Offa's Dyke, which is not far away either. There is also the Kerry Ridgeway, a 15-mile route through the hills of the Welsh borders, and strenuous hikes up to the Long Mynd and the famous Stiperstones – hikes that should wear out even the most indefatigable spaniel!

CONTACT Bishop's Castle, Shropshire SY9 5BN • 01588 638403 • thecastlehotelbishopscastle.co.uk
HOW MUCH? Double rooms £125–£210, less during the week. Dogs free.
ROOMS 12 bedrooms in the hotel – plus a cottage just across the road from the hotel where guests can stay self-catering or on a B&B package.

The Lygon Arms

Of all the handsome stone villages in The Cotswolds, Broadway is one of the most impressive, and it's here that you'll find the charming – and charmingly luxurious – Lygon Arms, an ancient coaching inn on the road from London to Wales. There has been a hotel here since medieval times, but most of what you see today dates from the 17th century, from the honey-coloured stone of the main façade to the vaulted Great Hall. Oliver Cromwell stayed here in 1651, and Charles I visited a few years before, and both their suites survive to this day. The hotel has 86 guest rooms – from 'Cosy' through 'Classic' to 'Deluxe' – which divide between the main building, the courtyard and nearby cottages. All are decorated in pastel shades with splashes of colour, period flourishes and a scattering of paintings. The Lygon is also particularly welcoming to dogs, who are allowed to roam the garden and most of the public areas, and many of the bedrooms are dog-friendly, with beds and treats thrown in for good measure. The hotel can also arrange for a dog-grooming session during your stay.

CONTACT High St, Broadway, Worcestershire WR12 7DU · 01386 852255 · lygonarmshotel.co.uk
HOW MUCH? Double rooms from £195 a night, dogs £25 a night.

The Fish Hotel

Deep in the heart of the Cotswolds, the rolling fields and wooded hills of the Farncombe Estate are home to a number of grand hotels, the latest of which – the Fish Hotel – is tucked into the hillside, with views of the valley below and a set of appealing rooms and suites decorated in a crisp and modern style. Divided between the Farmhouse, Coach House, Stables and Outhouse, the rooms are extremely comfortable; the grounds are also home to several 'Hilly Huts' with underfloor heating, hot tubs, en-suite bathrooms and wood-burning stoves, along with a number of treehouses, which have all the conveniences of the huts plus access by a rope bridge and a wooded setting. One of the treehouses is dog friendly, as are several of the hotel bedrooms, and hounds are also permitted in the bar and the lounge of the hotel and throughout the grounds, making walkies pretty much a cinch for lazy dog-owners. Dogs also get a bed, dog bowls, a towel and doggie treats. There is even a dog agility course for the energetic hound and the hotel can provide a special dog's dinner for particularly pampered pooches.

CONTACT Broadway, Worcestershire WR12 7LH · 01386 858000 · thefishhotel.co.uk
HOW MUCH? Double rooms from £150 a night, treehouses from £350, huts from £270. Dogs £30.

Colwall Park Hotel

The Malvern Hills' green wooded flanks rise spectacularly just to the southwest of Worcester: a quintessentially English landscape that inspired the composer Edward Elgar. The hills are famous for two things, the splendid medieval charms of Great Malvern's Priory Church and the steep but easy-to-follow footpaths that pattern the area, especially North Hill, making it a particularly good region to visit with a dog in tow. Located on the western side of the Malverns, just 3 miles from the priory, this hotel is an excellent base for exploring this beautiful region, its good-looking half-timbered façade giving a warm welcome and 22 light bright, individually decorated comfortable rooms, most of which are dog friendly and provide beds, bowls, towels and treats to their lucky occupants. Not only that, the hotel's restaurant is excellent, serving delicious food at affordable prices in an area where good restaurants are at something of a premium. The hotel's reception has walking packs detailing various routes, one of which starts from the hote, and also takes orders for packed lunches for hungry walkers.

CONTACT Colwall, Malvern, Worcestershire WR13 6QG
• 01684 540000 • colwall.co.uk
HOW MUCH? Double rooms from £80 a night, dogs
£10 a night.

Up Sticks Glamping

'Home comforts with the great outdoors right on your doorstep', is how Charlotte Taylor succinctly describes her family-run glamping site, set amid an apple orchard at the foot of the Malvern Hills. 'No rushing to the supermarket. Everything is here'. The 17-acre rural patchwork of meadows, hedgerows and natural ponds caters to every need. The glamping accommodation comprises 3 family-size safari tents each with fully equipped kitchen, sofas and proper beds. Throw in the bikes available to rent and the pub right next door and you quickly realise there's not a thing that you could want for. The attention to detail is exceptional. Fluffy towels are ready in your bathroom, there's a breakfast pack provided for your first morning, cool white wine awaits you in the fridge and the woodburner and firepit cast a warm glow as the sun goes down. They love dogs and offer a 'dog stay pack' which includes a crate, bowls and tether. Just as well – the Malvern Hills are on your doorstep, with footpaths and trails to die for (and onsite wash-down facilities for muddy paws and boots on your return).

CONTACT Birts St, Birtsmorton, Malvern, Worcestershire
WR13 6AP • 07713 670504 • upsticksglamping.co.uk
HOW MUCH? 2-night weekends from £350, 4-night
stays from £450. Full weeks from £650. Dogs £25.

OUT AND ABOUT
Four great walks with your dog

HAMBLETON PENINSULA This circular walk skirts Rutland Water's Hambleton Peninsula, home to the first ospreys to breed in England for 150 years and a popular location with everyone from dog walkers and birdwatchers to cyclists and and watersports enthusiasts. Visit between spring and autumn to see the ospreys hunting fish across the reservoir. **4.8 MILES**

HATHERSAGE This circular walk takes in some beautiful countryside around the pretty Peak District village of Hathersage. It's relatively flat and gentle by Peak District standards, with only a few small hills, and for the most part it follows well-made paths and lanes. However, there are three short stretches of road, one of which has no pavement – worth bearing in mind if your dog isn't great in traffic. **6 MILES**

MAM TOR & THE GREAT RIDGE This popular Peak District walk takes in the dramatic, windswept summit of Mam Tor, known as the Shivering Mountain, and traverses the Great Ridge that separates Edale from the Hope Valley. It starts and finishes in the village of Castleton and tags every major peak, including Hollins Cross, Back Tor and Lose Hill Pike. **6.6 MILES**

MONSAL TRAIL A traffic-free route through the spectacular limestone scenery of the old Midland Railway line – ideal for walkers, cyclists and even wheelchair users. The full trail extends for 8.5 miles but the stretch between Hassop and Headstone Viaduct is one of the easiest you can do, complete with listening stations along the way and passing through the 487m-long Headstone Tunnel – at the end of which the Headstone Viaduct offers spectacular views. **2 MILES**

THE OUTDOOR GUIDE

Barnsdale Lodge Hotel

A collection of low-slung, typically honey-stoned buildings around a central courtyard, Barnsdale Lodge is a long-established dog friendly Rutland hotel. It has 46 bedrooms, of which all those on the ground floor (around half) welcome dogs. There are also 17 very comfy self-catering lodges – Rutland Retreats – across the road, all of which are dog friendly too. Hounds get a welcome pack containing a bowl and a bed, chews and poo bags and a letter from resident pooches Coco and Maisie detailing fun doggy things to do. There are opportunities for off-lead walks in the hotel's own meadows, and you couldn't be much better placed for the glorious expanse of Rutland Water, where you can walk or cycle the path that circles the lake, enjoy the many watersports on offer or see the water on the stately Rutland Belle. Back at the hotel, the formal restaurant and light and airy conservatory are lovely and although they don't allow dogs, there's a very cosy dog-friendly bar where you can eat the same menu.

CONTACT Exton Lane, Rutland LE15 8AH •
01572 724678 • barnsdalelodge.co.uk
HOW MUCH? Double rooms £89–£149 a night. Dogs
£10 a night.

The Bull & Swan

Just outside the Lincolnshire market town of Stamford, Burghley House and Estate is best known for its annual horse trials. But there have been less wholesome times too: in 1684 the dissolute 5th Earl of Exeter founded The Honourable Order of Bedlam, an aristocratic drinking club that met at the Bull & Swan, behind ancient stone gables that have survived to this day. What's more, the erstwhile members of the Order have lent the pub's 7 comfortable bedrooms their names, or rather pseudonyms (the 'Badger', the 'Porcupine' and so forth). Each room is different, but they're all very comfortable, furnished with the same curvy dark furniture in a successful blend of traditional and contemporary styles. Each room has a decent-sized en-suite bathroom and dogs are very welcome – there is even a room-service menu for pooches. Downstairs, the pub serves everything from homemade Scotch eggs and doorstep sandwiches to steaks and fish and chips, and the grounds of Burghley House are perfect for walks with the dog – as is the footpath around nearby Rutland Water.

CONTACT 24 High St, St Martins, Stamford,
Lincolnshire, PE9 2LJ • 01780 766412•
hillbrookehotels.co.uk
HOW MUCH? Doubles from £110 a night. Dogs £20.

Nailcote Hall

Set in 15 acres of lush countryside, Warwickshire's Nailcote Hall is a former stately home dating back to the 17th century. Now it's a 4-star hotel and spa, and a very welcoming place, with oak beams, a priest hole and a comfy sofa or two. There are 49 rooms, most of them decorated in keeping with the character of the building, and well equipped with crazy-comfortable beds and great showers, TVs with Sky, wifi and tea- and coffee-making facilities. They're all of a good size and come with views of the lush countryside, the smell of fir trees and abundant peace and quiet. Dogs are welcome in the ground-floor rooms, which give easy access to the grounds and come with food and water bowls on their own feeding mat. Dogs are also welcome throughout the rest of the hotel except in the fine-dining restaurant, although you can eat with your dog in the bar. As regards location, you're well placed for the quaint town of Kenilworth and its castle, and the National Exhibition Centre is nearby, making it handy for trade shows, exhibitions, concerts, and – yes, dog lovers! – Crufts!

CONTACT Nailcote Lane, Berkswell, Warwickshire CV7 7DE • 024 764 66112 • nailcotehall.co.uk
HOW MUCH? Double rooms from around £109 a night., dogs £15.

Tiny Wooden House

If you've ever fancied spending a night on the set of 'Little House on the Prairie,' visiting Tiny Wooden House – a pair of wooden cabins designed to recreate the same sort of rustic idyll in what is by any standards a stunning Warwickshire location – might just be for you. Each abode offers all the comforts and proportions of a normal 2-bedroom house, but with a truly tiny footprint. Step inside and you'll find comfortable bedrooms, a kitchen finished with granite worktops, a separate bathroom and a verandah featuring an all-weather wood-fired BBQ that doubles up as a toasty wood-burner. Each home is set on the edge of a 100-acre arable field, facing unhindered views of the Warwickshire countryside, and, as the evening temperatures dip, the steaming water and crackling log fire of your wood-fired hot tub is a glorious way to see out the day. Finally, despite being only a few miles from Stratford-upon-Avon, the site is deep enough in Warwickshire's rural bosom to hear the county's agricultural heartbeat, yet it's within easy reach of the M40 and A423, so escaping here is a breeze.

CONTACT Grange Cottages, Snowford Hill, Long Itchington, Warwickshire CV47 9QE • 07774933717 • tinywoodhomes.webs.com
HOW MUCH? From £110 a night (min 2 nights), dogs free.

Cider Mill Cottage

A former cider mill converted into a delightful beamed cottage for two, amid lovely Worcestershire countryside.

Just a few miles northwest of Worcester, on the edge of the Malvern Hills Area of Outstanding Natural Beauty, this old beamed cider mill offers snug and cosy accommodation for two, or for a couple with a toddler or young child – and, of course, a well-behaved dog! It's been beautifully converted, and offers the perfect base for exploring a hugely attractive part of England, with Worcester, Malvern and the delights of the relatively unexplored Teme Valley on your doorstep. They love dogs in this part of the world and Cider Mill Cottage is a perfect off-the-beaten-track location for dog-walking, visits to dog-friendly cosy local pubs and other attractions that welcome four-legged friends.

Situated down a bumpy farm lane, about a mile from the main road, the cottage feels gloriously isolated, enjoying stupendous views over the surrounding countryside. It has a well-arranged open-plan living area, with a wood-burning stove, sofas, TV and DVD, a small dining area and a contemporary kitchen in which the original mill wheel (of the old cider press) has pride of place; the kitchen is ingeniously built around it. The kitchen is warmed by an Aga so you can really live out your country living fantasies – you are, after all, not far from the home of The Archers! Upstairs, there's a master bedroom with an antique double bed, along with a bright single room and a well-equipped modern bathroom, with more vintage pieces of furniture throughout. A welcome basket is provided on arrival, full of garden produce and homemade goodies.

Catherine, the owner, lives in the nearby main house, and is always on hand to advise on the best country walks or which pubs are dog friendly or serve the best food – and she'll also let you use her lovely swimming pool if you ask nicely. At the very least you should take a stroll through her gorgeous garden and make the most of the wonderful views from here over Worcestershire's patchwork of fields and lush green hills.

The nearby Teme Valley is a bit of a hidden gem, boasting quintessentially English countryside that is typical of this part of Worcestershire. There are lots of walks right from the doorstep, or you can follow part of the long-distance Worcestershire Way, which runs nearby on its route down to Malvern. Nearby sights include the local composer Edward Elgar's birthplace, just outside Worcester, the factory tours you can do of the Morgan Motor Company in Malvern and of course the city of Worcester itself, with its magnificent cathedral. You might start off thinking about a lovely weekend escape, but there's plenty to do and a full week here suddenly seems a rather attractive proposition, and is heartily recommended!

CONTACT Ayngstree, Clifton upon Teme, Worcestershire WR6 6DS • 07590 073084 • cidermill-cottage.co.uk
HOW MUCH? Seven nights from £410; short breaks and weekends available from £110.
ACCOMMODATION Two bedrooms – one double and one single – which suit a couple or a family with a young child (no children under 5).

Birdholme Glamping

Set amid 15 acres of prime Nottinghamshire countryside, it's questionable whether these 4 superbly endowed safari lodges are really glamping at all. Built by affable owners Peter and Holly Hinchley, in the middle of a young forest planted by Peter's father, these timber-framed lodges really do take things to a new level, with bamboo roofs beneath canvas tents, cosy living areas with wood-burners, comfy chairs and dining tables, proper bathrooms and well-equipped kitchens with an oven, a hob and fridge (where you'll find a bottle of bubbly to greet you on arrival). Sleeping 4 adults plus 2 little ones, they even have dishwashers, leaving you plenty of time to bask in your hot tub on the verandah and enjoy the views over the nearby lake. There's a smart TV, super-fast wifi and games and books for rainy days, and 2 of the lodges are dog friendly. A footpath leads fro the site to Leicestershire's Vale of Belvoir, plus there's a country park in nearby Cotgrave, from where you can follow the canal path all the way to Nottingham, 8 miles away, if you tire of country life. Not that it's likely!

CONTACT Birdholme Wood, Melton Rd, Stanton-on-the-Wolds, Nottinghamshire NG12 5BQ · 0115 850 0959 · birdholmeglamping.co.uk
HOW MUCH? Three-night breaks £620–£780.

Speedwell House

Situated in the pretty Derbyshire village of Castleton, deep in the heart of the Peak District, Speedwell House offers a variety of accommodation. It's a beautiful, award-winning 2-room boutique B&B but it also has a Barn and Stable each of which offers lovely dog-friendly and rather romantic self-catering accommodation for 2 people. These stone-floored, sympathetically restored properties are wonderfully cosy, kitted out with a mix of antique furniture, bespoke wooden beds and contemporary bathrooms that blends beautifully with the rustic stone walls and funky mirrors and fabrics; and with large flatscreen smart TVs, fast wifi, well-equipped kitchens (with dishwashers), they're right up to date too. Owners Mark and Hilary are on hand to help you make the most of your stay, with lots of tips on the best walks and pubs. Your dog will also thank you for choosing to come here, with beautiful views and invigorating walks in all directions: everything from a circular walk around the village taking in the ruins of Peveril Castle to trips further afield to Mam Tor, Edale and the Hope Valley.

CONTACT Buxton Rd, Castleton, Derbyshire S33 8WP · 07943 196256 · speedwell-house.co.uk
HOW MUCH? 2 nights from £260, 7 nights from £550, dogs £30 per stay. B&B rooms £90–£100 a night.

Pen-y-Dyffryn Hotel

Located right on the border of Shropshire and Wales, this lovely old Georgian country house hosts a characterful and very friendly family-run hotel in a great country location. The name means 'Head of the Valley', and it's an idyllic spot for both dogs and humans, well situated for walks into the surrounding hills and with an area of woodland next door, along with 5 acres of its own gardens and grounds. It has 8 rooms in the main house and 4 in an adjacent coach house, all traditionally furnished and very well equipped. Dogs are welcome in the coach house rooms, which have their own patios, and they receive towels, bowls, biscuits and treats (but you need to bring your own bed). There's a dog wash area with a warm water hose, dog shampoos and dog brushes, and hounds are allowed in all public areas up until 6pm. After that, you can leave them in your room while you dine in their rather good restaurant, which serves a delicious and well-presented menu, not to mention a hearty breakfast the next morning to set you up for exploring the countryside around.

CONTACT Rhydycroesau, Oswestry, Shropshire SY10 7JD • 01691 653700 • peny.co.uk
HOW MUCH? Double rooms from around £150 a night, dogs free.

The Peacock at Rowsley

Owned by Lord and Lady Manners of nearby Haddon Hall, the Peacock at Rowsley is a perfect place from which to savour this beautiful part of the Peak District and is within easy striking distance of the area's star turn, Chatsworth House and its languorous estate. Set in immaculately maintained grounds, the Peacock's main building, with its mullioned windows and stone gables, is firmly rooted in the 17th century, but the décor is a clever mixture of ancient and modern touches, and there's an elegant restaurant and cosy bar downstairs that are a joy after a long day's walking. Given the nature of the building, not one of its bedrooms is the same but all feature flatscreen TVs, iPod docking stations, DVD players and wifi. There are 14 guestrooms and 1 suite: most have large fireplaces, and comfy beds with big headboards (apart from a couple of four-posters). Dogs are welcome throughout – and with so many great walks possible from your doorstep, it would be a shame if they weren't; they certainly look the part flaked out in front of the Peacock's embracing hearths.

CONTACT Bakewell Rd, Rowsley, Derbyshire DE4 2EB • 01629 733518 • thepeacockatrowsley.com
HOW MUCH? Double rooms from £215 a night. Dogs £10 a night.

YORKSHIRE AND THE NORTHEAST

Is there a region with as much to offer the visitor as
North East England and the counties of Yorkshire,
Durham and Northumberland? Home to no less than
three national parks, its countryside is dramatic and
unspoiled, and the coastline a treat. No wonder they
call it 'God's Own Country'!

Low Mill Guest House

A truly special place to stay in a beautifully restored mill in the heart of the Yorkshire Dales.

'Small but special' is what one award citation said about Low Mill, and really it's bang on. They have just three guest rooms here, which keeps your stay on the intimate side. But what wonderful rooms they are, fashioned from an 18th-century watermill on the gushing riverside in Bainbridge in the heart of Wensleydale, four miles from Hawes. There's no mistaking the building's heritage – owners Neil and Jane have restored everything to working order, so the grindstones and cogs form a dramatic backdrop in the eye-popping guest lounge, while the wheel itself lies underneath the dining room (a tour by Neil, who did the work himself, is very much part of the experience).

There's also a story to tell in every lavishly appointed room – the old 'Store Room' sits under gorgeous beams, while the 'Kiln Room' retains its vintage ceramic floor tiles where the grain used to be spread to dry. And if you think you've been-there-done-that as far as boutique hotels go, be prepared to swoon at 'The Workshop', which is an absolutely massive space running the length of the building, complete with winding gear and pulleys, a wood-burning stove and free-standing copper bath.

Low Mill is a chic affair all round, from polished wood floors and exposed stone walls to cheeky fabrics and designer bathrooms, and it's ipod-docked, wi-fi-ed, flatscreen-TV-ed and fluffy-bath-robed up to its eyeballs. But style aside, there's comfort and fun here too, whether it's the deep bedside rugs or the leopard and tiger standing guard in the lounge. Dogs are welcome everywhere expect in the dining room, and Neil and Jane prefer it if you keep them off the beds and furniture. In another nice touch, half of the £10 a night they charge is donated to the local Blue Cross animal charity. The beautiful riverside garden is available for early morning walks with your dog (on a lead) and Low Mill's Wensleydale location means that there are more walks nearby than you can shake a stick at – in recognition of which there's a drying room for wet and muddy boots and paws. You can also explore by bike – 'Stage 1 Cycles' in Hawes offers bike hire – and Neil and Jane also have contacts with a travelling masseur, who can come and ease your aches and pains after a long day's walking or cycling up hill and down dale.

Luckily the breakfasts at Low Mill more than set you up for the day: strong on local produce, with eggs from the neighbours' hens, and offering everything from a sumptuous Full English to pancakes, omelettes and lots of other delicious things you might not expect. They also have a license to serve wine and beer, which you can enjoy on the outside terrace while you spot visiting herons. Low Mill won 'Food & Travel' magazine's 'Best B&B' award last year and we're not at all surprised. Long may they continue!

CONTACT Bainbridge, Leyburn, North Yorkshire DL8 3EF • 01969 650553 • lowmillguesthouse.co.uk
HOW MUCH? Store Room from £110, Kiln Room £130, Workshop £180. Dogs £10 a night, half of which is donated to the Blue Cross.
ROOMS Three luxury double rooms.

Broadgate Farm Cottages

A range of luxury self-catering cottages in East Yorkshire, each converted from charming period farm buildings.

Set in a prime location on the edge of the glorious Yorkshire Wolds, Broadgate Farm Cottages is home to a range of high-end dwellings situated on a 19-acre farmstead just two miles from the historic market town of Beverley. It's a gem of a rural spot, and it's no wonder that the owners have won numerous accolades in recent years, including the awards for best self-catering cottages from 'Remarkable East Yorkshire Tourism' in two out of the last four years.

Sleeping from four to 12, the characterful places to stay began life as period barns or farm buildings. Lovingly and skilfully converted using reclaimed natural materials and decorated using top-notch furnishings and opulent fabrics, each individually designed cottage is dog friendly and benefits from toasty eco-friendly central heating and a private garden or patio area. Stay in two-bed The Forge and enjoy a mix of oak and travertine flooring, a wood-burner, fully fitted kitchen and French windows overlooking the paddocks and Blackmeredale Bottom. Bigger groups should opt for capacious Cart House: with space for nine guests (and up to two children on put-me-up beds), underfloor heating and ground-floor bedrooms (all en-suite), it's a stylish choice and great for large parties too – as are the linked Barn House and Fold Yard, with a duo of sitting rooms and two wet rooms.

Whichever cottage you go for, you'll be greeted by wonderful views from the farm across the fields and a high level of quality throughout. What's more, spa treatments and private chefs are available to book, making stays even more special. Dogs are welcome in all the cottages and there's a small extra charge per dog; they prefer you to have a crate if you intend to leave the dog on their own, or they have an outside kennel you can use. The owners are also occasionally available for pet-sitting and they have contacts with a local dog-sitting/walking service. Above all, it's a tremendous location to enjoy with a dog, as the owners' terrier Coco will attest, with lovely walks close by in the Beverley Westwood and plenty of dog-friendly pubs.

Out and about, it's a mile to Walkington, a picturesque village with three inviting pubs, or for a scenic stroll, wander down onto the Westwood. Slightly further afield – just half an hour away by car – head to the beaches of Hornsea and Fraisthorpe, or visit Burton Agnes, an impressive Elizabethan stately home. Nature lovers won't want to miss Tophill Low – a haven for otters – while North Cave Wetlands is known for kingfishers and peregrine falcons. There are ample walking and cycling opportunities too, including the Minster and Wilberforce Ways. But at the end of the day it's back to the comfort and luxury of Broadgate Farm Cottages.

CONTACT Broadgate Farm, Beverley Road, Walkington, East Yorkshire HU17 8RP • 01482 888111 • broadgatefarmcottages.co.uk
HOW MUCH? Smallest cottages £536–£900 a week, largest cottage £1312–£2360 a week. Minimum stay 2 nights.
ACCOMMODATION 8 stylish self-catering cottages sleeping between 4 and 12 guests (High Barn is the Barn House and Foldyard linked).

Millgate House

A lavish yet extremely dog friendly B&B in a stunningly ornamented Georgian townhouse.

It's a pretty safe bet that you won't have stayed in a B&B quite like Millgate House before. Located just off the bottom of Market Place in the pleasant North Yorkshire market town of Richmond, this Georgian townhouse is a masterpiece of lavish, theatrical elegance sitting above a magical, sheltered walled garden with views down to the River Swale and its waterfalls. It's won almost every award going – the 'Good Hotel Guide' 'B&B of the Year' for 2011, for example – with visitors charmed and amazed in equal measure by a house that is positively stuffed with antiques and art. And not only does it have two extremely handsome resident whippets, but its dog-loving owners Austin and Tim welcome dogs in all their rooms and don't charge for them either. All they ask is that your dog is 'properly brought up', and that they are not left to roam freely in the garden or left unattended in their room for too long.

There are eye-opening curios and wonderfully ornate pieces at every turn in Millgate House. While each of the guest rooms is lovely in its own way, the ones overlooking the garden have the finest aspect. We also particularly like being able to step out of a free-standing Edwardian bath onto a Turkish rug, in front of a cast-iron fireplace. Meanwhile, in the glorious garden-view downstairs dining room, a splendid breakfast on polished mahogany tables is less a mere meal and more an experience. There is also a self-contained (and self-catering) romantic garden apartment with a lovely en-suite double, living room and open fire, which is also available by the night and similarly dog friendly.

All in all, you couldn't find a more comfortable place from which to explore Richmond and the countryside around, with walks in every direction. Try the 'Little Drummer Boy' walk, a five-mile circle from the market place back to Richmond's fascinating 10th-century castle, or explore Swaledale by following the river Swale as far as Easby Abbey, coming back by way of a disused railway. Austin and Tim have been at Millgate House almost forty years and have made it and its garden a place very much in their own image – charming, discreet and hugely likeable. Indeed the Sunday Telegraph described them as 'creative and cultured, with a strong dash of northern grit.' Trust us, you won't want to leave – and neither will your dog!

CONTACT 3 Millgate, Richmond, North Yorkshire DL10 4JN • 01748 823571 • millgatehouse.com
HOW MUCH? The Superking, Twin and Garden Apartment are all £165 per night. King double with private bathroom is £145. Two standard doubles with private facilities are £125. Dogs are free.
ROOMS Six beautiful guest rooms, plus a one-bedroom apartment for two people.

La Rosa

Described as 'more boudoir than boutique', this
hotel puts Victorian seaside fun and a certain amount
of romance centre-stage in 8 lovingly furnished
rooms occupying a building in which Lewis Carroll
often stayed. This elegant townhouse enjoys Whitby's
best views too, looking out over the harbour to the
ruins of Whitby Abbey on the opposite promontory,
and is a unique place to stay, with wacky décor,
retro furniture and fabulously sourced bric-a-brac
designed to evoke various dreams, themes and
schemes, from 'Arabesque' to 'Sacre-Coeur'. Dogs
are welcome in 4 of the rooms – specifically Lewis
(modelled on Lewis Carroll's study), Arabesque,
Little Red and Caravan – as well as in the top-floor
Crow's Nest apartment (which can sleep 6). They get
a doggy goody bag from Whitby's own 'Fuzzy Dog
Bakery', while breakfast for humans is delivered to
your door in a picnic hamper every morning. Four
of the rooms enjoy sea views, but even those that
don't have some compensation, from a huge bed to
a massive bath – and of course a very comfortable
hound dog!

CONTACT 5 East Terrace, Whitby, North Yorkshire
YO21 3HB • 01947 606981 • larosa.co.uk
HOW MUCH? Doubles from £125 a night, apartment
£250 a night. Dogs £10 a night.

The Feversham Arms

Cornerstone of much of Helmsley's reinvention
as a country resort, the town's Feversham Arms –
'the Fev' – calls itself 'a modern country inn with
good food and a great spa', and that pretty much
covers the essential facts. It's stylish and boutiquey
– just 33 rooms – without being uncomfortably
designer-like, so the contemporary country-house
rooms are nice and sensible, just like Helmsley
itself. The double rooms all face the street, while
suites get a wood-burner and direct access to
the gardens or a private balcony. There's a heated
outdoor pool and hot tub, while the Verbena Spa
offers everything from facials to exotic wellness
rituals. Dining is in the same modern Yorkshire
vein, with alfresco poolside lunches in summer
and afternoon teas in front of the fire pulling in
locals and passing tourists as well as guests. Most
of the rooms apart from the suites are dog friendly
and the hotel has a fair-sized country-pursuits
following. But this doesn't make it a toffs' hangout
– just that coming in with mud on your boots
won't throw everyone into a tizzy.

CONTACT 1-8 High St, Helmsley, North Yorkshire
YO62 5AG • 01439 770766 • fevershamarmshotel.com
HOW MUCH? Double ooms from £120 a night, £210
with dinner. Dogs free.

The Devonshire Arms

Must be a pub, with a name like that? Perish the thought! The Devonshire is an extraordinarily welcoming country house hotel set among the rolling acres of the Duke of Devonshire's Bolton Abbey Estate, just a few miles outside Skipton. It is grand, and there are portraits, antiques and mementoes that keep the ducal connection much in mind. But it isn't stuffy or even particularly formal, and there's a genuinely familiar welcome backed up by highly polished service. Its 40 rooms vary in size and aspect, but many have lovely rural views and dogs are allowed in most of them. Those in the original 18th-century wing have hand-carved four-posters, while the Wharfedale rooms have been more recently refurbished. Throughout you're talking elegant fabrics, excellent bathrooms and a keen sense of modern country style. Dining is similarly approachable, with seasonal tasting menus in the Burlington restaurant and an easy-going mood in the Brasserie and Bar. Over the road, the spa offers pool, treatments, sauna, gym and mountain bikes for guests.

CONTACT Bolton Bridge, Skipton, North Yorkshire BD23 6AJ · 01756 718100 · thedevonshirearms.co.uk
HOW MUCH? Double rooms from around £200 a night. Dogs £10 a night.

The Devonshire Fell

The boutique little sister to the Devonshire Arms offers just a dozen rooms in a more intimate setting in a small Edwardian hotel in Burnsall, not far from Grassington. We love the feel here since it's so unexpected, switching from traditional exterior to contemporary interior in the blink of an eye. It's a thoroughly modern experience all round inside the rooms – 'city chic in the countryside' they say – with bold colours, vibrant designs and stylish furnishings contrasting with the timeless rural views. Little extras make you feel special, from herbal teas to hot-water bottles in each room. Dogs are welcome in all rooms and on the lead throughout the rest of the hotel. There's a funky bar and conservatory and a sleek 2-AA-rosette restaurant, while if you drive down to Bolton Abbey you can use the Devonshire's health club and spa facilities. Closer to home, there are plenty of walks to be enjoyed through the moor and heathland of the Bolton Abbey estate, as well as numerous walks along the river, including to the ruins of Bolton Abbey itself.

CONTACT Burnsall, Skipton, North Yorkshire BD23 6BT · 01756 729000 · devonshirefell.co.uk
HOW MUCH? Double rooms from around £120 a night. Dogs £10 a night.

OUT AND ABOUT
Four great walks with your dog

INGLETON FALLS TRAIL This short loop from the village of Ingleton visits 4 stunning waterfalls and an ancient oak woodland on a good footpath which offers glorious views of the ancient limestone and slate base rocks that form the Yorkshire Dales National Park. Much of the trail has been designated as a Site of Special Scientific Interest by Natural England because of its rare plants, wildlife and geology. **4.3 MILES**

MALHAM COVE & GORDALE SCAR In a region of dramatic superlatives, Malham Cove takes some beating. Stroll a mile out from the village across lush green fields and following a babbling stream until you see the stupendous, limestone cliff, almost 100m-high, forming an enormous amphitheatre. Peregrine falcons soar above while steep rock-cut steps lead to the top of the cove, where you can continue to Malham Tarn and the canyon of Gordale Scar before circling back via the woodland pool of Janet's Foss. **8 MILES**

ROSEBERRY TOPPING This classic circular walk starts in the village of Great Ayton before climbing the hillside to the obelisk commemorating Captain Cook, who was born in nearby Marton. It then follows the Cleveland Way over Great Ayton Moor to Roseberry Topping – only 320m high but looking every inch a mountain. Affectionately known as the Yorkshire Matterhorn, its distinctive profile has inspired many young mountaineers. **6.3 MILES**

SYCAMORE & HOTBANK CRAGS GAP You'll find history every step of the way on the Hadrian's Wall National Trail, following sections of the legendary wall and taking in the remains of Roman settlements and forts. This short walk explores the most dramatic section of the wall, with its iconic sycamore tree. **6.5 MILES**

THE OUTDOOR GUIDE

Stow House

An exceptional boutique B&B in the heart of the Yorkshire Dales with magnificent views from every room.

A boutique bed and breakfast in the heart of the Yorkshire Dales National Park, Stow House occupies an artily (and artfully) renovated Victorian vicarage with magnificent views from every room. The project of a couple of escapees from London's media industry, it's an extraordinarily welcoming place to stay. Sarah and Phil renovated the place themselves and opened Stow House for business a few years ago as one of the most original and comfortable B&Bs for miles around.

The property sits in its own extensive grounds so is perfect for energetic hounds and their owners. Dogs are welcome in five of seven spectacular and exceptional bedrooms, each of which has unique modern artwork and a well-specified bathroom, most of them with large baths. The rooms have fabulous names, after the artworks that hang in each one – check out 'Like Wow Man' and 'Lovebirds', while our own favourites are the two bright modern spaces on the top floor of the building – 'Shotgun Clare' and 'Cowboy Balance' – with wood beams and big velux windows cut into the eaves. The rooms are all spacious and come with comfortable beds, underfloor heating, tea- and coffee-making facilities, good wifi and flatscreen TVs, DVD players, bath robes – and some have in-room standalone baths. The living room, snug/library and dining room downstairs all have woodburners. All Sarah and Phil ask dog owners is that they keep their dog on a lead when they're not in their bedroom and when they are to keep him/her off the bed and other soft furnishings.

They serve an excellent breakfast, freshly cooked to order, with home-made bread and granola alongside sausages and bacon supplied by the local butcher, and Sarah and Phil can also make packed lunches and an evening meal can be provided for larger groups. Should you fancy a drink, there's an honesty bar, or the powerful cocktails mixed by your hosts, come highly recommended.

Sarah, meanwhile, cannot help enough when you're settling in or need advice on the local area: Aysgarth Falls are just a short stroll away, and there are plenty of more challenging local walks as well as numerous country pubs that love dogs – for example the Wheatsheaf Inn in Carperby or the King's Arms in Askrigg, which featured as 'The Drovers' in the TV series 'All Creatures Great and Small' (as did the town). You're also in the heart of Wensleydale, and the cheese is made nearby; you can visit the factory and cheese shop at the Wensleydale Creamery in Hawes, and see the cheese being made before tucking into some afterwards in their restaurant and coffee shop. Wallace and Gromit would be jealous!

CONTACT Aysgarth, Leyburn, North Yorkshire DL8 3SR • 01969 663635 • stowhouse.co.uk
HOW MUCH? Double rooms from £115 to £185 a night, no charge for dogs.
ROOMS Seven double rooms, one of which can accommodate an extra bed.

The Traddock

In the North Yorkshire village of Austwick, not far from the bustling market town of Settle, The Traddock is a magnificent small family-run country house hotel – and one of the most luxurious dog-friendly places to stay in North Yorkshire. Canine friends are welcome in all of the 14 rooms and suites, and for a quick energy burn-off there are 2 large lawns in the hotel grounds, and of course a wealth of walking opportunities in the nearby Dales. Provided they are on leads in the hotel, dogs are allowed everywhere apart from the dining rooms of its 2-AA-rosette restaurant, but if you'd like to eat with your dog they happily allow this in the bar area provided you reserve a table – which you should definitely do as the food is majestic! Whichever room you choose, the décor is exquisite throughout and you can feel pampered with a selection of Molton Brown toiletries, tea- and coffee-making facilities, flatscreen Freeview TVs and fast wifi. Breakfast is a sumptuous buffet plus a range of hot dishes to set you up for walks into the national park, including the nearby Three Peaks and Malham Cove.

CONTACT Austwick, Settle, North Yorkshire LA2 8BY • 01524 251224 • thetraddock.co.uk
HOW MUCH? Double rooms fom £99 a night. Maximum 2 dogs per room, £5 each.

The Blue Lion

With the gorgeous Yorkshire Dales surrounding it, The Blue Lion is a Grade-II-listed building with a history as long as your arm, including being the last public house in England to have a 6-day licence, thanks to a previous landlady! Current owners Paul and Helen Klein have built a stunning reputation for the pub's food and accommodation, and one you can share with your dog too, with mutts welcome to stay in the 'Petite' doubles and the 'Classic' and 'Large Classic' doubles. There are 15 rooms in all, split between the main house and a converted stable building; Large Classics have a bath as well as a shower, while all the rooms have flatscreen TVs, free wifi and tea- and coffee-making facilities. Dog walking? Well, the Yorkshire Dales are right there, and there are walking maps available at the reception. On your return you and your dog are welcome to enjoy a drink in the cosy bar – provided the dog is on a lead – where you can also enjoy the pub's full menu. The food is great, quite traditional but all locally sourced and beautifully presented; the pub has won 'Dining Pub of the Year' 3 times recently.

CONTACT Main Road, East Witton, Leyburn, North Yorkshire DL8 4SN • 01969 624273 • thebluelion.co.uk
HOW MUCH? From £135 a night. Maximum 2 dogs per room, £15 per dog.

The Den at Husthwaite Gate

Tucked away to the side of a former railway station, this unique self-catering accommodation sleeps 6 in quirky ship-cabin-style sleeping pods and has the added bonus of a grassy space outside for a couple of tent pitches and an electric hook-up for a small campervan. It's well suited for friends' get-togethers or families, who can have the whole site to themselves, and has views across open countryside to the iconic White Horse on the Hambleton Hills and enough walks to wear out the most energetic hound. It's also thoughtful, quirky and green in equal measure: electricity is courtesy of the on-site wind turbine, the building is well insulated, and many items have been upcycled; there's also a high-spec kitchen, a smart TV, dishwasher and good wifi. The front door opens onto a sheltered lawn with a BBQ and firepit where you can watch the sun go down before retreating to your bed. There is a family bathroom and a separate outside shower and toilet cabin, plus a washhouse with a washing machine and tumble-drier. Overall it's a thoroughly comfortable and affordable place to stay in a wonderful location.

CONTACT Old Station House, Husthwaite Gate, North Yorkshire YO61 4QF • 07745 505807 • husthwaitegate.co.uk
HOW MUCH? £165 a night – 2-night minimum stay.

A Corner of Eden

Situated in one of the Yorkshire Dales' most undiscovered corners, this collection of 3 country cottages is well named, not only for its location in the beautiful Eden Valley but also because it really is the perfect spot form which to enjoy this glorious enclave of northern England. A derelict farm that was rescued by owners Debbie and Richard Greaves 15 years ago, it's relatively easy to get to – just a few miles off the M6 – but its location at the end of a private lane feels wonderfully remote and restful. All of the cottages are eco friendly and dog friendly – indeed they recently won the i newspaper's Staycation Award for 'Dog-friendly Accommodation of the Year'. They consist of a very comfortable Georgian farmhouse sleeping 8 people, a 3-bed barn with a wood-burning stove and its own hot tub and a 2-person cottage that's as romantic a retreat as you could desire, with a four-poster super-king-size bed and a cast-iron bath in the garden. There are 3 good dog-friendly pubs nearby, and any number of great walks on your doorstep in the lush Eden Valley and nearby Howgill Fells.

CONTACT EdenLow, Stennerskeugh, Ravenstonedale, Cumbria CA17 4LL • 01539 623370 • acornerofeden.co.uk
HOW MUCH? Weekends from £595, a week from £895.

The Carpenters Arms

In pretty little Felixkirk, just outside the market town of Thirsk, the Carpenters Arms is a clever marriage of country inn and destination restaurant – a village pub with a warm, welcoming feel, from its oak beams and stone floors to the deep colours and sparkling place settings. The enticing menu offers bistro classics, grills and game in season. Most of the veg and herbs – not to mention the flowers throughout the pub – come from the pub's own kitchen garden. There's also a garden room with log-burner and tables on the outdoor deck. If you feel spoilt rotten after your meal, wait until you see the rooms: they'll probably have to prise the key from your hands after a night in one of the glamorous garden suites, arranged around a landscaped courtyard, looking down over the Vale of York. There's underfloor heating, walk-in rain showers and sliding windows onto your own patio. The rooms are dog friendly, and you can eat with your dog in the bar – plus the North York Moors National Park and rolling Howardian Hills are on your doorstep.

CONTACT 1 Church View, Felixkirk, North Yorkshire YO7 2DP • 01845 537369 • thecarpentersarmsfelixkirk.com
HOW MUCH? Doubles from £80 a night. Dogs £10.

Warkworth House

You'd be hard-pushed to find a more dog-friendly place to stay than this family-run coaching inn situated in the picturesque Northumberland village of Warkworth, clutched within a loop of the river Coquet just a few miles south of Alnwick. The hotel has 14 guest rooms in all, including 3 extremely well appointed pet-friendly rooms on the first floor: all superior doubles with flatscreen Freeview TVs, wifi and tea- and coffee-making facilities. Room 3 has a shower and bath; room 4 a powerful shower, while room 8 has a traditional bath and a more traditional cottage feel with a four-poster bed. After one of many walks in the local area, you can enjoy something to eat from the menu with your dog at your feet in the lounge and later kick back with a couple of drinks in the cosy dog-friendly bar. Above all, the hotel's location couldn't be much better if you're travelling with a dog: Warkworth's dog-friendly beach is only a short walk away, and you could also try the 7-mile hike north to Alnmouth beach following the long-distance St Oswald's Way.

CONTACT 16 Bridge St, Warkworth, Northumberland NE65 0XB • 01665 711276 • warkworthhousehotel.co.uk
HOW MUCH? Doubles from £119 a night. Dogs £10.

Lord Crewe Arms

This much-loved inn on the Durham–
Northumberland border is an extraordinary building
with an extraordinary history – a 12th-century
abbot's lodgings that dominates the impeccably
preserved village of Blanchland. Inside it's all stone
corridors, soaring ceilings, heraldic shields and
majestic fireplaces; there are guest rooms in the old
abbot's residence and also in the restored miners'
cottages that flank the adjacent cobbled square.
While no two are the same, there is an updated
country-chic style throughout. Classed as 'Cosy',
'Canny' and 'Champion', all feature king-size
beds, robes and aromatherapy toiletries. Colours
throughout are earthy and muted, just like the
peaceful surroundings, where the loudest sound
you'll hear in the morning is the birdsong. The
hotel is well positioned for exploring and welcomes
pooches in 14 of the 21 rooms, where they'll find
a bed, bowl, towel and treats waiting. Although not
allowed in the excellent Bishop's Dining Room, you
can eat with your dog in the atmospheric Crypt bar
or in the Hilyard restaurant.

CONTACT The Square, Blanchland, Durham DH8 9SP •
01434 677100 • lordcrewearmsblanchland.co.uk
HOW MUCH? Double rooms from £139 a night. Dogs
£20 a night. Ask about their 'Pawsome Retreat' package!

St Valery

'The most pet-friendly accommodation in
Alnmouth' boasts the St Valery – and that's probably
right. Nevertheless the house dog Roxy has a
few rules for visiting friends, including keeping
on leads while inside and no dogs in the dining
room when breakfast is being served – all perfectly
understandable and not contentious. In any case it's
a very welcoming B&B, with a roaring fireplace
in the winter for dozing dogs and a summer place
to roost on the decking outside – naturally after
a stroll on the nearby dog-friendly beach. There
are 4 dog-friendly rooms on the ground floor,
including the wonderful St Benedict suite, with
a king-size bed and marble fireplace. Tea- and
coffee-making facilities are a given, and fresh milk
is delivered to your door each day. A good night's
sleep is virtually guaranteed underneath a silk-filled
duvet and Egyptian cotton linen, and you can top
off the evening with a drink from the well-stocked
honesty bar, waking up the next day to an excellent
breakfast made from as much local produce as
possible.

CONTACT 27 Northumberland St, Alnmouth,
Northumberland NE66 2RA • 01665 833123 •
stvaleryalnmouth.com
HOW MUCH? Doubles from £150 a night, dogs £20.

North Star Sanctum

Come for hot tubs, starry skies and warm and wonderful hospitality at this dog-friendly East Yorkshire retreat.

Time passes slowly at North Star Sanctum, a cluster of six meticulously kept East Yorkshire cabins that is the brainchild of rat-race refugee Simon North and his doctor wife, Rupal. Long sunrises and even longer sunsets dance over the flat fields around here, reaching out to the red-cliffed coastline, and on clear nights millions of stars are – as the name implies – visible from the comfort of your own private hot tub.

Simon wanted to do something completely different after leaving his corporate job, building these lodges on a site with a remote feel to an exacting set of specifications. Each is themed on a destination Simon and Rupal have visited on their own travel adventures, such as India ('The Raj'), and Morocco ('The Kasbah'). Provided with either one or two bedrooms, they are all beautifully finished, with fully equipped kitchens and huge floor-to-ceiling windows that open out onto your private patio, and wood-burning stoves complete with fire-lighting kits. Gowns and slippers are provided for manoeuvering between house and hot tub, there are toiletries in the bathrooms, and it's nice to know too that four of the six lodges welcome dogs.

Thoughtful little touches, like fresh eggs from Simon's hens and a chilled bottle of fizz in the fridge, make this faraway spot even more appealing – although it's not as far away from it all as it seems. You can cook up a feast in your lodge using produce you've bought locally, but for dinners out there's an extremely good dog-friendly local pub nearby, the Stag's Head Inn, just around the corner in the village of Lelley, where they serve superb steak pies, real ales and sublime desserts among many other things on an excellent pub grub menu.

There's also plenty to see and do nearby – country houses to explore, such as the amazing Jacobean mansion of Burton Constable Hall and Grounds, where they tolerate dogs pretty much everywhere except the main house; and the astonishing Bempton Cliffs RSPB reserve, where half a million seabirds reside between March and September, including puffins and their wonderfully named offspring, pufflings. You're also just a fifteen-minute drive from Hull, ten minutes from a number of appealing seaside villages and just over half an hour's drive from the delightful market town of Beverley.

It's the perfect spot, too, from which to explore the landscapes that have been so famously painted by the East Yorkshire artist David Hockney. Come for the hot tub, stay for the stars and leave with that fuzzy feeling you get from warm and wonderful hospitality.

CONTACT Humbleton Road, Fitling, East Yorkshire, HU12 9AJ • 07930 405530 • northstarsanctum.co.uk
HOW MUCH? 3-night stays £250– £350, 7-night stays £975–£1100. No other charges (pets, wifi, logs, charcoal, linen, etc).
ACCOMMODATION Six self-catering lodges with hot tubs, 4 of which are dog friendly.

Hawthorn Lodge

A mile or so outside the alluring market town of Richmond, North Yorkshire, the pine lodges at Flowery Dell are comfortable in the extreme – double-storied in some cases, with well-appointed accommodation for between 2 and 6 people on the edge of the Yorkshire Dales National Park. The natural wood throughout works wonderfully well, and the lodges are thoroughly Scandinavian too in the sense that they are equipped with saunas and in some cases hot tubs. Hawthorn Lodge sleeps 2–4 and is perfect for a romantic break in the country. It comes with a luxury king-size room with its own en-suite plus a twin room. There's a 4-person American therapy style hot tub on the balcony, a gas BBQ, a wood-burning stove (logs and firelighters available as an extra) and a beautifully equipped kitchen and sitting room with a 40-inch flatscreen TV that you can enjoy from the comfort of an Italian leather sofa. Most essentials are included, including wifi and a welcome starter pack of goodies so you can relax with a coffee while you're unpacking. Dogs are welcome for no extra charge.

CONTACT Hudswell Lane, Richmond, North Yorkshire
DL11 6BD • 01748 822406 • flowerydell-lodges.com
HOW MUCH? From £467 for a 3-night weekend to
£1255 a week in high season; dogs free, 2 maximum.

Forest Holidays Keldy

Like Forest Holidays' nearby Cropton site, this place has everything you need for a family holiday deep in the woods in one of England's most scenic corners. There are 59 cabins here, from the fabulous Golden Oak Treehouse, which sleeps 8, to Golden Oak Cottage, which sleeps 2. All the cabins are extremely comfortable and equipped with TVs and optional extras like wifi and fluffy robes; some are wheelchair-accessible and around half are dog friendly. The Forest Retreat is the hub of the site, with a café and bar, shop and children's play area; you can hire bikes and also book in with the Forest Ranger, who does wildlife-spotting and bushcraft tours of the site. What's also nice about Keldy is the host of activities and attractions on your doorstep, from the coast at Whitby and Scarborough to more woodland delights in Dalby Forest (where there's a Go Ape high-wire centre, among other things) and the North Yorkshire Moors Railway, which runs vintage trains from Pickering to Whitby. As for dogs, it would be hard to imagine having one and leaving it behind!

CONTACT Cropton, near Pickering, North Yorkshire
YO18 8HW • 03330 110495 • forestholidays.co.uk
HOW MUCH? Short breaks from £300, 7 nights from
£515. Dogs £15.

YHA Malham

If you favour walks through epic landscapes, then there's no better positioned property than this, situated in the heart of the Yorkshire Dales, a short distance from the Pennine Way and Yorkshire Dales Cycle Way. The hostel is in a quiet part of the village, right next door to 'Yorkshire's Favourite Pub 2019', the Lister Arms, and well used by hikers and families looking for a reasonably priced base. The hostel is a decidedly snazzy budget option for walkers and has both en-suite private and dormitory rooms and 2 dog-friendly camping pods outside, which can each sleep 2 people. There are views over the fields from the rooms, and budget meals and packed lunches are available from the restaurant, plus there's a kitchen for self-catering. Malham itself is a pretty village, and if the scenery which surrounds doesn't get you out, then your critter certainly will. You can follow the Pennine Way a mile north to some of the most spectacular scenery the National Park has to offer – the awesome limestone cliffs of Malham Cove, the glacial lake of Malham Tarn and the full-on canyon of Gordale Scar.

CONTACT Malham, North Yorkshire BD23 4DB •
0345 371 9529 • yha.org.uk
HOW MUCH? Dormitory beds from £13 a night, double rooms from £29, camping pods from £29.

Pegasus Cottage

A recently renovated fisherman's abode, Pegasus Cottage enjoys a perfect location by the sea, overlooking the pretty harbour at Craster, a small fishing village halfway up the Northumberland coast. Dating from the early 19th century, it's full of character, with stone walls and exposed beams, spectacular sea views, a cosy sitting room and 3 upstairs double bedrooms. The cottage has come a long way since fishermen lived here, and has all the mod cons you might need – wifi, a large flatscreen TV, DVD player, underfloor heating and a well-equipped kitchen. It also has a wood-burning stove and 2 bathrooms. A maximum of 2 pooches are welcome, and it would be a pity if they weren't, because the Northumberland Coast is made for walking. The walk north from Craster goes past the ruins of Dunstanburgh Castle to the big sandy bay and dunes of Embleton Bay; the walk south heads towards the seaside resort of Alnmouth, where there are more dunes and more beaches. Once back in Craster, you and your hound can enjoy dinner at the dog-friendly local pub, the Jolly Fisherman.

CONTACT Northumbria Byways • 01665 605541·
northumbria-byways.co.uk
HOW MUCH? From £789 to £1202 a week, short breaks £628–£1059. Dogs £25 each – maximum of 2.

Headlam Hall

The Robinsons understand Headlam. Situated between Darlington and Barnard Castle, the area around here has been farmed by the family for four generations, and they bring a passion and local knowledge for this Teesdale hamlet that you won't find in too many UK hotels. The family have also made Headlam Hall a haven for dogs, with 6 Mews rooms that are perfectly set-up for dog-owners and their furry friends, with direct access to the outdoors and their own designated car parking – perfect for easy access to the car. Each room is a good size and features either a shower-bath combined or a large walk-in shower, and dogs are also welcome in the Main Hall and Spa rooms. All rooms have flatscreen TVs, wifi, tea- and coffee-making facilities and Molton Brown toiletries. The 4 acres of the hotel gardens are perfect for some on-lead walking and there are off-lead walks on the village green. Eating with your furry friends is possible in the Library Bar, and dogs are also welcome in the Brasserie, Main Hall Lounge and bar, providing they are on leads.

CONTACT Headlam Hall, near Gainford, Darlington, Durham DL2 3HA · 01325 730238 · headlamhall.co.uk
HOW MUCH? Double rooms from £175 a night. Dogs free - maximum 2 per room.

Holdsworth House

Independently owned for around 400 years, this historic Jacobean manor house just outside Halifax in West Yorkshire is a thoroughly dog-friendly place to stay, with dogs allowed in many of its 36 bedrooms and everywhere else except the restaurant. Rooms are traditional in style and have tea- and coffee-making facilities, flatscreen TVs with Freeview, wifi and en-suite bathrooms with White Company toiletries. Dogs receive a treat on arrival and a blanket, bowl, poo bags and a 'Dog in Room' sign for the door; a member of the team may even be keen to take a photo of your pooch for the hotel's Facebook page. There's 24-hour room service and you can eat with your dog in the bar or leave them in your room while you dine in the 2-AA-rosette restaurant, which serves delicious seasonal, locally sourced food. Finally, the hotel's beautifully maintained gardens offer lovely on-lead walks, and you are close to some of Yorkshire's most dramatic countryside in Bronte Country to the north, where you can visit the Bronte Parsonage, and walk part of the long-distance Calderdale Way.

CONTACT Holdsworth Rd, Halifax, West Yorkshire HX2 9TG · 01422 240024 · holdsworthhouse.co.uk
HOW MUCH? Double rooms from £104 a night, dogs £10 a night.

The White Swan

A family-run inn, Pickering's White Swan is a boutique bolthole, with a bar and restaurant that serves great locally sourced food (try the seared lamb cooked in their charcoal oven) and a very comfortable set of rooms divided between the main building and the converted stables across the courtyard; there is also a very spick-and-span detached holiday cottage. Fabrics and décor are decidedly chic and sparkly throughout and the bathrooms get the thumbs-up too. You can choose between 'Vintage' rooms, some of which are more like suites and feature glam antique beds, and 'Hideaway' rooms in the stables, which tend to be larger. Dogs are welcome in the Hideaway rooms, which have porches for storing your dog's stuff. Dogs can dine with their owners in the bar or snug and they receive beds, a water bowl and treats on arrival and can even get a doggy sausage and bacon breakfast if they woof nicely. Not only that, the location is pretty much perfect, with lots of great walks on your doorstep – the hotel can provide maps and all sorts of tips on where to go.

CONTACT Market Place, Pickering, North Yorkshire
YO18 7AA • 01751 472288 • white-swan.co.uk
HOW MUCH? Double rooms from around £150 a night.
Dogs £12.50 per stay.

Tickton Grange

When the Whymant family came to this Georgian country house almost 40 years ago, it was dilapidated and unloved. Now it's one of Yorkshire's finest country house hotels, collecting multiple awards for its accommodation, food and highly personal service. The family renovated every inch of the building and there are 21 guest rooms spread across various buildings – the main house, the renovated stables and pump room, servants' quarters and workers' cottages. As you might imagine, no two rooms are the same, but expect country-house chic and plenty of welcoming touches, including handmade chocolates, fresh flowers and Bramley toiletries. Nothing's too much trouble, and service comes with a broad smile. Dogs are welcome in selected bedrooms, though not unfortunately in the public areas (including the excellent restaurant, Hide), but bed, towel, bowls and treats are provided. There are also 4 acres of gardens and 12 acres of fields and woodlands for walks, maybe with their resident spaniel, Bert. You also have the coast nearby, including dog-friendly beaches at Barmston and for part of the year at Bridlington.

CONTACT Tickton, Beverley, East Yorkshire HU17 9SH
• 01964 543666 • ticktongrange.co.uk
HOW MUCH? Doubles from £140 a night, suites £220.
Dogs £20 a night.

THE NORTHWEST

Is there a better place to run free with your dog than the peaks and fells of Cumbria and the Lake District? Along with the western fringes of the Yorkshire Dales and parts of rural Lancashire, the region is about as dog friendly as you can get, with oodles of great places to stay.

The Lodges at Artlegarth

Luxury lodges with hot tubs in the Eden Valley – as wonderful as it sounds!

If you're looking for your own private Eden, you might have just found it – well, Eden Valley in Cumbria anyway, which hereabouts amounts to the same thing. Jennie and Neil's six luxury log cabins – each with their own hot tub – sit in seven private acres of grounds at the foot of the Howgill Fells. They're just a mile's scenic walk away from the pretty village of Ravenstonedale, with the gorgeous, rolling Eden Valley on the doorstep, spectacular mountain views and not one but two national parks to explore if you can tear yourself away.

These are high-end, luxury lodgings for sure – all six come with a private hot tub, which looks out over fields and fells, spectacular sunsets and the darkest of dark skies. The self-catering lodges themselves are beautifully constructed in solid pine, and furnished in a contemporary country-chic style that's warm and welcoming. Kitchens and dining areas are not just an after-thought but spacious enough and fully equipped to rustle up anything from snacks, canapés and fizz to a full gourmet dinner for your family or group.

The three 'Bird' lodges (Curlew, Lapwing and Mallard) have a double, twin and a bunk-room, sharing one luxurious bathroom; the other three (Swaledale, Herdwick and Rough Fell – named after local sheep breeds, if you were wondering!) are substantially bigger, with three extra-large double rooms (two of which are en-suite) and one family bathroom. The bigger 'Sheep' lodges also tick many more of the 'luxury-in-the-country' boxes – so think high-spec open-plan living with floor-to-ceiling windows and a real log fire, smart TVs, borehole heating system and gas barbecue for your personal use. The owners will even book you an in-lodge spa treatment if you like.

All the lodges accept dogs, and there is plenty in the seven acres of grounds to keep all the family happy, from a woodland walk and play area to a wildlife pond, bird tables and even native red squirrels. There are also loads of great walks you can do in the countryside beyond, and it's a huge plus that the local village is just a mile away (down a quiet country lane or via a cross-country ramble), with the award-winning and extremely dog-friendly Black Swan by the river, along with an art gallery, public golf course, play park and tennis courts. Best of all, you're perfectly situated for both the Lake District and Yorkshire Dales national parks, so walking, cycling, country pursuits and wildlife-watching are all right on the doorstep. Kirkby Stephen is the nearest town, seven miles away, and it has a vibrant Monday market and a train station on the spectacular Settle to Carlisle Railway – itself another activity you can do with your dog.

CONTACT Artlegarth, Ravenstonedale, Kirkby Stephen, Cumbria CA17 4NW • 07548 668152 • lodgebreaks.co.uk
HOW MUCH? 'Bird' lodges, 3-night weekend/4-night midweek rates from £399–799, weekly rates from £599–£1299. 'Sheep' lodges, weekend/midweek rates from £799–£1599, weekly rates from £1,199–£2,598. Two dogs can stay for free.
ACCOMMODATION 'Bird' lodges sleep 4 adults and 2 children in bunk beds; 'Sheep' lodges sleep 6 adults and up to 3 children in travel cots.

Another Place, The Lake

A contemporary lakeside country house hotel that does everything just right.

If you're going to go to the trouble of updating a hotel in the Lake District – where there's lots of competition – you need to do it right, so kudos to Another Place, The Lake, which is handsomely sited on the shores of Ullswater. It's a stylish yet unstuffy sort of place, and is also properly dog (and family) friendly – the sort of place that has muddy wellies by the door, a great pool, guided kayaking and stand-up paddleboarding from its own jetty, wonderful wild swimming oportunities, as well as no less than 18 acres of grounds for all sorts of walks and adventures. But there are also romantic lake views, convivial public spaces and a great restaurant, which makes it a fabulous couples' retreat too, handy for exploring the less-visited northern Lakes and Eden Valley.

The guest rooms are split between the original Georgian country house and a new contemporary wing and they range from standard doubles to family suites, with lake views a premium in both locations. Sixteen rooms are dog friendly and you can leave your well-behaved dog in any of them, curled up on the dog bed that they provide; you'll also be given baby monitor tablets to keep an eye on your pooches when you're out! If you want a four-poster bed, high ceilings and an original feature or two, then the main house is for you, although even here the rooms have a light, modern touch. Other rooms and suites feel more contemporary, with a kind of nouveau-country style. Bluetooth radio, fridge and drinks flask are standard throughout, and we love the thought that has gone into the overall guest-friendly concept –

for example the addition of star-gazing beanbags under skylights.

Public areas flow seamlessly through both sections of the hotel in a kind of 'open-house' manner, and you can plonk yourself down in any number of places. As regards food, dogs are welcome in the area they call The Living Space – a Scandinavian-style café-bar with a family-friendly menu of burgers, salads, pasta and the like, which spills out onto a lake-view terrace. The Rampsbeck restaurant is a more grown-up place, where they do glorious things to locally sourced steaks, chicken, lamb and fish. The buffet breakfast is rather good, too.

Finally, the indoor pool is a real beauty – 20m long and with its own lake view; there's also a sauna, treatment rooms and an outdoor hot tub, plus of course the grounds and the Lakes beyond are perfect if you have a hound with you. There is kayaking and stand-up paddle boarding available on the lake, or you can drop the kids off at the impressive supervised kids' space. This is a proper resort hotel, done just right, in some of England's most attractive lakeland scenery – and it's dog friendly too!

CONTACT Watermillock, Ullswater, Cumbria CA11 0LP • 01768 486442 • another.place
HOW MUCH? Double rooms from £180 per night, family suites from £295–dogs £15 a night. Two-night 'Escape to the Lake' breaks, including dinner, from £200 per person.
ROOMS 40 rooms, including family-friendly suites and plenty of dog-friendly options.

The Wild Boar Inn

Away from Windermere's lake – and thus off the radar for many – the über-rustic Wild Boar springs a surprise, especially for those expecting a traditional lakeland inn. Yes, there are stone floors, oak beams, a real-ale bar and some lovely rural surroundings, and dogs are welcome throughout. But a keen sense of style – especially in 'feature' rooms – brings things bang up to date. Designers have gone to work on the bathrooms, so you might get a free-standing copper bath and a walk-out balcony overlooking the woods; other glam rooms have bespoke wallpaper, canopy beds, cast-iron wood-burners and bedside iPod docks, while outside you can work up an appetite in their 70-acre woodland, complete with 'green gym' exercise trail and private tarn. And appetite you will need to tackle the excellent restaurant, which makes a justifiable song and dance about its on-site smokehouse. Guests also get use of the leisure club at the sister hotel, Low Wood Bay, not far away near Ambleside, which is on the lake, so even out in the sticks you get the best of both worlds.

CONTACT Crook, Windermere, Cumbria LA23 3NF • 01539 445225 • englishlakes.co.uk
HOW MUCH? Double rooms £120–£300 a night, dogs £20 a night.

Old Dungeon Ghyll

Run by Neil and Jane Walmsley for almost 40 years, the Old Dungeon Ghyll, situated at the top of the Great Langdale valley, is a classic Lake District walkers' hotel. A visit to the hiker's bar here is a proper rite of passage for anyone in the Great Langdale area, and the 12 comfortable, traditionally furnished rooms upstairs have for decades provided a welcome refuge for Lake District hikers after a long day on the Fells. It has a slightly posher bar for residents, but overall it makes for a refreshingly old-school place to stay. Some rooms have private rather than en-suite bathrooms, there are no TVs in the rooms and there's not much in the way of a mobile or wifi signal to speak of. But then that is really the point of staying here, much like the excellent hearty food served throughout the day to fuel all that outdoor activity. Dogs are almost obligatory in what must be one of the national park's most scenic and active locations, and there's certainly no better view to wake up to – and no better place for an early morning walk with your hound.

CONTACT Great Langdale, Ambleside, Cumbria LA22 9JY • 01539 437272 • odg.co.uk
HOW MUCH? Double rooms from around £120 a night; dogs £5 a night.

Royal Oak Hotel

It's clear from the moment you step through the door that they truly love dogs at The Royal Oak Hotel; there are water bowls on one side of the porch and a bag of towels on the other. Once inside, dogs are welcome to join you anywhere in the bar area and there's a doggy 'Wall of Fame' right next to the bar. The hotel is in the heart of Keswick and there's a lovely park just a short walk from the door and dozens of dog-friendly shops and cafés throughout the town; Keswick enjoys a reputation for being one of the most dog-friendly towns in Britain and you'll find bowls and treats up and down the high street, and there are also numerous walks from the town up into the surrounding fells. The bar area is relaxed with comfortable, homely, décor and plenty of local beers and spirits on offer. If your dog would like to join you for breakfast then a special 'Sausage Breakfast' can be ordered to set them up for the day ahead. The bedrooms are crisp, smart and modern with lots of lovely local touches on the welcome tray and in the bathroom.

CONTACT Main Street, Keswick, Cumbria CA12 5HZ •
017687 73135 • royaloakkeswick.co.uk
HOW MUCH? Prices start at £117 per night for a
double room. Dogs £15 a night.

Holbeck Ghyll

From the moment you swing into the driveway, you know you have found the perfect place for four-legged adventures. Dogs are welcome in the lodges in the extensive grounds, and each has either a balcony or small terrace area, stunning views down over Windermere to the fells in the distance, and a bowl, bed and treat for your dog. The rooms themselves are crisp and modern, decorated using natural fabrics to create a comforting feel. Several also have a porch area for cleaning muddy dogs and boots after adventures on the fells. But it's not just your pooch that gets pampered here; there is an onsite spa offering a vast array of treatments and the main bar has oversized sofas and large armchairs to relax into to enjoy a pre-dinner drink. Your faithful friend is welcome to join you until 6pm, and although dogs are not permitted in the excellent restaurant, you can make arrangements for dinner (and breakfast) to be served in your room so you can all dine together. The staff are also quite happy for dogs to be left alone in their rooms but just ask that you let them know.

CONTACT Holbeck Lane, Windermere, Cumbria
LA23 1LU • 01539 432375 • holbeckghyll.com
HOW MUCH? Double rooms from around £150 per
night, plus £25 per dog per stay.

Randy Pike

A one-of-a-kind boutique bolt-hole featuring stunning suites with huge bathrooms.

There are boutique B&Bs – and then there are glorious, one-of-a-kind B&Bs like Randy Pike, the designer bolthole that's also the home of local restaurateurs Andy and Chrissy Hill. Situated on the outskirts of Ambleside, this former gentleman's hunting lodge enjoys a tremendous location, four miles north of Windermere at the heart of the popular Southern Lakes.

There are three suites in this grand house, and they are simply stunning ensembles featuring hand-carved beds, designer fabrics, rococo touches and absolutely massive luxurious bathrooms (variously described as nearly the size of Belgium, Luxembourg 'or another small European principality' – you get the idea, these are big bathrooms). Individual they most certainly are, but the suites do have some common features, with wonderful wooden floors and great views looking out over the woods around the building, and dogs are welcome throughout.

Andy makes his fab music collection available on the in-room iPod sound systems, there are drinks on arrival and all in all you couldn't be made to feel more welcome. There are also some lovely private gardens in which to stroll with your hound, which come complete with their own Dr Who Tardis, as well as a further place to stay, the amazing Juniper House. This is basically another spacious suite with a vast bedroom and views over the lake, equipped with an Alexa speaker, big squashy sofas, a minibar and Nespresso machine. The owners will bring breakfast to your door so you don't even have to move, and transfers are offered down to the owners' excellent Grasmere restaurant, the Jumble Room, which serves up hearty seasonal food in a relaxed and rather bohemian environment.

As for the location, Randy Pike overlooks some beautiful countryside from its hilltop location and is also within reach of plenty of attractions, including the local National Trust properties of Allen Bank in Ambleside, Wray Castle and Beatrix Potter's Hilltop Farm. Randy Pike is also close to some of the most magnificent lakeland fells, which offer some of the best walking routes in the UK – for you and your dog. It's a short walk through the woods to Blelham Tarn and the western shore of Windermere and you can also do a lovely walk following the shores of the lake and up to Hawkshead. They make no charge for dogs but Andy and Chrissy do like you to let them know if you're bringing the family hound!

There are plenty of B&Bs to be found around nearby Ambleside, and it's not unusual to find places that are dog friendly. But for a different kind of stay in glorious surroundings, Randy Pike really does stand out from the crowd.

CONTACT Low Wray, Cumbria LA22 0JP • 01539 436088 • randypike.co.uk
HOW MUCH? Doubles £200, weekends £225 – 2-night minimum at weekends, dogs free.
ROOMS 3 suites – Martindale, Vallelay and Dawson – featuring super-king beds plus the Juniper House suite in the garden.

Queen's Head Hotel

Sitting high on the sides of one of Cumbria's most ancient valleys and dating back to the 17th century, the Queen's Head's bright, crisp, interior belies its ancient roots, with a large and welcoming bar with warm fires and robust dinners through the winter and outdoor dining and lighter summer menus for the warmer months. Dogs are welcome in 8 of the 10 bedrooms and in all the public areas, and beds, bowls and treats are provided. Indeed being a dog-lover is seen as an essential qualification for working there; treats are on offer at the bar and dogs can expect to be spoiled rotten – according to the bar manager Mark, there's no such thing as 'too many dogs'. There's a dog shower outside to clean up muddy pooches and throughout the year the hotel hosts a number of dog-themed events, including a local 'Hound Trail' where a pack of hounds race around the hills following a laid-down scent. There's a small outdoor garden for late-night 'walkies', miles of stunning rambles right from the front door and a free leaflet detailing three dog-friendly hikes.

CONTACT Troutbeck Brow, Windermere, Cumbria
LA23 1PW • 01539 432404 • robinsonsbrewery.com
HOW MUCH? Double rooms from £80 a night. Dogs
£10 a night – 1 per room.

Lodore Falls Hotel

People have been coming to admire the waterfalls behind this hotel for centuries, and although the Victorians may have over-emphasized their size, they are still impressive, and from the lounge bar you can enjoy gloriously uninterrupted views of Derwentwater and Cat Bells. Dogs are very much welcomed here, with treats available on the bar and a 'Dog Dinner' available on the menu. You can dine with your dog in the dedicated lounges, there are ample grounds to exercise in and if you venture further afield and return home soggier than when you left, you can pick up a big fluffy towel from reception to dry off. Poo bags are also available from reception and there are bins dotted around the grounds. After a recent facelift, the hotel is bright and contemporary but still retains much of its historic charm, with cosy bedrooms with stunning views. Dogs are permitted in many of the rooms in the main hotel but not the new spa building. You can leave your dog unattended in your room; you'll be given an adorable 'Pooch in Room' sign to make housekeeping staff aware.

CONTACT Borrowdale Valley, Keswick, Cumbria
CA12 5UX • 0800 840 1246 • lakedistricthotels.net
HOW MUCH? Double rooms from £190 per night. Dogs
£10 a night.

1692 Wasdale

It's hard to imagine a more perfect setting than this western Lake District boutique B&B, which has stunning views over the Wasdale Valley. The old barn has been lovingly updated to provide a suite of stunning bedrooms, all furnished to an exceptional standard and with homely touches such as delicious biscuits baked by the owner, locally sourced toiletries and even beds and furnishings supplied by local traders. Dogs are allowed in 3 of the ground-floor rooms and there are two large fields on the doorstep where they can enjoy a good run. There's a stunning walk leading right from the door deep into the local countryside, as well as a vast array of other local trails just a short drive away. When you all return muddy and ready for a rest, you'll find a drying room to store your gear and a well-stocked honesty and snack bar to tide you over until tea time. Gosforth village is just a stone's throw away and has good pubs and restaurants. Perhaps the most enticing feature of all is the hot tub, situated just outside the farmhouse, with breathtaking views towards Scafell Pike and the Screes.

CONTACT Bolton Head Farm, Gosforth, Cumbria CA20 1EW • 01946 725777 • 1692wasdale.co.uk **HOW MUCH?** Double rooms from £160 a night. Dogs welcome by prior arrangement.

Coachman's Quarters

All right, you're not exactly sleeping inside Muncaster Castle, but it's near as can be – a unique B&B experience in the renovated coachman's lodgings around a cobbled courtyard, with the manicured castle lawns just a step away. In the evening, when everyone has gone home, you can sip a glass of wine in the Muncaster gardens and play at being to the manor born for a while. Rooms vary from cosy doubles to larger family rooms, with stone walls and exposed beams adding plenty of atmosphere and a well-equipped communal kitchen (both B&B and self-catering options are available). Dogs are allowed in 2 bedrooms as well as the communal lounge, and there is no shortage of space to exercise them. Residents enjoy free entry to the castle gardens, as well as discounted rates on castle tours and other attractions. There are plenty of walks from the door, including a lovely stroll down into Ravenglass with stunning views, the fascinating remains of Roman baths and the ever-popular Ravenglass & Eskdale Railway, to whisk you up into the heart of the stunning Eskdale Valley.

CONTACT Muncaster Castle, Ravenglass, Cumbria CA18 1RD • 01229 717614 • muncaster.co.uk **HOW MUCH?** Doubles from £90 a night, dogs £10 per stay.

Applegarth Villa

Hot tub delight, plus gorgeously chic rooms and suites in the heart of the Lakes.

Hot tub suites? Count us in at Applegarth Villa, a glam, adults-only five-star Lake District retreat up in Windermere village. The building is a bit of a gem in any case, one of those lovely Arts and Crafts mansions built by Victorian gents hankering after a country villa, complete with parquet floors and stained glass windows. As a hotel, it's perfectly formed and seriously stylish, with 15 individually fashioned rooms that go for bold colours, designer furniture, sumptuous fabrics, and super-smart bathrooms with underfloor heating and mood lighting. They start at 'deluxe' and go up to 'ultimate luxury' – which, in the case of the top two suites, means lavish apartment-sized spaces with the choice of either an enormous spa bath and private sun terrace or an 8-foot-wide circular bed in front of two panoramic bay windows. Every Victorian gents' villa had a coach house, which at Applegarth has been re-fashioned to offer seven new hot-tub suites – more stunning, boutique spaces, each with their own private terrace and tub and far-reaching views.

Choosing from this lot can be tough, but it may help to know that only three suites are dog friendly – Ultimate Luxury Room 1, which has a spa bath and lounge that opens onto its own sun terrace, and two luxury Hot Tub Suites, Harrop and Potter, which have their own entrances, private gardens and of course hot tubs. They don't charge extra for dogs, but they do provide well-behaved mutts with their own bed, bowl, treats and their own guide to the best nearby walks, many of which you can do right from your own front door.

The hotel is at the top of the village, which means there are sweeping mountain views from most of the rooms and suites. The great thing about Applegarth Villa is the location – away from the lake, for sure, but literally a minute's walk from the train station and a leisurely 20-minute stroll down to Bowness and the water. Plus it's only a quick jaunt on the open-topped bus along to Ambleside, which means you can leave your car at the hotel and avoid the busy roads and challenging parking.

The conservatory restaurant has the same outlook as many of the hotel's rooms, so breakfast is a joy on a sunny day, and there is everything from crepes to eggs florentine on the menu. The restaurant serves food that is good value and artfully presented, with plenty of local produce on a moderately priced Modern British menu. There's also a handsome oak-panelled bar with an open fire for cosier Lake District nights, though sadly your hound is not allowed in the bar or restaurant – really the only drawback for dog-owners that we could find.

CONTACT College Road, Windermere, Cumbria LA23 1BU • 01539 443206 • lakesapplegarth.co.uk
HOW MUCH? Ultimate Luxury Suite 1 £355, Harrop and Potter Hot Tubs Suites from £455. Dogs free.
ROOMS 15 double rooms in the hotel and 7 hot tub suites in the Coach House.

Hidden River Cabins

Beautifully designed log cabins with hot tubs set within ancient woodland on the edge of the Lakes.

We love everything about these luxurious log cabins – think Zach Klein's Cabin Porn for softies… Staying here, you have all the magic and romance of living in a cabin by a river amid an ancient forest without having to forgo too many 21st-century comforts.

Each cabin is beautifully crafted from a single tree trunk – and each has its own very gorgeous hot tub on a deck overlooking the river. There are modern bathrooms, contemporary wood-burners, fitted kitchens and TV with Freeview and a DVD player. We also like the fact that there is no internet or phone reception in the cabins: having to climb the hill to make a phone call or walk to the estate reception building for internet will wean you off your smartphones without making you feel completely cut off from the modern world. Finally, we also like that dogs are welcome (with a limit of up to 3 downstairs in each cabin) and that they provide dog treats on arrival and don't charge extra.

There are five cabins, but they are set far enough apart from each other to give the impression that yours is the only sign of human habitation for miles around. Inside, the décor and fittings have been carefully chosen to preserve the spirit of the exposed log walls – a glass-fronted wood-burner for gazing at the flames, brass bedsteads, stone-flagged floors and wooden furniture with clean contemporary lines. There are also fully fitted kitchens, complete with freezer, should you be lucky enough to need to store the day's catch. The cabins may sleep between six and ten, but the atmosphere within is intimate and

hygge enough for romantic breaks for couples. If you do fancy fishing – the river Lyne is famous for its sea and brown trout – there are rods for hire, and for a small extra charge you can rent a state-of-the-art barbecue on which to cook your catch.

Dogs on leads are also allowed in the reception and in the on-site restaurant, where if you don't feel like cooking at all, they serve a lovely menu based on prime local ingredients – fantastic smoked salmon, Westmoreland black pudding, Cumberland sausage and back bacon all make breakfast a treat.

There are plenty of good dog-friendly pubs nearby, for example the Golden Fleece in Houghton, a 15-minute drive away, which serves decent food. But the thing that makes these cabins most appropriate for dogs and their owners is the sheer number of walks you can do from your doorstep, along the river, through the woods and beyond; you are, after all, on the edge of the Lake District, which is probably the country's most dog-friendly region. Check out also nearby dog friendly attractions like the Honister Slate Mines.

CONTACT Hidden River Cottage, Longtown Carlisle, Cumbria CA6 5TU · 01228 791318 · hiddenrivercabins.co.uk.
HOW MUCH? Prices £190 a night for 2 people – 3-night minimum stay but 1- and 2-night stays sometimes possible.
ACCOMMODATION 5 cabins, 3 sleeping 6 in 2 double bedrooms and a double sofa bed, and 2 sleeping 10 in 2 double bedrooms, 2 twins and a double sofa bed.

OUT AND ABOUT
Four great walks with your dog

BUTTERMERE This classic glacial valley is home to three lakes and this lakeside walk does a full lap of one of them – Buttermere – through rocky tunnels and woodlands and some of England's finest mountain scenery. The walk has an adventurous feel, and you can lose yourself in beautiful woodlands and skim stones on the lake. You can see the battered remains of a yew tree Wordsworth wrote about on the bank of the Whit Beck behind the village hall. **4.4 MILES**

CAT BELLS With views over Derwentwater, Keswick and the surrounding fells, the classic route up Cat Bells is one of the best walks in the Lakes. Part of the skyline of Borrowdale, Cat Bells is technically a minor fell but feels like a proper mountain, with a perfectly shaped summit and a rocky scramble near the top. It appeals to a wide range of visitors and is often used as a starter peak for parents introducing their kids to hillwalking. **3.1 MILES**

GREAT GABLE There might be higher Lake District mountains but is there a more handsome one? Many walkers hike to the summit from Seathwaite in Borrowdale – an 8-mile return trip if you approach via Green Gable and descend past Styhead Tarn. But you can cut out a lot of the initial grunt-work by walking instead from Honister Pass (on a 6-mile route via Grey Knotts and Brandreth). **8 MILES**

TARN HOWS If the mountains seem too high, consider a stroll around Tarn Hows – thought by many to be one of the loveliest Lake District beauty spots. Owned by the National Trust, it takes around an hour to potter around. You can drive to Tarn Hows or simply walk up the country lanes and paths from Hawkshead or Coniston. **2 MILES**

THE OUTDOOR GUIDE

The Watermill

There's no mistaking the dog-friendly credentials of The Watermill; in fact you could go so far as to describe them as 'dog bonkers'. If the water bowls and dog-friendly accreditations in the windows don't convince you, then perhaps the bar might, with almost all the beers on tap being named with a doggy theme; a pint of Golden Retriever, or Bad Dog IPA is just the thing you need after a long day's walkies There are colourful dog portraits on the walls and even a special page in the bar menu dedicated to canine treats, plus a well-stocked doggy snack box on the bar. Dogs are welcome in the snug and inviting bar area and in all of the bedrooms, and for every dog that stays with them, The Watermill makes a donation to The Dogs Trust. The inn is tucked away in a quiet spot just a few hundred yards from the A591, with ample parking and within easy striking distance of dozens of beautiful walks, for example in the nearby Kentmere Valley. Or you could take a short drive up onto Scout Scar near Kendal for a stunning family friendly walk away from the busy crowds.

CONTACT Ings, near Windermere, Kendal, Cumbria
LA8 9PY · 01539 821309 · lakelandpub.co.uk
HOW MUCH? Double rooms from around £80 per night, dogs £7 a night.

Ryebeck Hotel

Tucked away in the foothills surrounding Bowness-on-Windermere, this hotel offers you space to unwind away from modern life, with plenty of room for you and your four-legged friend to stretch your legs. All dogs are welcomed with a bed, bowls and treats and there is no shortage of walks from the front door, with staff eager to direct you to the best routes. The hotel accepts 2 dogs per room and also welcomes them into the lounge, where you can have breakfast if you'd prefer not to leave your dog alone in your room. The lounge is spacious, with views of the grounds and oversized sofas to sink down into after a long day outdoors. Dogs are welcome in all ground floor rooms and the ample grounds are the perfect place for a quick leg stretch if you fancy a bit of a lazy day. With England's longest lake on your doorstep, there's lots to explore, and Windermere Lake Cruises welcomes dogs for free on all of their boats. Across the lake you'll find a lovely walk along the shores up to Wray Castle, with plenty of small beach areas perfect for picnics and a quick dip.

CONTACT Lyth Valley Road, Bowness-on-Windermere, Cumbria LA23 3JP · 01539 488195 · ryebeck.com
HOW MUCH? Double rooms from around £120 a night, plus £20 per dog per stay.

Eltermere Inn

Tucked away on the edge of this popular village, with easy access to all the local walks, this is a classic country house hotel with high ceilings and bedrooms that are tastefully decorated and offer a range of pricing options from the classic to a luxurious suite with deep roll-top bath. Up to 2 dogs are allowed in their 3 dog-friendly rooms (beds and bowls provided), and the ample grounds also offer the perfect spot for a quick breath of fresh air whenever you need it. Dogs are allowed in the bar area, which is comfortable and cosy with a large fire roaring away in the hearth throughout the winter months and a range of local beers and spirits available to warm you from the inside out. For something a little extra special, all guests also have free access to the spa at Langdale Estates, just five minutes' drive down the road, where you can enjoy a swim in the pool or simply chill out in the steam room. The Langdale Pikes offer full-day hikes for those with a sense of adventure, and the broad valley path alongside Great Langdale Beck to Skelwith Force is a perfect stroll for the whole family.

CONTACT Elterwater, Ambleside, Cumbria LA22 9HY •
01539 437207 • eltermere.co.uk
HOW MUCH? Doubles from around £145 a night. Dogs £15 per stay.

The Cuckoo Brow Inn

A gloriously cosy hideaway for you and your pooch, this old inn is buried away in Far Sawrey, just a hop, skip and a jump from Beatrix Potter's old home and a shortish stroll down to the ferry to Bowness. Nevertheless, you will truly feel as if you are a million miles from the modern world. Dogs are positively encouraged and allowed everywhere. On winter afternoons, the bar is a snug retreat with an open fire and assorted dogs snoozing around the legs of the nearby tables. During summer there is an outside seating area offering tranquil views of the surrounding hills. Dining is relaxed and the chef prides himself on sourcing as many ingredients as he can from within the county. The rooms are smart and contemporary, with deep baths and plenty of big fluffy towels. There is a range to choose from, including family rooms with bunk beds; dogs are allowed in bedrooms unsupervised and the welcoming reception area doubles as a small shop for any items you may have forgotten, including dog bowls. With loads of walks right on your doorstep there's plenty to wear out everyone.

CONTACT Far Sawrey, Ambleside, Cumbria LA22 0LQ •
01539 443425 • cuckoobrow.co.uk
HOW MUCH? Double rooms from £99 a night. Dogs £10 per stay.

The Yan

This family-run hotel offers boutique rooms and hearty food in a gorgeous Lakeland location.

It means 'Number One' in local dialect, and there's a good chance that The Yan will be number one on your agenda after spending a night or two here, or even just eating in the excellent downstairs restaurant. Part of the successful Broadrayne Farm business, which also includes a glamping site and a set of comfy holiday cottages, this brand-new restaurant with rooms is their latest venture. A short hop north of Grasmere, midway between lakes Windermere and Ullswater in the heart of the Lake District National Park, it occupies a lovely old slate-roofed set of country outhouses which enjoy wonderful views over the surrounding landscape and is decorated in a contemporary yet rustic style that will make anyone feel at home. It's an eco-friendly conversion too, with lots of recycled materials and wood upcycled into headboards and suchlike.

The seven upstairs guest rooms are each individually decorated in a crisp and unfussy modern style and come in various shapes and sizes, as you would expect in a historic building like this; there are three standard cosy doubles, a couple of more spacious deluxe rooms (with a double bed and sofa bed) that will easily accommodate a family of four, and two rooms that welcome dogs, one standard and one deluxe – a nice thought in what is so obviously a dog-friendly environment. All of the rooms are equipped with smart TVs, tea- and coffee-making facilities, good wifi and super-king-size beds with good quality linen (which can also be configured to sleep three if need be). The bathrooms are crisp and modern and come with rainfall showers and backlit heated mirrors that run

the length of the room. Towels are provided for dogs but you'll need to bring your dog's bed.

Downstairs there's a comfy open-plan lounge decorated in a similarly contemporary yet cosy country style, and the restaurant, which serves hearty British food from 3pm till 9pm every day at great prices – just the sort of food you need after walking the fells, including a choice of sumptuous sharing platters as well as a range of delicious breakfast dishes. Dogs are welcome in the restaurant and lounge as long as they are on leads (that are attached to their owners!). The Yan's owners Dave and Sally are usually around, as is their daughter Jess, who is the hotel's general manager, while her husband and chef Will oversees the kitchen. There's a pub within walking distance too, and lots of walks from the front door of the hotel, plus Grasmere is about 15 minutes away on foot. All the family can advise on where best to head for, and they'll make you up a packed lunch for the day if you order it in advance.

All in all, then, it's a thoroughly family affair, offering beautiful, very well-priced boutique rooms and great food in a gorgeous location that's perfect for short breaks with a dog. A winning formula if ever there was one!

CONTACT Broadrayne Farm, Grasmere, Cumbria, LA22 9RU • 01539 435055 • theyan.co.uk
HOW MUCH? Doubles £90–£130 a night, dogs £20 a stay.
ROOMS Seven guest rooms, including 2 dog-friendly doubles.

Alston House

Alston House has long been a hotel but we like the direction that current owners Mike and Carol have taken the place, with a welcoming café and restaurant as its hub and 7 dog-friendly rooms upstairs that are popular with the passing bike-and-hike trade (Alston is on the Pennine Way and C2C routes). Nothing is too much trouble, and it's a soothing experience all round – earth-tone décor, gorgeously soft beds, cafetiéres with proper coffee on the tea trays. A deep sleep is guaranteed in tiny Alston, which is Britain's highest market town. Three of the rooms have lovely baths – room 1 at the back in particular has a rather singular bathroom fitted into a very bijou space but still manages to offer a huge stand-alone slipper bath for soothing away aches and pains, while another has an impressive roll-top bath. Breakfast is a hearty affair, from croissants and fresh fruit salad to the full monty, after which you can retrieve your boots from in front of the fire, your kit from the drying room or your bike from the cycle store and start the day on the trail all over again.

CONTACT Townfoot, Alston, Cumbria CA9 3RN • 01434 382200 • alstonhousehotel.co.uk
HOW MUCH? Double rooms £65–£90 a night, dogs £20 a night.

The George & Dragon

Clifton's George and Dragon makes a great base for touring around Penrith, Ullswater and the Eden Valley. The old Georgian inn – part of the local Lowther Estate – looks age-old traditional from the outside, but inside it's zippy and modern, with lovely, compact rooms that mix pretty fabrics, mod cons and paintings and antique furnishings from the Lowther collection to great effect, and also welcome dogs. Bathrooms are nice and bijou too, many with either walk-in showers or roll-top baths, and all in all it's a very handsome place to stay. Dogs can eat with you in the bar but not the restaurant downstairs, which is a real country gourmet's delight, with almost everything sourced from the local Lowther Estate – fish from the river, veg from the kitchen gardens and meat from the cosseted Lowther herds. Choose from venison medallions on mash, fell-bred lamb or oysters from the Solway coast or the signature twice-baked cheese soufflé. There's also a lovely sunny courtyard and garden where you can chew the fat with your hound.

CONTACT Clifton, Penrith, Cumbria CA10 2ER • 01768 865381 • askhamhall.co.uk/george-and-dragon/
HOW MUCH? Double rooms from £100 a night, dogs £10 a night.

The Midland Hotel

An icon of Art Deco design, the Midland
Hotel is beautifully positioned on Morecambe
promenade, with superb views across the Bay to
the Lake District fells. Built in the 1930s when
Morecambe was in its seaside heyday, it cut a
sad figure until just a few years ago, when it was
sympathetically and rather wonderfully restored,
and its clean angles and cool sweeping lines and
many of its original Art Deco features brought back
to life. These include a collection of marvellous
friezes and sculptures by Eric Gill, brought together
with bold modern touches that suit the building
perfectly. Among these are the excellent restaurant
and terrace with to-die-for views over the Bay,
and the very colourful, ultra-modern Rotunda
cocktail bar. As for the bedrooms, they are starkly
contemporary, but with plenty of nods to their
1930s heritage, and the views again are superb, not
least those from the six magnificently cool roof-top
suites. Dogs get a bowl and a bed and are allowed in
the bar downstairs, and Morecambe Bay has plenty
of opportunities for a good walk or two.

CONTACT Marine Road West, Morecambe, Lancashire
LA4 4BU · 01524 424000 · englishlakes.co.uk
HOW MUCH? Double rooms with breakfast £125–
£460, dogs £20 a night.

The Inn at Whitewell

Situated in the heart of the Forest of Bowland,
the Inn at Whitewell is a lovely spot to escape for
a while, surrounded by miles of stark, stunning,
moorlands. It feels like the middle of nowhere
but actually it's the middle of everywhere – the
nearest village, Dunsop Bridge, has a phone box
that officially marks the geographic centre of the
United Kingdom! The Inn dates back to the 14th
century and is warm and inviting. During winter,
fires blaze in assorted hearths and in summer there
is a stunning patio area to take in the magnificent
views. Dogs are allowed in all the bedrooms and
every other area of the inn apart from the dining
room and there is no extra charge for bringing
them with you; beds and bowls are available on
request and they're very flexible on numbers, just
call ahead if you have more than one. Should you
wish to breakfast or dine with your dog, that can
be arranged either in the bar, lounge or in your
room. With plenty of walks right from the door and
wholesome, hearty, meals to come back to, this is
the perfect retreat at any time of the year.

CONTACT Whitewell, near Clitheroe, Lancashire
BB7 3AT · 01200 44822 2 · innatwhitewell.com
HOW MUCH? Prices from around £140 a night – dogs
free.

YHA Hawkshead

A glorious setting for both dogs and humans – at an affordable cost.

Midway between Windermere and Coniston Water, in the heart of the southern Lakes, this grade II-listed Regency-style building enjoys a glorious setting overlooking tranquil Esthwaite Water and is perhaps the ideal location for family-friendly activity breaks on a budget – or just an affordable holiday in the Lake District. Even by YHA standards, Hawkshead is unusual for the sheer variety of accommodation it offers, which varies from the usual dormitory beds and private rooms in the hostel itself to a choice of dog-friendly tipis, glamping pods, cabins and camping pitches in the grounds outside.

Among many other facilities in the hostel, there is a spacious lounge, a dining room, a self-catering kitchen and a games room, and all facilities are of course open both to those who opt to stay in the hostel itself or those who camp or try one of the hostel's glamping options. The three tipis are fully kitted out with bedding and can sleep four people on mattresses. They have a partly carpeted wooden floor and a lockable chest in which you can store your belongings and also use as a table. There's eco-friendly solar lighting and two comfy bean bags for you to chill out on during the day. There are eight camping pods, including a standard pod sleeping three and a large pod sleeping four (on a double futon and two single beds), both of which have heating and an outdoor seating area, plus there's a large cabin that can comfortably sleep 4–5 people and is perfect for a family, with a double bed with a single above and a set of two bunk beds. Finally, there are ten bell tents on the front lawn, each kitted out with a double futon and three single futons plus

all bedding, and also the campsite, which is situated in the Victorian kitchen garden, a picturesque spot surrounded by woodland with a stream running alongside. It can accommodate up to ten family-sized tents and a couple of smaller tents, and campers have full access to the same facilities as glampers, including the self-catering kitchen and indoor showers and toilets, which are just metres away.

All in all, Hawkshead is an ideal base for a cheap, dog-friendly family and activity holiday in The Lakes, great for walking and cycling in nearby Grizedale Forest and with easy access to the southern fells and Lake Windermere. Finally there's a lovely, stile-free route you can walk with your dog that takes in some spectacular Lake District scenery. It's a pleasant and easy stroll from the hostel to Hawkshead village. From there, progress to Low Loanthwaite and then through some woodland and meadows, around the top of Blelham Tarn, and finally on to Wray Castle – a mock-Gothic castle on the shore of Windermere where dogs are also welcome. It's a five-mile round-trip and a great way to wear out your wolf!

CONTACT Ambleside, Cumbria LA22 0QD·
0345 371 9321· yha.org.uk
HOW MUCH? Dormitory beds from £10 per person, private rooms from £25 a night, camping from £8 per person, tipis from £49 a night, pods £29 a night, bell tents from £59 a night.
ACCOMMODATION 106 beds in a selection of dormitories and private rooms, some en-suite, plus a variety of glamping options.

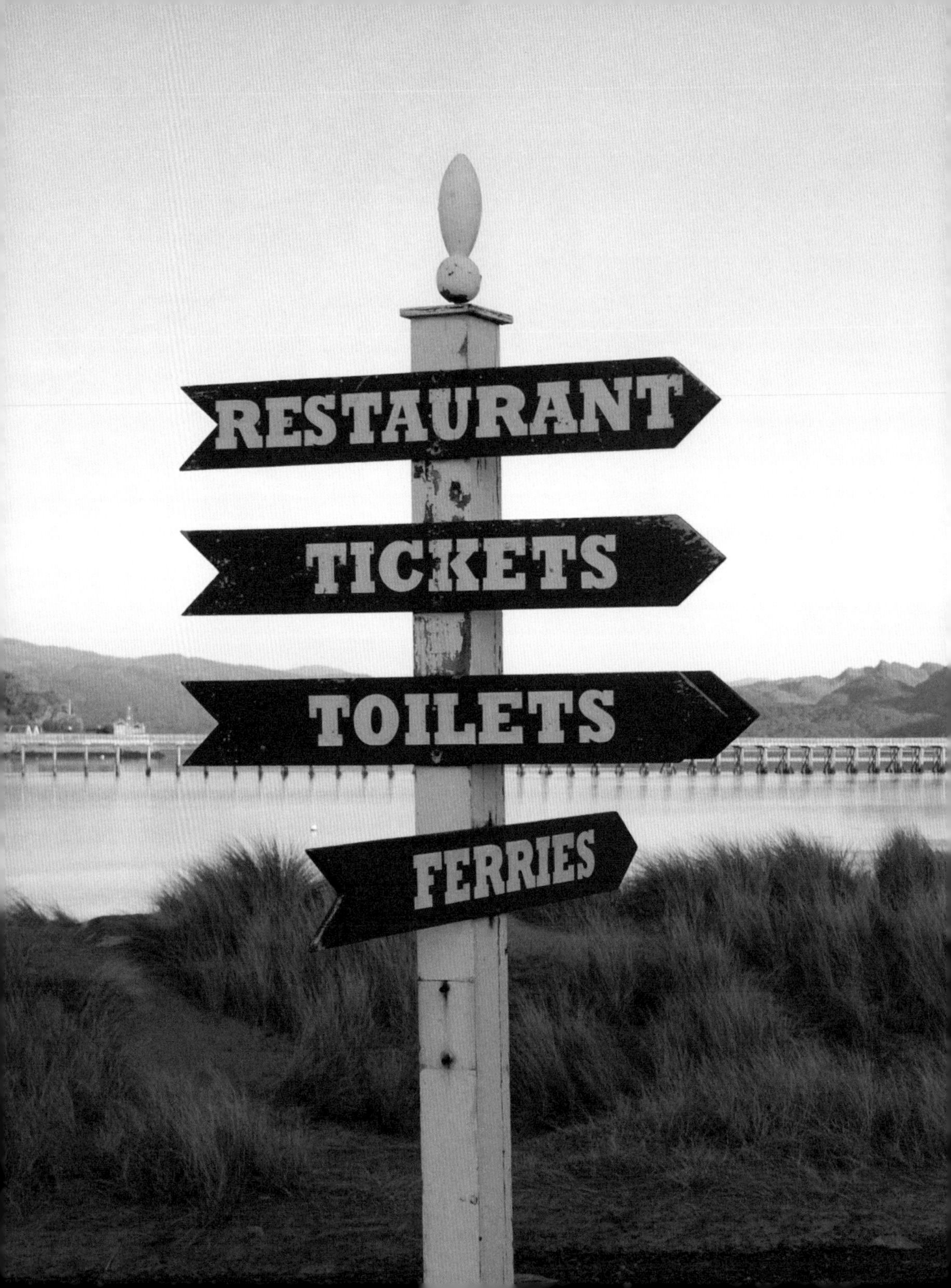
RESTAURANT
TICKETS
TOILETS
FERRIES

WALES

Dripping with mystery and legend, Wales is one
of Britain's most beautiful natural playgrounds,
with an impressive range of beaches, valleys,
rolling hills and jagged mountains. Catch it on
a good day, when the sun is beaming and the
clouds sparse, and you might forget you're in the
UK at all.

Forest Holidays Beddgelert

Adventurous holidays with dogs in the heart of the Snowdonia National Park.

Situated in a part of Wales drenched in myth and legend, Forest Holidays Beddgelert (pronounced 'Bethgelet') is perhaps the cabin holiday group's most intimate and certainly its most tranquil location, just outside the pretty village of the same name in the heart of the Snowdonia National Park.

It's a terrific place to come on holiday, with just sixteen cabins dotted throughout the woods here, and tucked away to the degree that this leafy glade can feel like your own secret hideaway. The Colwyn river wraps around one side of the site, while on the other you can hop onto one of the steam trains of the Welsh Highland Railway, which whisk you up to Caenearfon or down to Porthmadog through some of the UK's most picturesque mountain scenery.

Above all, it's a perfect place to return to after exploring the wonders and wilds of Snowdonia, with one, two and three-bedroom cabins that are equipped with everything you need, including hot tubs that are the perfect place to relax after a hard day's hiking before getting cosy in your cabin and watching the stars through the large floor-to-ceiling windows. Some of the cabins are dog friendly, so the whole family can come, while at the centre of the site, the Forest Retreat and Bakehouse has a café and bar, shop and play area, bikes for hire and the chance to go wildlife-spotting and do some bushcraft activities with Forest Holidays' very own Rangers.

For all the excellent facilities, however, it's the location that really steals the show here. Beddegelert would be an appealing village

wherever it was located, but it's in the very heart of the Snowdonia National Park, surrounded by magnificent mountains, rivers and lakes, and – in case you're interested! – was also the inspiration for the stories of Rupert Bear. The village has an attractive, bustling feel, with plenty of shops and restaurants, and is on the wonderful Welsh Highland and Ffestinog Railway so it's easy to get to other intesting places. For nearby walks, the hill of Moel Hebog (Welsh for 'bare hill of the hawk') offers a gentle ascent, or there's the foot of Snowdon (Yr Wyddfa) a couple of miles away near the village of Rhyd-Ddu, which is also on the Welsh Highland line.

Further afield, you can travel from one scenically sited castle to another, or take the Ffestinog Railway from Beddgelert to Blenau-Ffestinog or Porthmadog. From there it's easy to reach the unique and very memorable fake Italianate village of Portmeirion, built by eccentric architect Clough Williams-Ellis between 1925 and 1976 using endangered buildings from all over Britain, and famous for the cult TV series 'The Prisoner', among many other things.

CONTACT Beddgelert, Gwynedd LL55 4UU • 03330 110495 • forestholidays.co.uk
HOW MUCH? Short breaks from £300, 7 nights from £515. Dogs £15.
ACCOMMODATION 16 cabins, sleeping from 2 to 6 people, some with hot tubs.

Fforest Fields

You couldn't get closer to the heart of rural Wales than the holiday cottage and yurts of this delightful family farm, situated just outside Llandrindod Wells in the midst of the green hills of Powys. Some people come back here year after year – to walk, fish, canoe or swim, or just to commune with nature. The cottage sleeps 5 comfortably, in a double bedroom, a twin and a small single; it's beautifully furnished and has a log fire for chilly evenings as well as a pretty front garden and a sun-trap BBQ area at the back. Their lakeside yurts are cosily decorated with cushions, rugs and lanterns and have room for 4 people in a double bed and 2 pull-out futons, and rates include all bedding, a log-burner with a stock of wood, BBQ and firepit. You also get your own kitchen, with a 2-ring burner, crockery and utensils, and an eco-toilet. The farm is equipped with an underfloor-heated shower block and an on-site shop, but perhaps best of all you and your dog have access to hundreds of acres of farmland, plus 2 lakes for fishing, swimming and paddling, with a small beach and a jetty with kayaks.

CONTACT Hundred House, Llandrindod Wells, Powys LD1 5RU • 01982 570406 • fforestfields.co.uk
HOW MUCH? Cottage £75–£100 a night, minimum 3-night stay. Yurts £77–£120 a night for up to 4 people.

Y Granar

Deep in the heart of mid-Wales, this spacious, open-plan beamed studio for two is a dog owner's dream. Not only does it offer a generous doggy welcome pack, containing leads, guest dog tags, bowls and treats for up to 4 dogs, it also has a unique four-poster dog bed, where small and medium-size dogs can be left to lie. There is also a small enclosed grass paddock that is home to a range of dog agility equipment, and access to 2 acres of bluebell woods, river bank and grassy meadows. The pasture may sometimes have sheep and requires dogs to be on lead, but the woods and river bank are perfect for any number of lead-free walks you can do from your door. As for humans, the stunning interior has a kitchen and seating area, underfloor heating and a king-sized four-poster bed below a set of skylights that make it ideal for stargazing – plus there's an outside deck with garden chairs from which you can enjoy a location that feels far from civilisation. Despite that, you're only a mile from the busy market town of Tregaron, and the beaches of Cardigan Bay are only a half-hour drive away.

CONTACT Tregaron, Ceredigion SY25 6NL • 03332 020899 originalcottages.co.uk
HOW MUCH? £448– £695 a week.

Tal-Y-Waun

Owned by the same people who run the lovely Gwern Gof Isaf farm campsite in the heart of Snowdonia, this fabulous holiday cottage is perfect for walkers, nestled in the Ogwen valley and giving easy access to the mountains of Capel Curig and Tryfan – slopes that were famously a training ground for members of the 1953 Everest expedition. The cottage has 5 bedrooms – 2 doubles, 3 singles – and 2 bathrooms, a nicely furnished sitting room and a dining room with large table fashioned out of the old dairy. Dogs are welcome and it has wifi, a wood-burning stove, central heating and a well-equipped if small kitchen. There is also a washing machine, a couple of TVs, a DVD player and a games room for rainy days – not that unusual in this part of the world. It really couldn't be cosier, but the main attraction is its position, with Capel Curig nearby and Glyder Ridge and Carneddau mountain ranges offering scenic climbs. Less energetic folk can make do with the lovely but less ambitious walk along the old road between Capel Curig and Bethesda.

CONTACT Capel Curig, Betws y Coed, Conwy Ll24 0EU • 01766 830306 • talywaunholidaycottage.co.uk
HOW MUCH? From £420 for a 3-night stay to £980 for 7 nights.

St Curig's Church

It's fair to say you've probably never stayed anywhere quite like St Curig's. The church was deconsecrated in 1992 and converted by current owner Alice Douglas, and the results of her labours are an astounding blend of modern style and religious heritage, with the added bonus of an outdoor hot tub among the tombstones in the garden. The views over Snowdonia's mountains are incredible, and you'll also get a good view of Brecon – not the Welsh town but the family dog, of course. Alice doesn't charge anything extra for dogs and there are walks directly from the church, both in the mountains and the nearby forest. There's a drying room with a washing machine and a store for bikes or kayaks, a well-equipped kitchen on the mezzanine level, and a dining room and lounge area in the apse, which provides an atmospheric environment for tinkling the grand piano or playing an impromptu game of pool. But these are all activities for a rainy day, and the real reason people come here is to explore the nearby hiker's paradise, Capel Curig.

CONTACT Capel Curig, Gwynned LL24 0EL • 07980 619139 • stcurigschurch.com
HOW MUCH? 2–6 night breaks £1890–£5490, 7 nights £3990.

Slate Mountain Glamping

Family-sized, hillside safari tents for dogs and humans in the spectacular heart of Snowdonia.

Snowdonia's lofty peaks may steal all the coverage, but at this North Wales tourist attraction it's the mountain range's subterranean scenery that draws you in. Situated in the very heart of the Snowdonia National Park, Llechwedd Slate Caverns is a fascinating interactive experience that tells the story of the region's slate-mining heritage. At its height, the Welsh slate industry employed more than 17,000 men, with over half a million tonnes extracted annually. Little wonder then that nearby Blaenau Ffestiniog has long been known as 'the town that roofed the world'.

Now visitors to this multi-award-winning attraction can immerse themselves in North Wales' industrial past – albeit in the utmost of comfort. First opened in summer 2018, six high-end safari tents are the latest additions to the thriving Slate Caverns site. Situated on a car-free hillside (luggage is delivered to your tent), overlooking the vast mine and quarry complex, these glamping units promise a stylish stay, with fantastic views across Snowdonia. The tents each accommodate up to five people, with a couple of smaller ones for families of four. King-size beds and cannily crafted bunks ensure a good night's sleep, while the en-suite bathroom (complete with electric showers and a proper loo) and fully equipped kitchenette make it just like home. Wood-burning stoves are provided, along with barbecues, firepits and a spacious verandah, so it's still possible to feel like you're enjoying a holiday in the Great Outdoors, plus dogs are welcome as long they are on a lead at all times and don't climb on the furniture or bedding.

The Slate Caverns complex comprises a host of fun-filled and illuminating attractions. The Llechwedd Deep Mine tour takes guests on a guided trip below the surface via a narrow-gauge cable railway, the steepest in Britain. The caverns are brought vividly to life courtesy of the knowledgeable guides with a little help from some state-of-the-art audio visuals. Hold on tight for The Quarry Explorer off-road adventure as you traverse the man-made mountains and cavernous craters in a military truck, while Zip World cranks up the adrenaline another notch with Titan, Europe's largest 4-person zip line – the closest you can get to skydiving without jumping out of a plane.

Location-wise, The Slate Caverns score pretty high on the 'singular settings' scale, and it's a testament to the draw of the place that most people would be clamouring to go glamping here even without the added bonus of the impressive array of attractions on the doorstep. Poised in the heart of this iconic national park, with red kites circling overhead and some of the clearest night skies around, a stay here offers the essential Snowdonia experience, and then some.

CONTACT The Slate Caverns, Blaenau Ffestiniog, Gwynedd LL41 3NB · 01766 830306 · llechwedd.co.uk
HOW MUCH? From £120 to £180 a night, depending on the time of year.
ACCOMMODATION Six safari tents, 4 of which sleep 5 people and 2 sleep 4 people.

Graig Wen

Succumb to the tranquil hills of Graig Wen. Smart, sustainable and quite simply lush.

Graig Wen is one of the smartest operations in the book – it's not only a glamping and camping site but has four self-catering cottages too, and we love the fact that well-behaved dogs are welcome pretty much everywhere, not to mention the fact that the charge they make for dogs on the campsite is donated to a local animal sanctuary.

On the glamping side, there are two cosy yurts – a small one sleeping two and a larger one with room for five – and a bell tent sleeping four, while a couple of other 'pop-up yurts' move around the site according to the season. There's also 'Jones', a romantic shepherd's hut that can comfortably accommodate two or a young family of four, with a double bed and two bunks that can swing down when needed. Built by local craftspeople, it has – like the yurts – a wood-burning stove (a basket of logs is provided), a kitchenette with a gas hob and fridge and crockery and cutlery, and the double bed is covered with a sheep's wool duvet. Isolated and sheltered among dense woodland, both the yurts and shepherd's hut offer total privacy from the main campsite, and the beautiful Mawddach Estuary Trail is just a short walk away through the woodland and meadows.

The great thing about Graig Wen is that there's so much to do nearby, with or without your car. Intrepid walkers could tackle Cader Idris, the spectacular mountain behind the site. Bikes are available to hire and using the estuary cycle path you can cycle all the way to Barmouth without even seeing a road – and virtually the entire route to Dolgellau in the other direction is road-free, too.

If glamping isn't for you, then you have a choice of some grown-up rooms in their Slate Shed B&B or family breaks in their splendid holiday cottages. Ty'r Adar (which sleeps 5 people) means 'House of Birds' in Welsh, due in part to the fact that you can drop off to sleep at night listening to the hooting of owls in the trees outside; three others (Pine Cottage, Little Haven and Small Barn), each sleep between 2 and 6. They're all beautifully furnished and very up to date, with flatscreen TVs, DVDs, dishwashers and more. Yet they're cosy too – Ty'r Adar has a wood-burning stove and sumptuous Welsh blankets. They do ask that dogs aren't left unattended in the cottages or glamping accommodation but they can put you in touch with an excellent doggy day-care centre if you're visiting somewhere that is not dog friendly.

Finally it's worth knowing that the guys at Graig Wen are ambassadors for the Snowdonia Dark Skies Reserve and they promote various special events pertaining to this in the latter part of each year. Weather permitting, it's not a bad time to come for a spot of stargazing and howling at the moon!

CONTACT Arthog, near Dolgellau, Gwynedd LL39 1YP • 01341 250482 • graigwen.co.uk

HOW MUCH? Yurts from £60 per night, shepherd's hut from £85 a night, cottages £50–£115 a night – minimum stays apply at all. Camping pitches adults £7–£9, children £3–£4; under 5s free. Dogs £10.

ACCOMMODATION 4 yurts, a shepherd's hut, and 4 cosy cottages, plus around 30 camping pitches.

Felin Geri

Set in the idyllic wooded Ceri valley, the safari
tents at Felin Geri provide the perfect opportunity
to take a step back and live life at your own pace,
in a 24-acre paradise of woodland, water and
wildlife. They welcome well-adjusted dogs who
have the river to play in and loads of space to run
around. Each tent has an open-plan living space
with sectioned-off sleeping areas for up to 6–8
people. Good quality linen, duvets and towels are
all included, and there's a covered verandah on
which to enjoy a sundowner while watching the
local wildlife. There's also a well-equipped kitchen,
a cool box to keep things cold and a shower room
and toilet at the back of each tent. A wood-burning
stove keeps you warm while doubling up as an
oven, and a series of battery-powered hurricane
lamps provide the light you'll need to play the board
games that come with each tent. All of the tents also
have private hot tubs and there is a traditional Welsh
cottage for those not up for glamping. They also
have a state-of-the-art telescope for stargazing in
what are some of the UK's darkest skies.

CONTACT Cwmcou, Newcastle Emlyn, Ceredigion
SA38 9PA • 01239 712856 • felingeri.co.uk
HOW MUCH? Short breaks from £450 for 4 nights;
£560 for 3 nights at weekends; 7 nights £980–£1350.

Smuggler's Cove Boatyard

Situated in a former slate works overlooking the
Dyfi Estuary, Smugglers Cove Boatyard has been
offering moorings and acting as a hub for local
sailors for years. But these days it's more than just a
boatyard, with camping pitches on the riverbank, a
glamping boat on the foreshore and 2 self-catering
holiday cottages – 5-bedroom Chapel House
and 2-bedroom Quarry Cottage – which can be
rented as a single let. With room for 14–18 people
in 7 bedrooms and a couple of sofa beds, it's an
ideal venue for family reunions, celebrations and
get-togethers – a rustic and cosy pair of cottages
with central heating and a wood-burning stove.
Dogs are welcome, and there is lots of space to run
around and an outdoor tap and drinking bowls
for thirsty hounds and dirty paws. You can launch
your own boat or canoe or enjoy the private beach,
from which you can swim or just watch the boats
bobbing about. You also can stride out into the hills
behind on numerous footpaths, or visit Aberdyfi
beach at the far end of the estuary, an expanse of
golden sand and dunes, much of it dog friendly.

CONTACT Frongoch, Aberdyfi, Gwynedd, LL35 0RG •
0800 023 6489 • smugglerscove.info
HOW MUCH? From £1395 to £1895 most of the year;
short (3–4-night) breaks from £995. Dogs £25 per stay.

Parkway Hotel & Spa

There's a lot to like about this friendly, privately owned hotel just north of Newport in Cwmbran. Situated in a low-slung modern set of buildings, it has 80 very comfortable guest bedrooms of all shapes and sizes, many of which have been recently refurbished, and it has recently diversified by adding a shepherd's hut in its extensive grounds. It also has a well-equipped spa featuring a heated pool, sauna, steam room and gym. The rooms are very well appointed and come with the sorts of facilities you expect in a decent four-star – speedy wifi, TVs, tea- and coffee-making facilities, air-conditioning, robes and en-suite bathrooms. The Garden Suites, with private patios, are dog friendly, as is their very cosy shepherd's hut, which is frankly a cut above most glamping, with an en-suite bathroom, underfloor heating and a wood-burning stove. Dogs are provided with beds, treats and a special canine menu for dinner, and although the hotel's excellent 2-AA-rosette restaurant is not open to canine chums, you can eat in the bar or lounge, and the grounds offer easy off-lead walks.

CONTACT Cwmbran Drive, Cwmbran NP44 3UW · 01633 871199 · parkwayhotelandspa.com
HOW MUCH? Garden suites from £190 a night, shepherd's hut £195 a night, dogs £30 a night.

Under the Oak

Set in a corner of a traditional Monmouthshire family farm, Under the Oak provides a luxury glamping experience, with just 3 safari tents either side of a large pond, and views stretching out to the rolling Welsh hills. Sheep and cattle are generally your nearest neighbours and buzzards and red kites soar overhead, yet Cardiff is just a 30-minute drive away. The tents have every conceivable comfort, including a Welsh box bed and a hot tub filled with natural spring water, heated by a wood-burning stove. Dogs are welcome and provided with a basket, blanket and bowl. Owners Lydia and Richard provide lots of homely touches – fluffy towels, comfy cushions and a kitchen well stocked with plenty of basics. Each tent offers a spacious and comfortable place in which to unwind, and a wood-burning stove throws out heat on chilly Welsh nights. Outside, a well-sheltered verandah is perfectly placed for a spot of star-gazing, and there's a table and chairs for alfresco dining. The mountain above the farm offers excellent walks and panoramic views across to the Bristol Channel.

CONTACT Pen y Waun Farm, Mountain Rd, Bedwas, Caerphilly, Monmouthshire CF83 8ER · 07886 477930 · undertheoakglamping.co.uk
HOW MUCH? 2-night breaks £260–£340. Dogs £25.

OUT AND ABOUT

Great walks with your dog

ABERPORTH CLIFF PATH   Aberporth is a pretty village clinging to the hillside on the West Wales coast, and this tarmac cliff path is part of the Wales Coast Path, with stunning views out to sea and quite a variety of dog-friendly cafés and pubs along the way. 1.3 MILES

BEDDGELERT This walk from Beddgelert explores an ancient landscape of wizards, dragons and kings, taking in the ancient hill fort of Dinas Emrys, and starting with Gelert's Grave on the banks of the Afon Glaslyn – Beddgelert's most famous landmark. Just don't share the story of the loyal dog Gelert, mistakenly killed by Prince Llewelyn, with your pet! . Keep your eyes peeled for gold nuggets! 4.8 MILES

FOEL ISPRI   TThis easy walk is cut into the valley side, with stunning views of the Mawddach estuary, Barmouth viaduct, Dolgellau and the Arans. The route follows a flat track known rather dramatically as The Precipice – a former tramway that once led along the hillside to the now abandoned goldmines at Foel Ispri. The ruins of some mine buildings still remain along with a few connecting paths and tramway beds. Keep your eyes peeled for gold nuggets! 0.5 MILES

GLAMORGAN COAST PATH The Glamorgan section of the Wales Coast Path delivers sweeping views, hidden coves and dramatic cliff edges. There are plenty of places to start but the most popular is Ogmore-by-Sea, a stunning coastal town with a heck of a beach. You could also walk to Dunraven Castle from Southerndown, which includes Dunraven Park's green hillsides and epic coastal views. While in Southerndown, grab a pint at the dog-friendly Three Golden Cups. 14 MILES

THE OUTDOOR GUIDE

Cosy Under Canvas

Award-winning dome glamping with hot tubs and firepits in a Welsh woodland.

Twisting and turning along the winding country lanes, surrounded by undulating green and yellow fields deep in the heart of the Welsh/English borders countryside, it's almost impossible not to get childishly giddy about what treats await you at Cosy Under Canvas. As you slowly roll into the carpark, offload your bags into the wheelbarrow kindly provided for you, and walk along the wooden pathway across a wildflower wetland, it quickly becomes apparent that you've arrived somewhere quite special. Owner Emma has been running Cosy Under Canvas for 12 years now, and her experience and attention to detail resonates throughout the site – from the little welcome boards with your names written in chalk to the homemade cakes left out for your arrival. And dogs are very welcome too!

There are seven pitches, spread out in a small private woodland and cleverly hidden from each other by the trees, and they consist of five spacious geodesic dome tents – Holly, Oak, Beech, Hazel and Rowan – and two cosy domes – Willow and Ash. All welcome dogs (you just need to bring your own bed) and come with their own wood-fired hot tub, firepit, chiminea, compost loo, indoor wood-burning stove, sheepskin rugs, super comfy double or king-size beds, raised double futons, wood and kindling, lanterns and tea lights. There's a 'cosy corner', which is filled with board games and activities for kids, a 'cosy lounge' with comfy chairs, beanbags and low tables for chilling out, and a large communal sheltered kitchen with full recycling facilities and equipped with everything you could possibly need for cooking up a storm over a campfire. There's also fresh drinking water and a handful of gas stoves in case the rain puts a dampener on things. The two communal showers are heated by the large wood-fired Aga in the kitchen – a nice communal touch, as it relies on everyone chucking in a log from time to time to make sure the water stays hot – but if you fancy a proper power shower (heated by a biomass boiler) then pop up to the main house. With all these green credentials, it's no wonder that Cosy Under Canvas is also the proud owner of a much-coveted gold Green Tourism Award.

All in all, Cosy Under Canvas is a woodland retreat like no other. The kids will never want to get out of the hot tub, and couples will only want to cosy up with each other next to the fire and stare up at the starry dark skies above. You're also close to the literary haven of Hay-on-Wye, where as well as plentiful bookshops, there are lots of organic food shops, antique and secondhand gems to keep you occupied for a full day. Hay is also situated within the 520 square miles of uninterrupted and truly outstanding natural beauty of the Brecon Beacons National Park.

CONTACT Dolbedwyn, Newchurch, Kington, Powys HR5 3QQ • 01497 851603 • cosyundercanvas.co.uk
HOW MUCH? Domes from £130 to £796 depending on the season and time and length of stay.
ACCOMMODATION Five spacious domes and two cosy domes all sited on raised decks. Dogs £15 per stay.

The Slate Shed

A peaceful boutique B&B in the glorious Snowdonia National Park.

The folks behind the glamping and camping and cottages at Graig Wen also run a lovely boutique B&B, The Slate Shed, housed in what was once a Victorian slate-cutting mill. There are five rooms, all of them dog friendly and decorated in a bright, contemporary style and equipped with flatscreen TVs, good wifi, posh toiletries, lovely Welsh wool blankets and bath robes. You are welcomed with chocolates and a drink, and you can soak up the fabulous views over the Mawddach estuary during your stay; the Brán or Miri Mawr rooms have the best views – intriguingly they are all named after obscure Welsh pop stars!

In short, it's a great place to come with your dog, with tremendous walks from your doorstep and dog-friendly beaches just a short drive away. The estuary path leads to dog-friendly pubs and the owners can put you in touch with a doggy day-care centre nearby if you want to head off somewhere that doesn't accept dogs – for example to take the train up Snowdon. Dogs also get a welcome treat and a towel on arrival.

What about humans? Well, the rooms are cosy and have very comfortable beds, and the breakfasts are yummy, with everything sourced from local farms or friends and family – and they'll deliver a breakfast hamper to your room if you're feeling lazy. Meanwhile, everyone is welcome to enjoy the spacious communal Caban area, with its stunning views, honesty bar, books, maps and games to pass the time on rainy days.

There's tons to do in the local area, from hiring a bike in the village of Dolgellau and cycling to the local pub to hitting the nearby beaches, just five minutes away. Tackle Cader Idris, the spectacular mountain right at the back of Graig Wen, or explore a stack of challenging mountain-bike trails at nearby Coed-y-Brenin, around five miles north of Dolgellau. You can climb up the waterfalls at Arthog, visit Cregennan Lakes or from your doorstep walk directly through the property's own surrounding 45 acres of wild woodland and meadows to the Mawddach Estuary and the 9.5-mile-long Mawddach Trail, which follows the old rail line to the southern edge of the estuary. The George III pub is a good place to stop off for a pint and something to eat, and, as you would expect in such a scenic location, it is thoroughly dog friendly. Further afield, Harlech Castle, Portmeirion and the Ffestiniog Steam Railway are within easy reach, plus the Slate Shed and the area around it is also a fabulous place for star-gazing, with some of the most seriously dark skies in this part of the Snowdonia National Park.

CONTACT Arthog, Dolgellau, Gwynedd LL39 1YP • 01341 250482 • slateshed.co.uk
HOW MUCH? Double rooms £90–£130 a night. Dogs £10.
ROOMS Five en-suite rooms, including one accessible ground-floor room with wet room.

Top Of The Woods

Carefree Welsh glamping with acres of space, excellent walks and a beautiful woodland on the doorstep.

Top of the Woods is part of Penralt Farm, a quaint 18th-century farmstead with chickens scratching around outside and three pet Kunekune pigs, plus farm sheds that are home to housemartins and a rare breed of bat (the farm hosts seven of the UK's 17 bat species). The site has won sustainable tourism awards for the past two years running, and is a thoroughly eco-friendly place to stay, with a variety of glamping styles to choose from – four fully furnished geodesic domes (complete with log-burners), four luxury safari lodges and nine spacious pioneer camps. It's all pretty high-spec, but the feeling and style is very definitely back to nature – star-gazing and guitars around the campfire are fine, gadgets and noise not so much.

Dogs are welcome everywhere, and the rules are pretty simple: they must be kept under control and preferably on a lead on-site, but that's about it; they always have doggy treats and water in reception on arrival, and blankets and poo bags are available if you need them. As dog owners themselves, owners Soo and Jon also have lots of advice and recommendations on things to do with your dog while you're here, for example the walks you can do through the adjacent 325 acres of Ffynone Wood.

Every tent has proper beds, with good-quality linen provided, cooking facilities, their own barbecue, dining equipment, cool box, lantern, rugs and cushions. The safari lodges also have a fully equipped kitchen, dining tables and benches, plus a welcome pack containing things like coffee, bread, milk, candles and a basket of logs. The pioneer camps and nature domes feature a 2-burner hob, plus a dining table and benches. A Dutch Barn serves as a covered picnic and meeting area for the whole site (which also has regular camping pitches), with tables, hammocks, phone-charging points and a stash of games. There is also a freezer and a microwave, while the main courtyard area has hot showers and flushing toilets, washing-up sinks and free wifi. The pioneer lodge and safari lodge meadows also have their own hot showers and compost toilets.

Soo and Jon offer farmhouse breakfasts at weekends and also host dinners in the evenings, and a mobile fishmonger visits twice weekly, plus there are usually other activities going on, from bushcraft sessions and storytelling to their excellent and very special 'Woof Weekend' in May, when dogs and their owners get even more pampered than usual.

Finally, Top of the Woods enjoys an undeniably great location, right in the heart of Pembrokeshire, and handy for the Pembrokeshire Coast. Even with all these attractions on your doorstep, you may find you spend more time on the site than you meant to, delving into the woods and picnicking in the sun. There's a lot to explore – so why would you want to ever leave?

CONTACT Penrallt Farm, Boncath, Pembrokeshire SA37 0EP • 01239 842208 • topofthewoods.co.uk
HOW MUCH? Pioneer Lodges £80–£105 a night. Nature Domes £90–£120. Safari Lodges £110–£135. Dogs £5 a night – 2-night minimum stay.
ACCOMMODATION Pioneer Lodges, Nature Domes and Safari Lodges sleeping 4–6 people.

Treberfedd Farm

A beautiful array of eco-friendly self-catering accommodation in a very special part of Wales.

A working organic farm with Hereford cattle and Llanwenog sheep, Treberfedd Farm in Ceredigion's lush Aeron Valley is a special spot, with a series of enticing holiday cottages and stylish eco-cabins in a beautiful hilltop location just a 15-minute drive from the sea at Aberaeron and New Quay. Treberfedd has four pin-neat cottages sleeping anything between 5 and 9 people, and two unique octagonal eco-cabins in a flower-filled meadow for some extremely luxurious glamping. The cottages range from a lovely four-bedroom farmhouse to a couple of converted barns and a picture-perfect thatched cottage. Each has rustic charm in abundance, but they are also well equipped with modern amenities, with fully fitted kitchens, open-plan living areas, underfloor heating, TVs and DVD players and decent wifi. Three of the cottages have hot tubs and there's a night-time darkness here that makes it perfect for stargazing.

The cottages all take dogs, as does one of the two eco-cabins. These are unique octagonal creations, circular inside, with large windows all the way round that look out over the valley. The interiors are bespoke and completely original, and actually more spacious than you might think, with an open-plan kitchen, large dining table and a super-king-size bed that makes the most of the panoramic views down the valley, along with fold-down bunk beds for the kids. The unique design of the cabins not only blends into the landscape but also serves a practical purpose, with robust insulation provided by the grass on the roof and sheep's wool in the walls, while no fewer than 16 scots pine trees, visible from the interior, hold up the roof. Underfloor heating powered by the farm's wind turbine and solar panels also helps to keep the place warm all year round, and one of the eco-cabins has a wood-fired hot tub.

Treberfedd is a perfect place for both a romantic holiday for a couple and a large family gathering, with a private dining room (with optional chef) that can be hired with group bookings. The location is perfect too – not only with scenery to die for but also loads to do in the surrounding area, whether it's visiting the nearby coast, mountain-biking in the Cambrian Mountains or just hanging out on the farm: they have a playground, sandpit and climbing wall, and they've recently added a wood-fired pizza oven on site for guests to use as well. You can also follow the two-mile farm trail through the meadows and woods, along which you can meet some of the farm's own animals. They've been breeding cattle, sheep and chickens here for hundreds of years, and in that respect nothing much has changed on the farm. We're just lucky that current incumbents Jack and Eleanor decided to share it with the rest of us!

CONTACT Dihewyd, Lampeter, Ceredigion SA48 7NW • 01570 470672 • treberfedd.co.uk

HOW MUCH? Cottages from £352 a week in low season to £1050 in summer. Cabins from £350 a week in low season to £810 in summer. Short breaks from £199 all year round.

ACCOMMODATION The 2 eco-cabins sleep a family of 4, while the various cottages sleep between 5 and 9 people.

The Felin Fach Griffin

'The simple things in life done well' is their motto, and it's perfectly suited to this rather special inn, situated on the edge of the Brecon Beacons National Park, which has 7 very comfortable rooms above a restaurant that is one of the best in the region. The rooms all have big beds, wifi, Roberts radios, homemade biscuits, fresh flowers and posh toiletries (no TVs!). Breakfasts are delicious and a good indicator of dinner, which features seasonal dishes and ingredients from the Welsh borders. Dogs are welcome in all rooms, the bar and at a special out-of-the-way table in the restaurant. They're also well catered for everywhere else, from the entrance, where you'll find baskets of clean towels, to your room, laid out with blankets and bowls, all at no extra charge. There's also a help yourself 'K9 Cupboard' stocked with blankets, bowls, treats and extra poo bags and a hose to rinse off those paws. Meanwhile there's no shortage of things to do, from lots of great walks to book-browsing in Hay or just pottering around nearby Brecon, Abergavenny or Crickhowell.

CONTACT Felin Fach, Brecon, Powys LD3 0UB •
01874 620111 • felinfachgriffin.co.uk
HOW MUCH? Double rooms from £142.50 a night,
£202.50 with dinner. No charges for dogs.

The Falcondale

You can't help but start to unwind as soon as you set eyes on the Falcondale, which hoves into view a mile or so outside the pretty university town of Lampeter – a Grade II-listed country house perching atop the Teifi valley, surrounded by glorious walking country, With 17 beautifully decorated bedrooms, furnished with luxurious beds, great showers and deep baths, TVs, tea- and coffee-making facilities and homemade shortbread, it's a comfortable place to stay and has a cosy bar and 2-AA-rosette restaurant. It's also about as dog friendly as it gets: hounds get a welcome pack including food, a towel, blanket, bowls and poo bags; a dinner of chicken, rice and vegetables, with a chewy ear for dessert, can be added for a fiver. Dogs are allowed everywhere but the restaurant but you can eat the same menu in the conservatory, guests also have their own, dog-friendly lounge on the 1st floor. You'll find ample circular walks from the hotel and plenty of dog friendly beaches nearby – Cai Bach, Cwmtydu, Aberaeron and Poppit Sands. Not only that, dogs stay free during National Pet Month - every April.

CONTACT Falcondale Drive, Lampeter, Ceredigion
SA48 7RX • 01570 422910 • thefalcondale.co.uk
HOW MUCH? Double rooms from £135 a night. Dogs
£10 a night.

The Grove of Narberth

You can have it all at this fabulous little Pembrokeshire hotel, which provides understated luxury and fine dining in beautiful surroundings. It has 25 rooms and suites in total – 14 in the hotel itself and 11 in the cottages in the grounds – all of them large, elegant and comfortable, and provided with Sky TV, tea and coffee, telephone, hairdryer and wifi, cast-iron baths and monsoon showers. Dogs are welcome to stay at 5 of the cottages but not inside the hotel proper. Expect a bed, blanket, bowl, treats and bags waiting for you. But food is the thing here, and whatever you order will likely come fresh from the kitchen garden or a local producers, with Welsh beef and lamb, fish and local cheeses always featuring on the menu; water comes from the Grove's own spring – sparkling or still. Dogs can also dine by reservation in the snug of the Artisan Rooms for breakfast, lunch and dinner – and a doggie dining menu is also available. Best of all, there are 26 acres right outside to race over and roll about in, and the nearby sandy beaches and also the wooded slopes of the Preseli Hills await.

CONTACT Molleston, Narberth, Pembrokeshire
SA67 8BX • 01834 860915 • thegrove-narberth.co.uk
HOW MUCH? Double rooms £175–£235 a night, suites
from £285. Dogs £20 a night.

The Druidstone

The Druidstone is a national treasure: a weather-beaten Georgian house, with a walled garden, poised on the cliff above one of Pembrokeshire's loveliest beaches. But it is the people who make a hotel great and Druidstone excels in this: it's family run, the staff are delightful, and it has everything you need in a hotel – wonderful breakfasts, good bar meals, proper kids' teas, a bar that stays open late and fabulous views out to sea. The only drawback is that in summer it gets booked up months ahead. The hotel proper has just 11 rooms but there are also 5 cottages around the gardens, including a tiny eco-hut, powered by wind and solar. Dogs are allowed everywhere except the main dining room, which means you'll need to eat in the bar, or outside if the weather is good. Dogs are allowed on Druidstone's fabulous beach, reached in 10 minutes from the hotel, and the Dru (as everyone knows it) is slap-bang on the Pembrokeshire Coast Path – one of the best walks anywhere in Britain. Easy local walks also take you to Little Haven (with a fine dog-friendly pub, The Swan) to the south, or north to the surfers' beach of Newgale.

CONTACT Druidstone, Broad Haven, Pembrokeshire
SA62 3NE • 01437 781221 • druidstone.co.uk
HOW MUCH? Prices from £85 a night to £200 for
luxurious en-suites. Dogs go free.

SCOTLAND

With more than 800 islands and 10 percent of Europe's coastline,
Scotland is diverse, deep, and very hard to pin down. Its major
cities – Glasgow and Edinburgh – can hold their own with any
in Europe, but it also boasts some of the most remote and wild
landscapes in Europe. Come here to walk and to wonder.

Crispie Estate

Stay on a stunning Scottish country estate right by Loch Fyne and the Mull of Kintyre.

Only in Scotland could you find somewhere like the Crispie Estate, where 120 acres of pristine coast and ancient forests are yours for the duration of your stay. It's only a couple of hours' drive from Glasgow, yet is a stunning location: you can sail, walk, cycle, kayak, swim or just explore the place on foot, and there is even a motor boat moored in the bay for guests' exclusive use as per RYA certificate requirements. There are two places to stay on the Estate: historic Crispie House, which sleeps 16 people, and Crispie Lodge, a smaller, more contemporary affair which can accommodate eight people. Both properties enjoy the use of their own private grounds and their own private beach, and Crispie House has an indoor swimming pool and games room. Only Crispie House is dog friendly, with a maximum of two dogs accepted free of charge. Just turn up, throw away the car keys...and tune out.

Crispie House is a lovely rambling old place with no less than seven bedrooms – a perfect venue for a large group of family or friends celebrating a special occasion or who just want to get away from it all in the Scottish Highlands. There's a large sitting room and dining room, an indoor heated swimming pool, sauna and a games room. It's light-filled and spacious in summer, while roaring open fires, lounging sofas and cosy rugs are the perfect antidote when the weather turns cold.

Dogs are welcome throughout the house, there is a warm utility room where they can dry off and the owners provide dog towels for extra drying assistance. Although they prefer dogs to stay off the furniture, they do provide throws for the sofas, along with a little doggy welcome pack with beds, water bowls, bio-degradable poo bags and treats.

Crispie House is also a fabulous place to exercise your dog: it's at the end of a three-mile road, so the surrounding area is very safe. To the left is extensive woodland, and there is a large garden at the front that leads down to Loch Fyne. At any time of year the views across the loch to the Mull of Kintyre are stunning, while outside the lawn sweeps directly down to the beach. Otherwise amble through the woods, fish, swim or cycle – or just relax and enjoy the views.

You could spend most of your time exploring the area on foot; there are a number of dog-friendly pubs and restaurants in the surrounding areas, Portavadie is accessible on foot for most of the year and everywhere else is accessible by car or boat. But there are lots of more energetic activities on hand too, for example exploring the nearby waters in the estate's own motor boat, or learning to sail at the nearby Tighnabruaich Sailing Club. You could also play golf at the Kyles of Bute club. However, it's not every day you get to spend time on your own private estate, so we wouldn't blame you for staying put!

CONTACT Kilfinan, Tighnabruaich, Argyll & Bute PA21 2ER • 07951 912469 • crispie.co.uk
HOW MUCH? From £2500 to £4500 for a week's stay.
ACCOMMODATION Crispie House has 7 Bedrooms and 4 Bathrooms and sleeps 16.

East Cambusmoon

Luxury eco-friendly accommodation in beautiful National Park countryside yet within easy reach of Glasgow.

An environmentally aware self-catering oasis just back from the banks of Loch Lomond, East Cambusmoon Farm is a five-acre smallholding that is handily tucked into the heart of the Loch Lomond and Trossachs National Park. The savvy couple who run the cottages – Deborah and Steve Macken – have experience in renewables and have learned lessons from their success in fashioning their own home on clean and green lines. The result is spectacular, with fabulous insulation, solar panels, heat and hot water provided by a ground-source heat pump and no less than three charging-points for electrical vehicles, and two very different cottages joined at the hip to share their magical green touch.

The two-bedroom Old Dairy is the original property and the four-bedroom Curlew Cottage the young upstart, with larch cladding and white render. You won't find a radiator in either, rather underfloor heating on the ground floors, which is usually enough to make things snug, although there are wood-burning stoves on hand if need be. Both cottages are open, airy spaces bathed in light and bringing a bit of the beautiful surrounding countryside inside as well. It works so well and is such a cosy hideaway that even if the weather is damp you won't mind too much.

Neat touches include some welcome (homemade and local) provisions, free unlimited wifi and a trampoline in the barn that helps keep active wee ones happy if it rains. It's all brilliant and compelling proof that a low-carbon footprint and a responsible attitude to the environment doesn't mean sacrificing comfort or style. You can rent the cottages individually, for couples or for families, or together they can accommodate up to 14 people in some style, with four bathrooms, an en-suite loo, plenty of patio space, and toys, games and books for young children. They also welcome two dogs in each cottage – which is just as well given the walks to discover in the surrounding countryside.

As you might expect from a property located in a national park, the local area offers plenty of opportunities for outdoor activities, from Munro-bagging, golf and mountain biking to a much more leisurely walk up neighbouring Duncryne Hill, with its spectacular loch and hill views. Deborah and Steve can advise on the best dog walks and cycle routes and have maps you can borrow as well having a clean-down area for when you return – handy for bikes, dogs, muddy boots, whatever. The dramatic fortification of Dumbarton Castle is just a 20-minute drive away, as are the whisky distilleries of Glengoyne and Auchentoshan. Glasgow and its myriad attractions, meanwhile, lie just forty minutes to the south.

CONTACT Gartocharn, Dunbartonshire G83 8RZ • 07905 093997 • lochlomondcottage.com
HOW MUCH? Old Dairy: 3 nights from £340; Curlew Cottage: 3 nights from £510.
ACCOMMODATION Two cottages – the 2-bedroom Old Dairy and 4-bedroom Curlew Cottage.

The Bonham

One of Edinburgh's longest-running boutique hotels, The Bonham has contemporary style, individuality and understated chic. This was one of the city's first boutique hotels and following a recent re-furb remains a thoroughly stylish place to stay, with original art on the walls, excellent service and attention to detail, and one of the better hotel restaurants in the city. It's good to know, too, that all of the hotel's 49 rooms accept pooches, and dog beds and bowls are available on request. Dogs aren't allowed in the restaurant but you can enjoy the same menu in the bar, and there are walkies close at hand in nearby Drumsheugh Gardens. You're also very close to the unique Water of Leith, which flows through the city centre from the Scottish National Gallery of Modern Art, through the former mills and mill workers houses at Dean Village, to Stockbridge and eventually leads to the sea at Leith. Overall, if you're looking for a place to stay in Edinburgh that can comfortably accommodate both you and your four-legged friend, you couldn't do much better.

CONTACT 35 Drumsheugh Gardens, Edinburgh
EH3 7RN • 0131 2266050 • thebonham.com
HOW MUCH? Double rooms from around £109 a night,
dogs £30 per stay.

Mackays Hotel

A privately owned town centre hotel, right up in the far northern Highlands of Scotland, Mackays has cosy rooms, a nice restaurant and bar, and ever-present owners who attend to every detail and make sure all of their guests are happy. It's not the poshest place you'll ever stay in but it will definitely be one of the most welcoming and comfortable, and – situated, as it is, on what is officially 'the shortest street in the world' according to the Guinness Book of World Records – is at the centre of the small coastal town of Wick and the heart of the local community. It also has 2 resident hounds, Max and Bria, who ensure that dogs and their owners always get a warm welcome. There are 30 rooms in all, refurbished in contemporary style with comfortable beds and tea trays with local shortbread, and a series of self-catering apartments where they accept dogs who are also allowed in the main lobby and bar, where you can eat the same menu as is served in the hotel's excellent restaurant as well as enjoying their huge collection of Highland malt whiskies.

CONTACT Union St, Wick, Caithness KW1 5ED •
01955 602323 • mackayshotel.co.uk
HOW MUCH? Double rooms from £119 a night;
apartments £136, townhouses £240; dogs £15 per stay.

Monachyle Mhor

This stylish hotel may be easy to get to from Scotland's Central Belt, but, hidden down a quiet glen, it feels a million miles away from anywhere. They are serious about food here and offer their own cookery courses, as well as farming their own sheep, cattle and hens. On arrival, check out their kitchen garden, where the aroma of herbs and array of vegetables will build up your appetite for dinner. This will feature quite a lot of the garden's produce alongside the likes of Perthshire lamb and Scrabster-landed monkfish in a 5-course extravaganza that showcases Scotland's culinary larder to the full. Meanwhile, the accommodation is as ambitious and impressive as the cooking, with suites laden with oversized beds and stand-alone baths. They have 14 rooms in all, 5 in the main house, some with loch and mountain views, and 9 courtyard rooms, which have views over the mountains and farm. They accept dogs in some of the courtyard rooms, and indeed are so dog friendly that even guests without dogs are encouraged to take dogs staying at the hotel out for a walk – and there is plenty of opportunity for that!

CONTACT Balquhidder, Lochearnhead, Perthshire FK19 8PQ • 01877 384622 • mhor.net
HOW MUCH? Suites with breakfast from £195 a night. Dogs £10 a night.

Auchrannie Resort

The Auchrannie Resort on the Isle of Arran has for years managed to be all things to all people: a family-friendly place to stay made up of an original old-world luxury hotel, a more modern annexe and a series of luxury lodges. It has a swathe of leisure facilities, including 2 swimming pools and an excellent spa awash with myriad treatments and a superb chill out room, all amid extensive tree-filled grounds. Wherever you decide to stay, the resort is surrounded by sweeping mountains and the sea is just a short distance away. They have no less than 3 restaurants to choose from – Scottish tapas at eighteen69, the Cruize Brasserie and Brambles seafood grill, and you can dine with your dog in the Waterside bar as well as in the lounges of eighteen69 or in any of the guest lounges in the spa. On sunnier days you can chill out on the Cruize Balcony, Brambles terrace or the outside spaces next to the spa. Meanwhile, dogs receive treats on arrival, towels are provided for muddy paws and the grounds are large enough for even the most inexhaustible hound!

CONTACT Auchrannie Rd, Brodick, Isle of Arran KA27 8BZ• 01770 302234• auchrannie.co.uk
HOW MUCH? Double rooms from around £139 a night, dogs £10; retreats/lodges from around £250, dogs £30.

Cairngorm Lodges

Homely, well-furnished, eco-friendly lodges deep in the woods of Aberdeenshire.

There's something special about waking up deep in a forest: sleeping in the woods engenders a cosiness that can't quite be replicated anywhere else, and the truth is that staying in a wooden lodge in some of the Cairngorms National Park's deepest, darkest woodland is about as far away from most people's day-to-day existence as it's possible to get. That is perhaps why the enterprising folk up here founded Cairngorm Lodges, which offer the chance to get away from it all in some of the finest natural scenery the UK has to offer. Situated on the 750-acre Blelack Estate in Aberdeenshire, they started with the repair and renovation of just one building, an existing 'Woodcutter's Cabin', which was such a success they decided to build four more lodges from scratch, each in its own secluded forest location.

It's a real get-away-from-it-all break, with no wifi, no reception building or additional facilities; just the lodges, and the woods. Which means it's a perfect place to visit with a dog – indeed it would be a crime to come here without one! The lodges are very well equipped and they allow up to three dogs per lodge; the only rule being they're not allowed on the beds. Each lodge has two bedrooms – one double, one twin, so is perfect for a family of four; they each have a sitting room/kitchen and bathroom, outside decking with a barbecue and are heated by a wood-burning stove and lit with low-energy lighting, and logs are laid on in generous supply. Everything is done with the environment in mind: the lodges are built from sustainable wood and the forest sustainably managed. They recycle everything, and perhaps most importantly are passionate about preserving the local flora and fauna, encouraging dragonflies, running bee-keeping courses and offering lots of advice on where to spot local wildlife. Red squirrels are daily visitors to the lodges and there are red deer in the woods and beyond, and among an abundance of birdlife you will be able to spot kestrels, sparrow hawks and pine martens: all good reasons to be circumspect about when you decide to let your dog off its lead.

All the lodges are dog friendly and the forest has a multitude of marked paths that would take weeks to walk – plus there are plenty of hill and mountain walks beyond, with no less than 24 'Munros' easily accessible from the site. It's a fabulous area for horse-riding and in particular mountain-biking, with some great mountain bike routes through the forest. It's also not far to the mountain-biking centre of Tarland Trails, and bike hire is available at Cycle Highland in Ballater, a few miles southwest of Cairngorm Lodges. All in all, we reckon this could be the perfect place for both an active holiday and a peaceful contemplative one – or, even better, a mixture of the two!

CONTACT Logie Coldstone, Aboyne, Aberdeenshire AB34 5PQ • 07583 436040 • cairngormlodges.com
HOW MUCH? The 4 newest lodges cost £555–£815, depending on the time of year; short breaks £410–£500. The original Woodcutter's Lodge is £460–£650 a week, short breaks £348–£455.
ACCOMMODATION Five lodges, each sleeping 4 people.

Log Cabin Scotland

Well-appointed wooden lodges in a spectacular woodland location on the shores of Loch Awe.

Beautifully located on the edge of Loch Awe, in the wilds of western Scotland, these log cabins offer a fabulous chance to get away from pretty much everything if that's what you're keen to do. Their location in the heart of the Inverliever forest (indeed the tiny village of Dalavich is itself a Forestry Commission creation) is perfect for both waterside and woodland holidays: each lodge enjoys fishing rights on the loch (Scotland's longest and renowned for its trout fishing), and where the water ends, the forest begins, with all manner of scenic walks and cycle routes and any amount of wildlife to spot along the way, from red squirrel and deer in the woods to osprey and otters on the loch.

As for the lodges, there are four in all, each with its own secluded space (at least a quarter-of-an-acre) so that you would hardly know the others were there. They vary in size, sleeping from 4 to 6 people, and you can choose between a woodland or waterside location, but all come complete with open-plan living area with kitchen, 2–3 bedrooms, family bathroom, wood-burning stove, and large verandah, a TV and DVD player and free wifi – plus they are all pet friendly, so you can bring the family hound along as well. Best of all, though, are the eco-friendly wood-burning hot tubs. Fern Lodge is deep in the woods by a babbling brook but still only 150m from the loch; while the other woodland lodge – Orchy – is 250m from the shore. The other two – Crannog Lodge and Lochside Lodge – both overlook the water. They're all fully insulated, double-glazed and warm and cosy at any time of year, but obviously sitting in the hot tub enjoying a glass of wine while looking out over the loch on a summer's evening is pretty hard to beat.

There's no question that it's a wonderful place to bring a dog and all of the cabins are particularly welcoming to canine friends, with walks galore on your doorstep.

You could first of all try the waymarked Tall Trees Trail down to the loch, or stroll through the Barnaline Oakwoods and visit Avich Falls, or, with a bit more time on your hands, pick up the Inverinan Trail through the nearby forest to the gorge of Abhainn Fionn. Once back, you could repair to the excellent and very friendly Lochview Grill for food and drink – dogs are welcome in the bar. Or you could try the Kilchrenan Inn: you'll need to drive here (it's around 7 miles away) but it's a slick and contemporary country pub that is dog friendly and serves an excellent locally sourced and very moderately priced seasonal menu.

CONTACT Dalavich, Argyll & Bute PA35 1HN• 07706 122034 • log-cabin-scotland.co.uk
HOW MUCH? 2 nights £250–£370, 3 nights £300–£575, 4 nights £395–£645, 7 nights £495–£895. Prices include all linen and 3 bags of logs for the wood-burner and hot tub.
ACCOMMODATION Fern Lodge sleeps up to 6 in 2 bedrooms and a sofa bed; Lochside Lodge sleeps 6 in 3 bedrooms; Crannog Lodge sleeps 4 in 2 bedrooms. Orchy Lodge sleeps 5 in 2 bedrooms.

Lower Polnish

A beautifully renovated Scottish bolthole by the sea that makes the perfect romantic, dog-friendly escape.

A traditional Scottish blackhouse dating back to 1750, Lower Polnish is an open-plan, one-bed property set on the almost entirely uninhabited 3500-acre Ardnish peninsula on the west coast of Scotland. It's a truly remote location, the peninsula pushing out like a blunted thumb towards the islands of Muck, Rum and Eigg in a patchwork of thick pine and oak forests, white sandy beaches and ruined crofts, but don't let that put you off, it's well worth the journey and truly the definition of a rural retreat – a bolthole with no internet or phone reception where you can get away from it all, relax and put city life out of your mind.

You can only get here by leaving your car in the parking space and walking the last 300 metres, down a steep wooded valley and across a babbling burn. You'll need to carry all of your provisions (including food and drink) down the track too. The house is relatively newly renovated and is spread across a single level. It's lovely and light, and a stone's throw from the sea. There's a wood-burning stove sitting at one end firing out warmth (replacing the spot where cows would have once lived in winter) and a brand new sitting room in a glazed conservatory offering panoramic views of what is by any standards breathtaking scenery. Sit in here with a hot brew or a glass of wine and take it all in. You may even spot some local wildlife, so make sure you bring your binoculars. The brand-new kitchen and bathroom complete the picture, giving you everything, in fact, that you need for a quiet, stress-free break for two – plus of course a dog, for whom it might just be the ideal holiday spot.

You might not want to leave the cosiness of the cottage, indeed the views from the conservatory may be all you need. But if you are tempted out, the peninsula is a walker's paradise. Bring your dog and amble along the private foreshore. There's a lot to explore, and with no neighbours nearby, apart from the seals and white-tailed sea eagles, it's a pretty secluded spot. It's populated mainly by herds of deer, who roam a landscape that's made up of bare hills, patches of forest, several lochs, a fabulous coastline and a pure white sand beach, interspersed with the ruins of a hundred abandoned houses that testify to how hard life once was here. After a day out discovering the area, you'll look forward to getting back to the comfort of the cottage. A piece of advice? Don't forget to check out the dark skies for stars on a clear evening.

CONTACT Ardnish Peninsula, Scottish Highlands PH38 4NA · ardnish.org/polnish
HOW MUCH? £525–£675 a week.
ACCOMMODATION A cosy 1-bedroom cottage that comfortably sleeps 2 people.

Big Sky Lodges

These eco-friendly pine lodges are a perfect base for this corner of the Highlands – and they're dog-friendly too!

If you're looking for a Highland holiday with a difference, then Big Sky Lodges may be just what you're after – six Scandinavian-style, solid pine log cabins set in glorious countryside across the water from Inverness. They're called 'Big Sky' for a reason. Situated on the so-called Black Isle between the Cromarty and Beauly Firths, this isn't classic mountainous Highland territory as such, but rich, crofting land, known for its exceptionally mild climate and a landscape of rolling, forested hills and meadows where the views stretch as far as the eye can see.

The lodges are set on their own 17 acres of this unspoiled paradise; some have balconies, where you can enjoy midge-free mild evenings or have your breakfast each morning while watching the numerous red kites catch their own. The lodges themselves are things of beauty in their own right, pretty much wood throughout – sustainable Finnish pine – so very eco-friendly, and exceptionally comfy: perfect bases for both interacting with the nature outside or hunkering down when the weather is poor.

Each lodge has a wood-burning stove and three double or twin bedrooms, two or sometimes three bathrooms and a large living area and fitted kitchen. They have central heating, dishwasher, washing machine, flatscreen TV and DVD, and free wifi, as well as books, DVDs and stuff for rainy days. Stays include bed linens and towels and posh toiletries. All bookings include tea, coffee, hot chocolate, fresh milk and tasty teacakes. They also offer additional Scottish breakfast packs on request. Proprietor Ailsa is on hand to tend to all your needs and requests, and all the lodges except Rowan are dog friendly – just as well, as it would be a sin to do the walks in the nearby woods without a hound in tow. All doggy bookings receive a welcome hamper with water bowl, treats, poo bags, garden stake and cable and a cosy blanket. They accept up to 2 dogs per lodge and just ask that dogs aren't left unattended while their owners are out – but with all this glorious countryside all around, why would you do that?

If you want to explore further afield, the Black Isle itself is worth investigating – Cromarty is a pleasant town and nearby Chanonry Point is a popular place to spot dolphins. Plus you're just a short drive from Loch Ness in one direction, Speyside and Aviemore in another, and the pleasant towns and countryside around the Dornoch Firth to the north.

CONTACT Drynie Park, Muir of Ord, Inverness-shire IV6 7RP • 07796 546861 • bigskylodges.co.uk
HOW MUCH? Prices from £360 for 3-night stays.
ACCOMMODATION Six Scandinavian style lodges, each comfortably sleeping 6 people.

Craig Cottage

A unique off-grid cottage, on the banks of one of Scotland's most remote sea lochs.

Situated on one of western Scotland's most beautiful yet least visited lochs – Loch Etive – this comfortable self-catering holiday cottage is the perfect answer for anyone seeking a properly remote, off-grid place to stay that's also not too hard to reach. Down a forest track on the western side of the long crooked Loch Etive, two miles from any sort of proper road, it's accessible by car (preferably but not necessarily a 4-wheel-drive), or by sea, but that's about it. Once here, it's about as peaceful and remote a spot as you could find in the UK, yet you're only a two-hour drive from Scotland's most populated region.

A single-storey stone cottage right by the water's edge, Craig Cottage has just two bedrooms – one double, one twin – so it's an ideal place for a family of four looking for somewhere to spend a week without phones and Facebook. There is no mains electricity, only a generator to provide lighting; the kitchen stove and fridge are powered by gas, and heat comes from the wood-burning stove in the sitting room, which provides the hot water that fills the radiators, keeping the house warm and cosy at all times. There is plenty of free wood and kindling, and also plenty to gather, and both bedrooms have lovely views of the loch and big comfy beds with new mattresses and good quality linen. There's a family bathroom and the loft has been converted to a play den for the kids – plus there are lots of books and other activities throughout the property for wet-weather days. Outside there's a garden, but really the entire landscape here is yours to enjoy pretty much as far as the eye can see.

The property is dog friendly, and it's hard to imagine a better place to bring your dog on holiday – wild and untamed, with fast-running rivers, native forests, and of course the loch itself, much of which is inaccessible by road. There's plenty to explore nearby. You could visit the Falls of Lora, where the loch flows into the sea, take a boat tour from Dunstaffnage or hire a boat on the loch from Taynnuilt –while at the opposite end, Allt Easach and Glen Etive are delightfully unspoiled, with plenty of opportunities for kayaking and wild swimming. There are also a number of points along the shore from which you can launch your own boat or kayak.

You can also just stay put and enjoy the cottage, in which case you should probably put your dog on a lead – the woods nearby are home to roe, fallow and red deer; there are otters in the loch and pine martens visit the house almost daily. You can also swim from right in front of the cottage or further up the loch in a shallow bay. And if you end up missing city life, it's worth knowing that Oban is just a half-an-hour's drive away. Otherwise, just hunker down and enjoy the cottage – there aren't many places in the UK like it.

CONTACT Craig Cottage, near Bonawe, Oban, Argyll & Bute PA37 1RL • 07918 873586 • etivecottages.co.uk
HOW MUCH? Price per week £500–£600.
ACCOMMODATION The cottage comfortably sleeps 4.

Loch Melfort Hotel

By dint of its unspoiled nature and bountiful littoral, many hotels on Scotland's west coast boast spectacular views, but romantic Loch Melfort Hotel arguably has the best of the lot. This cosy, family-run hotel sits way out west in the wilds of Argyll, enjoying a vista alive with sprinklings of islands and sunsets as warm as the welcome from owners Calum and Rachel Ross. The rooms in the characterful main hotel are our pick (there are comfortable lodge rooms too), and some are designated dog friendly, with pooches getting a welcome pack with towels, a bowl and tasty treats. Downstairs there's a bistro, lounge and restaurant, all of which you can eat in with your dog. Local produce is to the fore, with the seafood and an excellent wine list a highlight. Outside, with 17 acres of grounds to explore, it's ideal for rambles with your four-legged friend. A wee path leads down to their boathouse, where the intrepid can go for a swim in summer, while the big attraction nearby is Arduaine Gardens, which are handily pet friendly too. Fido will have the time of his life!

CONTACT Arduaine by Oban, Argyll & Bute PA34 4XG •
01852 200233 • lochmelfort.co.uk
HOW MUCH? Double rooms with breakfast from £80 a
night. Dogs £10 per stay.

Forest Holidays Strathyre

Situated in the Queen Elizabeth Forest Park, just outside the appealing Perthshire town of Callander (so-called 'gateway to the Highlands'), this is one of Forest Holidays' most scenic locations, in the heart of the gorgeous Trossachs. But it does what all their sites do so well – tames the wilderness while still enabling you to feel in touch with nature. So basically, you can make your holiday as outdoorsy, as relaxing or as challenging as you like. There are 45 comfortable cabins spaced out around the site, either with a loch view or in a forested glade. Each sleeps between 2 and 8 people and some welcome dogs. All the cabins are extremely well equipped, with full kitchens and some with log-burners, while a hot tub on the deck adds a bit of style. The site's Forest Retreat hub has a café and bar, shop and play area, bikes for hire and wildlife-spotting and bushcraft activities. Beyond, there are loads of sights and adventures to choose from – birdwatching trails, high-wire fun at the nearby Go Ape or visiting the nearby village of Aberfoyle, which gives access to some of the best Trossachs walking trails.

CONTACT Callander, Perthshire FK17 8HF •
03330 110495 • forestholidays.co.uk
HOW MUCH? Prices from £300, 7 nights from £515.
Dogs £15.

Cromlix Hotel

It's rare to find an award-winning five-star hotel that goes out of its way to welcome dogs. But what else would you expect from an establishment owned by dog-loving tennis star Andy Murray, whose seriously luxurious hideaway is on the outskirts of his home town of Dunblane. Proper thought – and money – has gone into making this feel every bit a luxurious Scottish country house retreat, with accommodation spread across 10 bedrooms, 5 suites and a one-bedroom gate lodge, all decorated in their own individual style. They share views of the grounds and the tennis courts (but, of course!) and come with Egyptian cotton bed linen and Penhaligon toiletries. Impressively, dogs are welcome in any room or suite, although they are not allowed in the public areas, including, sadly, the Chez Roux Restaurant. The expansive grounds make up for this, giving dogs plenty of room to enjoy themselves while you take in lungfuls of glorious fresh air. Bowls, towels and beds can be arranged for dogs, too.

CONTACT Kinbuck, near Dunblane, Perthshire FK15 9JT • 01786 822125 • cromlix.com
HOW MUCH? Double rooms from £250 a night. No charge for dogs – maximum 2 per room.

Four Seasons Hotel

Enjoying a spectacular setting in the Trossachs and Loch Lomond National Park, this hotel is famous for the fact that The Beatles spent a couple of nights here in 1964. You can stay in one of the main building's bedrooms or head up the forested hillside to the nearby chalets, which come with Bose speakers, vintage CD players, tea- and coffee-making facilities and en-suite bath/shower rooms. Dogs are as welcome here as world-famous popstars and get a welcome pack with a treat, bedding and bowls; dog-sitting and dog-walking services are also available – just ask about the 'Pet Butler' service. There is a canine menu for hungry dogs, while for humans the 'Seasons View' restaurant offers all-day dining, and there's also the Tarken Bistro and Terrace; both are pet friendly. Numerous activities are available at the local watersports centre; you can even follow in the footsteps of the Fab Four and take a boat out. Dogs also love the old railway track behind the hotel, where you can walk for miles. The view, though, is the thing here: fit for a rock star – and, of course, your prized pooch.

CONTACT St. Fillans, Perthshire PH6 2NF • 01764 685333 • thefourseasonshotel.co.uk
HOW MUCH? Double rooms with breakfast from £85 a night – dogs free.

Comrie Croft

In the heart of deepest Highland Perthshire, Comrie Croft, run by a co-operative of like-minded environmentally aware individuals, is no mere campsite. Yes, they take tents, but they've also got Norwegian katas, an on-site Tea Garden and a superb bike shop for exploring the network of trails that snakes up the Croft's wooded hillside. First-timers might feel most secure down in the main camping field by all the facilities, but more adventurous souls will want to push on up into the forest, where secluded pitches have their own campfires and there are 4 of 7 of their so-called katas – Swedish tipis with wood-burning stoves and a sleeping area strewn with animal skins. They also have a 3-bed Farmhouse on-site and a Bunkhouse with shared dormitory accommodation. Dogs can camp with you and stay in the katas and are also welcome in the Farmhouse, and there are loads of great walks nearby, and fabulous scenery in all directions. Indeed, with a very well-stocked shop on-site too, there's precious little need to leave the Croft at all if you don't want to – and why would you?

CONTACT Braincroft, Crieff, Perthshire PH7 4JZ •
01764 670140 • comriecroft.com
HOW MUCH? Katas £229 per weekend, £99 per week night. Dogs £5 per stay, 2 dogs maximum per kata.

The Crofthouse

The perfect Highland retreat for a large group of friends, The Crofthouse is situated on a working farm in an exquisite Highland location and sleeps 8 people in comfort. Visitors are made to feel very welcome here, and the farm is dog-friendly too. The Crofthouse itself is almost Scandinavian in feel: pine-clad, with a large open-plan living area, a family room that sleeps 4 and 4 further beds in 2 separate spaces in the loft. It's no slouch when it comes to facilities, with underfloor heating, wifi and flatscreen TVs. And remember, it's a farm, so you can watch farmer Roy's herd of Highland cattle from your balcony. Crofthouse guests can even use the new Crofthouse Studio free of charge. Here you can dance, draw, do a spot of yoga, hold a small-scale meeting or meditate as you take in the stunning wood and mountain views. The location isn't far from Aviemore, with all its activities and funicular railway. Nighttime can reveal some truly spectacular starry skies, and for dogs – well, it would be hard to imagine a better place when the time comes for walkies!

CONTACT Uvie Farm, Newtonmore, Inverness-shire
PH20 1BS • 07811 322722 • myhighlandcroft.co.uk
HOW MUCH? Monday–Thursday £144 a night, Friday–Sunday £166 a night. July–August from £786 a week.

Laggan

As remote a spot as any you'll find in the British Isles, Laggan is an off-grid cottage situated in a particularly inaccessible part of the remote Ardnish peninsula. You can only get here by boat, and even then only when the tides allow; it has no electricity; there's a very limited mobile reception and of course no broadband or phone; and you're a half-day's walk from your nearest neighbour. If this sort of thing appeals, however, you can be sure that there are few other places that can deliver quite so much peace, space and solitude, and of course they could hardly not welcome dogs! It might be remote but it's not primitive: oil lamps provide light, it has heating, and there is a fridge, cooker, hot water heated by a very efficient wood-burning stove – and a radio for listening to the shipping forecast. There are also 2 comfortable bedrooms plus a box room, so if needed it can sleep 5 people. You obviously have to be very organised about provisions – it's a 3-hour hike to borrow a cup of sugar – but the boat (with outboard) is there for your own private use, and it's only a 10-minute journey across to the mainland.

CONTACT Ardnish Peninsula, Scottish Highlands PH38 4NA • ardnish.org/laggan
HOW MUCH? £950 a week.

Osdale Cottages

Most of the Isle of Skye comes with sensational views as standard but the panoramas from these 2 renovated sheep farmers' cottages have to be among the best on the island, tucked beneath the flat-topped outcrops of Macleod's Table and looking out over the Cuillin Ridge and the sea loch of Dunvegan. Reached by way of a farm track, it's a special place even by Skye's exalted standards – 2 holiday cottages, the Farmhouse and the Byre, rentable separately or together. The former is a stone-built 2-bed cottage with an open-plan living area, a wood-burner and underfloor heating, plus a utility room with a washing machine and a boot room for coats, muddy boots... and muddy dogs, who are especially welcome at both cottages. The Byre also has 2 bedrooms, ground-floor underfloor heating, a large kitchen, a double-height living room heated by a wood-burner and a utility room with washing machine. Both cottages are perfect places for walking, cycling and generally exploring Skye – for example Dunvegan Castle and the nearby Duirinish and Waternish peninsulas.

CONTACT Isle of Skye IV55 8WQ • 07712 820494 • osdalecottages.com
HOW MUCH? From £550 to £850 a week; short stays from £385.

Roulotte Retreat

Romantic wee gypsy caravans and a cosy cottage in the heart of the Scottish Borders.

Always thought you had a bit of gypsy blood in you, or are you just a little caught up in the romance of drifting around the world in a traditional hand-carved wooden caravan? Well Roulotte Retreat may just be for you. The same goes for yoga lovers and just plain lovers at this seriously sexy retreat in the Scottish Borders which offers yoga, walking, nearby horse-riding, cycling, and is an ideal, mainly adults-only getaway for two, or for groups of friends, and also accepts dogs.

There are seven sumptuous roulottes (traditional French wooden caravans) to choose from, six of them sleeping two people and one for up to four persons, and one of them – Rosa Bella – welcomes dogs. Each roulotte has its own highly individual colour and decor scheme, and all are immaculately hand-finished and boast bags of character. There are just enough creature comforts, like a proper en-suite shower and toilet, but no TV, leaving you free to focus on relaxing in your cosy hideaway in a wildflower-strewn meadow. Two of the roulottes, Gitana and Zenaya, have their very own eco hot tubs so that you and your beloved can soak under the stars – and you can see plenty of those in the dark skies in this part of the world – with a glass of bubbly in hand.

Roulotte Retreat is also home to a dog-friendly self-catering cottage, Horseshoe Cottage, which welcomes 2 well-behaved dogs and can sleep up to four people. It can be rented along with with Ruby, a gaily painted bowtop Romany caravan that sleeps two in cosy comfort. Tucked away in their own wild woodland section of the garden, the cottage and caravan have lots of room: the cottage has a large sitting room and a double and twin bedroom and comes well equipped with a dishwasher and washing machine, wood-burning stove, TV and DVD, while Ruby is a wonderfully cosy option for two after a little more privacy. Children are also allowed to stay in the cottage but not Ruby.

The guys at Roulotte Retreat also host yoga and relaxation breaks and can arrange beauty treatments and massages as well as small intimate weddings for couples looking for something more unusual for their special day. Filled with light by day and cosily lit by night. their 1950s wooden Studio is a perfect space for events, workshops and celebrations.

Finally, despite the remote, away-from-it-all feel, Roulotte Retreat is pretty easy to get, just three miles from the extremely pleasant Borders town of Melrose, with its quaint streets and ruined abbey. There are lots of good walks nearby, including the long-distance St Cuthbert's Way and other routes into the surrounding Eildon Hills, along with all sorts of other outdoor activities.

CONTACT Bowden, Melrose, The Scottish Borders TD6 0SU • 0845 094 9729 • roulotteretreat.com
HOW MUCH? £105–£165 a night in high season, dogs £10 a night.
ACCOMMODATION 7 roulotte caravans, one of which is dog-friendly, plus a 2-bed cottage and caravan, sleeping up to 6 people.

Trigony House Hotel

An ultra-relaxed country house hotel with a great restaurant and spa that's also dog friendly!

Deep in the green, rolling countryside of Southwest Scotland, this extremely comfortable 18th-century house is as tranquil a place as you could imagine. Owner and chef Adam Moore and his wife really get that peoples' needs are much more straightforward than hoteliers sometimes think: a comfortable room with a decent bed, great locally sourced food and the ability to quickly relax and feel at home. The facilities are good, with a dedicated spa, and dogs are welcomed like old friends and provided with beds, towels and bowls, a map of walks and gourmet treats. Small wonder that Trigony House has recently been named 'Best Dog-Friendly Hotel in the UK'!

Trigony House has the facilities of a luxury hotel but an atmosphere that's more redolent of your best Scottish friends' country house – if, that is, your friends are superb cooks and extremely keen gardeners. Throughout, the emphasis is on quality rather than quantity, with just nine guest rooms, all spacious and nicely furnished in a classic style, with the primary focus on comfort. Beds have hand-sprung mattresses and Egyptian cotton sheets; all rooms come with a butler's tray brimming with homemade shortbread, good coffee, tea and hot chocolate; and they all have good wifi, Freeview TVs and DVD players. The bathrooms are decent sizes and well appointed, with either a mixed bath/shower or a separate shower and Scottish Ishga toiletries. The larger rooms have a small sitting area, and the largest, the Garden Suite, has a separate bath and shower and its own conservatory and garden. Most either have views over the gardens and Lowther Hills to the east or the Kier Hills to the west, while one has views over the woodland behind the hotel and the ruins of a Roman Fort.

Service throughout is gracious and as unobtrusive as you wish, both in the hotel and restaurant and in the garden spa, which is small but perfectly formed, with a lovely wood-fired hot tub and Finnish sauna and offering a range of holistic treatments, including various massages and the usual facials, manicures and pedicures. They also offer Japanese Reiki, not just for you but for your dog too – something that perhaps expresses what this hotel is about better than words can. Finally the restaurant serves food that is not only delicious but highly local, with milk from a nearby organic dairy, fish and seafood from the Solway Firth and Galloway beef and lamb from an award-winning local butcher. Breakfast includes Ayrshire bacon and sausages and amazing local black pudding; the veggie breakfasts are great too, as are the veggie options on the main menu, which like many of the dishes are based on ingredients from their walled kitchen garden and greenhouse.

CONTACT Closeburn, Dumfries and Galloway DG3 5EZ · 01848 331211 · trigonyhotel.co.uk
HOW MUCH? Double rooms with breakfast £125–£145 a night; Garden Suite £170 a night. £9.50 per dog per night. Maximum 2 dogs per room (negotiable).
ROOMS Eight spacious double rooms with en-suite bathrooms plus a suite with private garden.

OUT AND ABOUT

Four great walks with your dog

FAIRY POOLS This short walk on the rugged west coast of the Isle of Skye visits one of the most magical places in Scotland: the stunning waterfalls of the Fairy Pools. Set near Glen Brittle, with the island's Black Cuillin mountains as a backdrop, the blue-green waters of the river Brittle's pools are a magnet for wild swimmers who love the ice-cold, crystal-clear waters of the Allt a' Choire Ghreadaidh. **4.5 MILES**

GREAT GLEN WAY The Great Glen Way makes for a very pleasant, relatively flat route if you're after a spot of gentle walking over several days that takes in lots of great natural sights, passing Loch Oich and Loch Ness and for much of the time following the Caledonian Canal through some of Scotland's most majestic scenery. It's a lovely path to dip into; indeed for weekend walkers and dog-lovers, it's hard to imagine a better long-distance path in the UK. **77 MILES**

LOCH LOMOND & THE TROSSACHS On the eastern side of Loch Lomond on the famous West Highland Way, take a water bus from Balmaha to Inchcailloch Island, where you can take one of 2 paths – the low path, a gentle woodland walk, or the summit path, a steeper climb. Each takes about the same time but don't forget to stop and enjoy the views. **4.2 MILES**

WILDCAT TRAIL In the stunning scenery of the Cairngorms, the 10km 'Wildcat Trail' takes in the River Spey and stunning views of the surrounding mountains. There are 6 points around Newtonmore where you can join the trail, and it's easy to follow thanks to the wildcat symbols along the way. The trail crosses crofting land where livestock may be kept, so keep dogs under close control. **6 MILES**

THE OUTDOOR GUIDE

Dog-Friendly Destinations

Dog-Friendly Places

MILSOM®

*Not only are Milsom Hotels a great place to eat, drink and stay, they also offer the perfect breaks with your dog. Plenty of walks on the doorstep, such as the riverside walk from **Maison Talbooth** and **Milsoms in Dedham** or along the promenade to the beach in Harwich, while **Milsoms Kesgrave Hall** is set in over 40 acres of woodland so easy for an early morning stroll at the start of the day. Sausage is always on the menu for breakfast and one of our hotels will even 'dog sit' while you are having dinner!*

How can it be a family holiday if you have to leave a member of the family behind? A third of people take their pets on holiday with them, and why not? There are hundreds of pet-friendly cottages out there, in wonderful areas that your dog will just love to explore.

We pride ourselves on being able to provide accommodation for both you and your pet, and with well over half of our portfolio being dog-friendly, you'll have plenty to choose from. We are sure your perfect property is at the tip of your fingers.

Many of our properties have dog-friendly perks, whether it be a welcome pack including all the essentials or some advice on where you'll find the perfect walk. It might be that we take several pets in one property or provide a bed for them too.

The Outdoor Guide
FIND IT - SHARE IT - LIVE IT

The Outdoor Guide

Inspired by Julia Bradbury's love of walking, The Outdoor Guide believes passionately in the value of enjoying a healthy life outdoors — providing routes for both complete beginners and experienced hikers, plus an ever-growing collection of accessible walks for wheelchair users and families with buggies.

This is a site for people who love getting out, lacing up a pair of muddy boots and discovering the Great Outdoors!

www.theoutdoorguide.co.uk

Cool Places

Britain's Coolest Places to
stay, eat, drink... and more!

Based on recommendations on
the Cool Places website, this is a
lavish full-colour guide to more
than 200 of the very best places to
stay in the UK – everything from
boutique hotels and designer B&Bs
to chic country cottages and luxury
glamping sites.

Whether you're looking for a glam
country getaway, a seaside holiday,
a family break or a romantic treat,
put yourself in the trusted hands
of Cool Places and find your perfect
UK place to stay.

Price £18.99

Acknowledgements and credits

DOG FRIENDLY BRITAIN – COOL PLACES TO STAY WITH YOUR DOG

Published in the UK by Cool Places & Punk Publishing,
81 Rivington Street, London EC2A 3AY
© Cool Places Ltd 2020
www.coolplaces.co.uk
A catalogue record of this book is available from the British Library
ISBN 978-1-906889-71-5

CREDITS

Editor: Martin Dunford
Assistant Editor: Lauren Ash
Contributors Kate Bendix, Alice Brown, Chris Coe, Martin Dunford, Lottie Gross, Phil Lee, Robin McKelvie, Beth Pipe, Andrew White. Thanks also to the many other UK writers who have contributed to Cool Places over the years.
Design & layout: Diana Jarvis and Kenny Grant
Proofreading: Leanne Bryan

THANKS

To Caroline Osborne for last-minute words and wisdom, Daisy and Lucy for everything, Lauren for patience beyond the call of duty, Diana Jarvis for design and photography, soup and biscuits, Kenny for the original design, Leanne for proofreading, Mike and Ali for hospitality and finally Busby & family and of course Sonny for special walks. And to all the people and businesses that make Cool Places so special.

SALES

UK Sales: Compass IPS Limited, Great West House, Great West Road, Brentford TW8 9DF; 0208 326 5696; sales@compass-ips.london
Printed and bound in Great Britain by Bell & Bain Ltd, Glasgow
This book has been printed on paper made from renewable sources.

PICTURE CREDITS

Images used are used with permission from the property owners, the establishments or the photographers, including the following:
Cover photographs: Lord Crewe Arms (front); Watergate Bay, © Rebecca Kathryn (back); South Place Hotel, The Falcondale, Walcot Hall, © Olivia Moon Photography (front flap); Walcot Hall, © Olivia Moon Photography (back flap).
p1 The Eastbury Hotel & Spa, Dorset
pp2–3 The White House, Norfolk
p4 The Greyhound Inn, Oxfordshire
p6 The Old Coastguard, Cornwall; Sonny, London (© Martin Dunford); South Place Hotel, London; The White House, Norfolk.
p8 Milo, Bailliffscourt Hotel & Spa (© Lottie Gross)
pp10–11 Busby, Whitstable © Andrew Day
pp12–13 Bailiffscourt Hotel & Spa

pp14–15 Barnsdale Lodge, Rutland
pp16–17 Ziggy, Cornwall (© Hayley Spurway)
p18–19 South Place Hotel, London
pp20–21 Randy Pike, Cumbria
pp22–23 The Greyhound Inn. Oxfordshire
pp24–25 Cosy Under Canvas, Powys
pp26–27 Pack Holidays, Norfolk
pp28–29 Byron Apartments, Devon
pp30–31 Walcot Hall, Shropshire (© Indie Love Photography)
pp32–33 Ampthill Park, Bedfordhsire (© Diana Jarvis)
p39 Elephant Hotel (Benjamin Stuart Photography)
pp 54–55 Bluebell Wood, Lydhurst Cottages, West Sussex
pp 66–67 Russell in the Dunes, Cornwall (© Rebecca Vickerstaff)
pp 96–97 Boots, Tistocker's Cabin, Someset
pp112–113 The Swan at Lavenham, Suffolk
pp126–127 Pack Holidays, Norfolk
p141 Oak Tree Cottages (© Phil Mynott Photography)
pp142–143 Thorpe Cloud, Derbyshire (© Diana Jarvis)
pp152–153 Malvern Hills, Worcestershire (© Diana Jarvis)
p158 Birdholme Glamping (© Alex Wilkinson Media)
pp160–161 Embleton Bay, Northumberland (© Diana Jarvis)
pp170–171 Bamburgh, Northumberland (© Diana Jarvis)
pp184–185 Another Place, The Lake, Cumbria (© Nicodem-Creative)
p190 Old Dungeon Ghyll (© Steve Partridge)
p198 Hidden River Cabins (© Nikki Paxton Photography)
pp200–201 Another Place, The Lake, Cumbria (© Sideways)
pp210–211 The Slate Shed, Gywnedd
pp222–223 Clywedog reservoir, Powys (© Diana Jarvis)
p229 Top of the Woods (© Tom Harper)
pp234–235 Dog on Boat, Laggan, Ardnish Peninsula
pp260–261 Dog and Stones, Laggan, Ardnish Peninsula

SMALL PRINT